Fundamentals of Microeconomics

Fundamentals of Microeconomics

Cecilia Danton

MURPHY & MOORE

www.murphy-moorepublishing.com

Published by Murphy & Moore Publishing,
1 Rockefeller Plaza,
New York City, NY 10020, USA

ISBN: 978-1-63987-248-0

Cataloging-in-Publication Data

Fundamentals of microeconomics / Cecilia Danton.
p. cm.
Includes bibliographical references and index.
ISBN 978-1-63987-248-0
1. Microeconomics. 2. Economics. I. Danton, Cecilia.
HB172 .F86 2021
338.5--dc23

For information on all Murphy & Moore Publications
visit our website at www.murphy-moorepublishing.com

MURPHY & MOORE

Contents

Permissions

Index

Preface

The branch of economics which deals with the behavior of individual firms as well as consumers in decision making and allocation of resources is known as microeconomics. Microeconomics studies the individual agents themselves as well as the interactions between these agents. Various mathematical tools such as exponential functions, derivatives and statistics are used in microeconomics. The key focus of microeconomics is on analysing the market mechanisms which establish the relative prices among goods and services and allocate limited resources. Various theories have been put forward by different economists over time such as the consumer demand theory, production theory, opportunity cost, price theory and cost-of-production theory of value. Game theory is another important subject studied under microeconomics. It is used to understand how information and information systems affect an economy and economic decisions. Using these theories, the failure of market to produce desired results is also studied under microeconomics. The topics included in this book on microeconomics are of utmost significance and bound to provide incredible insights to readers. This book is compiled in such a manner, that it will provide in-depth knowledge about the theory and practice of microeconomics. It will serve as a valuable source of reference for those interested in this field.

Given below is the chapter wise description of the book:

Chapter 1- The area of study which deals with the behavior of individuals and firms while making decisions related to allocating scarce resources is known as microeconomics. A few of the basic theories studied within this discipline are cardinal utility theory, indifference curve theory and revealed preference theory. This is an introductory chapter which will introduce these aspects of microeconomics.

Chapter 2- Theory of costs states that the costs of a business are responsible for determining its supply and spending. Some of the major theories of cost are traditional theory of costs and modern theory of costs. This chapter has been carefully written to provide an easy understanding of these varied theories of cost.

Chapter 3- The quantity which the producers wish to sell is referred to as the supply and the quantity that the customers want to buy is termed as the demand. The aim of this chapter is to explore the various aspects of supply and demand such as supply curve, law of supply, demand curve and law of demand. These topics are crucial for a complete understanding of the subject.

Chapter 4- The situation wherein different economic firms contend for obtaining goods which are limited by varying the elements of the marketing mix is termed as competition. Some of the different types of competition are perfect competition, oligopoly and monopoly. The diverse applications of these types of competition have been thoroughly discussed in this chapter.

Chapter 5- The theories of firm primarily state that a firm exists and takes decisions in order to maximize profits. A few of the prominent theories of firm are Baumol sales maximisation model, Williamson's model of managerial discretion, Robin Marris' model of managerial enterprise, etc. The topics elaborated in this chapter will help in gaining a better perspective about these theories of firm.

Indeed, my job was extremely crucial and challenging as I had to ensure that every chapter is informative and structured in a student-friendly manner. I am thankful for the support provided by my family and colleagues during the completion of this book.

Cecilia Danton

Microeconomics: An Introduction

The area of study which deals with the behavior of individuals and firms while making decisions related to allocating scarce resources is known as microeconomics. A few of the basic theories studied within this discipline are cardinal utility theory, indifference curve theory and revealed preference theory. This is an introductory chapter which will introduce these aspects of microeconomics.

Meaning, Scope and History

In the present-day sense, Economics is a subject whose study helps individuals, groups, nations and even international organizations make important choices for material welfare, both short-term and long-term, under limitations or constraints of resources. Under its widespread umbrella comes the individual or the household going to the market, the firm trying to make profits, the village growing into an industrial town, the less developed country striving for development, multinational organizations and the world economy in general.

Evolution

Even though the term Economics had not come into usage then, there was thinking on economic issues in Western Europe in the 16th to late 17th centuries that go by the name Mercantilism or merchant-like thoughts. It emphasized the role of the government in following policies leading to a positive Balance of Trade, was thought to be the index of the country's prosperity. In the second half of the 18th century, there emerged economic thoughts that go by the name Physiocracy. It emphasized the role of land and agriculture in ensuring a country's prosperity. The Mercantilists had focused on trade and commerce and accumulation of gold and silver. The Physiocrats focused on productive work, leading to the generation of agricultural surplus.

In the third quarter of the 18 th century, with the publication in 1776 of An Inquiry into the Nature and Causes of the Wealth of Nations by Adam Smith, Classical Economics was born. Britain was beginning to experience the Industrial Revolution. Smith emphasized Division of Labour or Specialization as the source of productivity or efficiency in factories contributing aggregatively to the nation's wealth or prosperity. J.B.Say, T.R. Malthus, David Ricardo and J.S.Mill enhanced his ideas and added their contributions to this new body of thought. They came from different professions but all of them had an aggregative approach, took a long-run perspective and made sweeping generalization. Together with Adam Smith, they constitute the Classical economists. Towards the end of the 19th century, there developed a new approach, which has come to be called Neo-Classical. Economists began to study economic issues on a more individual level, asking how the price and quantity of specific goods (and services) were determined in the market, and how firms set their wages, maximizing their profits and minimizing their costs. The canvas became smaller, the conclusions less sweeping. Instead of the aggregates, the units became marginal or incremental. Instead of the entire nation, the individual consumer or producer became the focus of interest.

Decisions depended on a rational weighing of costs and benefits leading to a balance or equilibrium. It is this equilibrium that became the most important objective rather than the wealth of nations, that is, growth.

Menger, William Stanley Jevons and Alfred Marshall are foremost among these new thinkers who came to be called 'marginalists' or Neo-Classicals.

Marshall's Definition of Economics

Marshall's Principles of Economics, the pioneering work of Neo-Classical tradition, provided the following definition of Economics: "a study of mankind in the ordinary business of life; it (Economics) examines that part of individual and social action which is most closely connected with the attainment and with the use of the material requisites of wellbeing. Thus it is on one side a study of wealth; and on the other, and more important side, a part of the study of man."

This definition established the character of the subject as for a long time to come. Economics studied human beings as they go about their everyday life.

Robbins's Definition

In 1932, in Lionel Robbins' Essay on the Nature and Significance of Economic Science, Lionel Robbins highlighted another aspect of the subject, choice under conditions of scarcity. "Economics is a science which studies human behavior as a relationship between ends and scarce means which have alternative uses."

First, resources or means of production (land, labour, capital goods such as machinery, technical knowledge) are scarce or limited. Secondly, what is applied to the production of a certain commodity or service is unavailable for the production of another, alternative one. But human wants for the consumption or use of goods and services (food, clothing, housing, education, entertainment) are countless and unlimited. So people or organizations must choose among them. Economics is the study of how people (or organizations) can choose to use the scarce or limited resources to produce various good and services and distribute them to various members of society for them to consume. Contemporary Economics is largely built upon this Robbinsian understanding of Economics.

Is Economics a Science or an Art?

If we look at the above two equally famous definitions, we see that while Marshall regards it as a 'study of mankind', which is what Humanities is, Robbins sees it as a Science. Most universities award Bachelor of Arts and Master of Arts degrees for the study of Economics. In contrast, the London School of Economics offers BSc and MSc degrees to its students of Economics.

Indeed the scope of Economics is so wide that it is difficult to label it as either science or art. It is perhaps a mixture of both.

As Nobel Prize winner Paul Samuelson put it, "Not only is Economics at once art and a science, economics as a subject can combine the attractive features of both the humanities and the sciences".

But even if the epithet 'science' is given to Economics, it remains a Social Science. It is, to use Marshall's words, 'the study of mankind', of people as members of a society or nation or economy, acting and interacting among themselves in the complex process of production and exchange, consumption and distribution.

There is, of course, the concept of a Robinson Crusoe Economy where the country has just a single person performing all the economic activities by himself. The name is borrowed from the title of a book by Daniel Defoe on a man shipwrecked on an island. But this is merely an analytical tool to facilitate the understanding of the complex reality of an actual economy. Essentially, the subject Economics is social in character.

Is Economics Positive or Normative?

In 1953 Milton Friedman, in his Essays in Positive Economics, said that economists should not be Normative, that is, pass moral strictures or make 'value judgments'.

They should be Positive, that is, make propositions or statements such as: 'If the price of a commodity goes up, its quantity consumed falls, other things remaining the same' rather than: 'You stupid consumer! Don't go on buying more and more of this commodity when the price of it was going up.'

Even policy prescriptions or recommendations should be expressed in a calm, categorical way, such as: 'If there is inflation and the government prints more notes, the inflation is likely to get aggravated', instead of: 'The government should not do a mad thing like printing more notes when there is inflation in the country.'

What Subjects does Economics Relate to?

Mathematics and Statistics are tools of Economics, used for theoretical as well as empirical study. Pioneers like Alfred Marshall used verbal exposition as well as graphs to make their points, say, about the Demand Curve or the various Cost Curves. But in contemporary times it is impossible to study Economic Theory without knowledge of Mathematical Techniques such as geometry, algebra, calculus, set theory, matrices. However, Samuelson assures that it is only for "the higher reaches of economic theory" that mathematics is needed. For a general understanding, it is enough to be alert and informed. ".. Logical reasoning is the key to success in the mastery of basic economic principles, and shrewd weighing of empirical evidence is the key to success in mastery of economic applications."

Economics is both theoretical and empirical. For empirical analysis, the application of Statistics to Economics has led to the emergence of Econometrics. Most contemporary research in Economics is with the help of Econometrics.

Political Science too helps in the study Economics which originally was called 'Political Economy'. Knowledge of history and geography too are essential for a grasp of Economics. Sociology and History too are related areas. Economic History and Economic Geography have developed as subjects in their own right.

Other subjects or courses that have emerged from Economics are: Commerce, Business Economics, Business Administration, and Business Management. Undergraduate courses in Commerce and Business Economics compulsorily include courses/papers in Economics.

Microeconomics

In Greek, the words 'micro' and 'macro' mean small and huge, respectively. Microeconomics is the branch of Economics that studies economic issues in small, individual details, as if under a microscope. In contrast, Macro-Economic studies economic issues in aggregative and overall forms, looking at the broad picture. Classical economists like Adam Smith, J. B. Say, and David Ricardo had been concerned with the nation or the country as a whole, and drew their conclusions on an aggregative basis. Their analysis was more macro than micro in nature.

Neo-Classical economists like Alfred Marshall, Menger, W. S. Jevons were concerned with households and firms as individual rather than aggregative entities and used 'marginal' (small additional or incremental) units in their methodology. The 'margin' was the concept they used in their technique of study. The old-fashioned Neo-Classical theory of Marginal Utility, for example, says that the price of a commodity is decided by the additional 'utility' that a small additional unit of it yields. Microeconomics is Economics using the perspective of small, micro units.

The Term Macroeconomics

So far as modern Macro-economic (as distinct from Classical Economics which was macro in character), It started with John Maynard Keynes, after the Great Depression of the 1930s. During this Depression, both Europe and America suffered along with their colonies in various parts of the world. There was accumulation of unsold stock, closure of production units and widespread unemployment, both employers and employees were affected. Keynes analyzed the phenomenon in terms of Aggregate Demand falling short of Aggregate Supply and argued that under such circumstances if the Government of a country played an active role and stepped up its own expenditure, Aggregate Demand would be boosted and Depression corrected.

This was the beginning of modern Macroeconomics. Later John Hicks, Milton Friedman, Lucas and others have developed Macroeconomics to a very-well developed body of thoughts with many policy implications.

Micro Vs Macro

Is there any issue of Microeconomics versus Macroeconomic? Is either of the two more fundamental or important? Most universities make the students first take a course in Micro Economics and then go on to Macroeconomics. However some universities are now offering both courses in the same semester or academic year.

So far as undergraduate and even post-graduate studies are concerned, it is essential for students to first grasp the concepts of Microeconomics and then go over to those of Macroeconomics. For example, the concept of the 'margin' is first learnt through Marginal Utility, Marginal Rate of Substitution, Marginal Productivity etc. and only subsequently used through Marginal Propensities to Consume and Save. The concept of Consumer Equilibrium has to be learnt prior to its application in the box diagrams used, say, in the Heckscher-Ohlin Theorem of International Trade Theory.

So far as public policy making (governmental or even corporate) is concerned, Macroeconomics is more relevant. However, as Paul Samuelson has emphasized, that there is no essential opposition between Macroeconomics and Microeconomics. "Macroeconomics deals with the big picture – with the macro aggregates of income, employment, and price levels. But do not think that microeconomics deals with unimportant details. After all, the big picture is made up of its parts." He has also pointed out that both subjects are "vital" to the understanding of the subject.

Basic Areas of Microeconomics

Microeconomics falls into several broad areas:

- Consumer Choice and Demand: This deals with how an individual consumer (person or household) chooses what quantities he/she should buy at certain market prices so as to maximize satisfaction, i.e., how a Demand Curve or function is arrived at, for the individual and for the Market.

- Production – Cost, Revenue and Profit: This relates to how a productive unit, say, the firm, chooses, on the basis of cost considerations and revenue prospects, what quantity to produce and sell so as to maximize profits, i.e., how a Supply Curve or function is arrived at both individual and Market levels.

- Market - Structure and Strategy: Markets can be of various forms or structures, beginning with Perfect Competition, Monopolistic Competition, Oligopoly, Duopoly, Monopoly and , Monopsony). In addition to standard tools of Geometry and Calculus, Game Theory is often used to analyze the various strategies suitable for the various markets. So after the analysis of Consumption and Production, comes the analysis of Markets.

- Factor Payments, Risk and Uncertainty: This relates to the determination of payments for the various factors of production, such as rent, wages and profits, in terms of marginal productivity, reward for risk-taking etc.

- Welfare Economics: This relates to the maximization of satisfaction or welfare for the society rather than the individual. It encompasses situations of Market Failure, caused often by Externalities, as well as problems caused by information that is Asymmetric.

- International Trade: Like two or more individuals, countries too can come together in relations of production and exchange. This inter-national trade too is analyzed in Microeconomics, beginning with the theories of the Mercantilists and Adam Smith to more modern ones. The treatment however is different from that of Open Economies in Macroeconomics, say, by Mundell-Fleming.

Basic Economic Problem

The fundamental problem in economics is the issue with the scarcity of resources but unlimited wants. Economics has also pointed out that a man's need cannot be fulfilled. The more our needs are fulfilled, the more wants we develop with time. By definition, scarcity implies a limited quantity of resources. As a result of scarcity, there is constant opportunity cost. Opportunity cost means that if you use your resources to consume a particular good, you cannot consume any other good with the given resource. Therefore, economists are concerned with dealing with the optimum allocation of resources in society to make the usage of these resources efficient as well as practical.

What to Produce?

No country can produce all the goods because there are limited resources available to them. Therefore, a choice has to be made between the different types of commodities that a country can produce with its available resources. For instance, a farmer who has a piece of land can produce either wheat or rice. Similarly, the government of a country needs to decide where to allocate its resources whether in consumer goods or defence goods or both, if both, and then what will be the proportion of allocation of resources in the two categories of goods.

How to Produce?

This economic problem is concerned with the technique of producing a commodity. This problem arises only when there is more than one way of manufacturing goods. The techniques of production can be classified into two broad categories:

- Labour Intensive techniques (extensive use of labour).

- Capital Intensive techniques (extensive use of machinery).

Labour intensive technique is known to promote employment, whereas capital intensive techniques promote growth and efficiency in manufacturing.

For Whom to Produce?

All wants of people in a society cannot be satisfied. So, a decision has to be made on who should get the amount of total output of goods and services produced. Society decides on the amount of luxury and standard goods that have to be produced. The further distribution of these goods directly relates to the purchasing power of the economy.

How Market Mechanisms Solve the Basic Problems of an Economy?

All the three kind of economies, Capitalistic economy, Socialistic economy and Mixed economy, solve the basic problems of an economy in two methods:

- Free price mechanism.

- Controlled price system which is also called State intervention.

The Basic Problem of an Economy and Free Price Mechanism

A system of guiding the decisions of individuals within an economy through the price which is determined with the help of market forces of demand and supply is called price mechanism. This system is free of any government intervention. When the market equilibrium is reached by market forces of demand and supply, i.e. the quantity supplied becomes equal to the quantity demanded, then the price of a commodity is determined. Price mechanism also facilitates the determination of resource allocation, consumption and production as well as determining the level of savings and factor income. This method mostly takes place in a capitalistic economy.

The Basic Problem of an Economy and State Intervention System

This system is defined by administering the fixed prices of every commodity. In a socialist economy, the government plays a vital role in determining the price of commodities. Ceiling price or floor price may be introduced by the government to regulate the prices of certain commodities.

Examples of the Economic Problem

Consumers

Households have limited income and they need to decide how to spend their finite income. For example, with an annual income of £20,000, a household may need to spend £10,000 a year on rent, council tax and utility bills. This leaves £10,000 for deciding which other food, clothes, transport and other goods to purchase.

Workers

Householders will also face decisions on how much to work. For example, working overtime at the weekend will give them extra income to spend, but less leisure time to enjoy it. A worker may also wish to spend more time in learning new skills and qualifications. This may limit their earning power in the short-term, but enable a greater earning power in the long-term. For example, at 18 a student could go straight into work or they could go to university where they will hope to gain a degree and more earning power in the long-term.

Producers

A producer needs to remain profitable (revenue higher than costs). So it will need to produce the goods which are in high demand and respond to changing demands and buying habits of consumers – for example, switching to online sales as the high street declines. Producers will need to constantly ask the best way of producing goods. For example, purchasing new machines can increase productivity and enable the firms to produce goods at a lower cost. This is important for fast-changing industries where new technology is frequently reducing costs of production. Without firms adapting to how they produce, they can become unprofitable. Firms may also need to make long-term investment decisions to invest in new products and new means of production.

Government

The government has finite resources and its spending power is limited by the amount of tax that they can collect. The government needs to decide how they collect tax and then they need to decide whom they spend money on. For example, the government may wish to cut benefits to those on low income to increase incentives to work. However, cutting benefits will increase inequality and relative poverty.

Cardinal Utility Theory

Demand of a good refers to the quantity which the consumers can buy at different prices and at different level of money income. Here it is important to differentiate between the desires/ want for a commodity with the ability to buy it. The desire of a person to buy is something which he wants to buy but whether he can buy that or not depend on the money income which he has. Hence demand is not a want or desire to buy something; it is the ability of a person to buy different things at different prices given his money income.

Demand depends on various factors like the price of the good; the price of the other related good, income of the consumers, taste and preferences of the consumers, government policies etc. but the main problem for a consumer is to determine how much quantity of each good to buy and at what price in their current income?

The answer lies in the Theory of consumer behavior. According to theory of consumer behavior/demand, a consumer always consumes and demands that much quantity of a good which maximizes his utility. Here, by utility we mean the satisfaction derived from a commodity, which is even there before consuming that commodity, but it can only be felt after consuming the commodity; in fact utility is the only thing which induces a person to consume a good. Hence the level of satisfaction comes only after consuming the good. But the next question is how to measure the utility? For this there are two schools of thoughts. One was given by the neoclassical economists as the Cardinal utility theory and the other was given by the modern economists as the ordinal utility theory.

Cardinal utility approach was originally given by Marshall. According to him, utility can be measured in utils, where utils is a scale like 1,2,3, and so on where one can measure his level of satisfaction or utility. Whereas, ordinal utility approach was given by Hicks where the utility cannot be measured in cardinal approach rather it could be measured in terms of ranks or orders. For instance, the highest satisfaction/utility level would be given the highest rank and the lesser satisfaction/utility could be given lesser rank in terms of measurement of utility and so on.

Theory of consumer behavior attempts to seek the consumption of goods which maximize consumer's utility. It also helps a consumer in his decision making about how to allocate his consumption expenditure on different goods so that his total utility could be maximized. But before moving ahead in the theory of consumer behavior based on cardinal approach it is important to know the assumption of this approach.

Assumptions

- Rationality: A consumer is always rational i.e. he always prefers more of goods and services to derive maximum utility. Thus he always buys the commodity which gives him maximum utility first and then he buys the least utility giving commodity at the end.

- Finite money income: The consumers have limited money income which they spend on the purchase of all the goods and services for their living. Thus they allocate this income as their consumption expenditure on all goods and services.

- Cardinal utility: The utility derived from the consumption of each good is measureable in terms of utils which is in turn equal to the money a consumer is willing to pay for it i.e. 1 util = utility of 1 unit of money.

- Constant marginal utility of money: The utility of each unit of money spent on buying the good remains the same i.e. one.

- Diminishing marginal utility: According to this, utility derived from the consumption of each successive unit of the good diminishes. As we consume more of a good the utility derived from each successive unit of it decreases (although the total utility from the consumption of the total quantity of good increases). This is also known as 'Gossen's first law'. Note that here each successive unit of the good is homogeneous in nature.

- Additive utility: According to this, the utility derived from the consumption of all goods and services is additive in nature. Therefore, the utility function of a basket 'n', comprising of various goods and services, is represented as follows: $U = f(x_1, x_2, x_3, ..., x_n)$.

  Here, $x_1, x_2, x_3, ..., x_n$ are the quantity of different goods and services consumed by the consumer with his limited money income.

  Now based on this, the total utility function of n items is additive and can be written as: $TU = U_1(x_1) + U_2(x_2) + U_3(x_3) + ... + U_n(x_4)$.

Concept of Total Utility and Marginal Utility

Total utility refers to the sum of utility derived from the consumption of each unit of a good. Since as per the cardinal approach utility can be measured, hence Total utility can also be measured in utils and in monetary terms. Algebraically: $TU = U_1 + U_2 + U_3 + ... + U_n = U_N$.

Marginal utility is defined as the utility derived from the last unit consumed. It is also defined as the utility derived from the consumption of each successive unit of the same good. More precisely, Marginal utility is the change in the total utility due to an additional unit consumed. Algebraically:

$$MU = \Delta TU/\Delta Q$$

$$\text{Or, } MU = TU_n - TU_{n-1}$$

Where, TU_n is the total utility derived from the consumption of n units of a good and TU_{n-1} is the total utility derived from the n-1 unit of the same good. This can be explained with the help of the following table.

Quantity (in units)	Total utility (in utils)	Marginal utility (utils)
0	0	-
1	40	40
2	70	30
3	90	20
4	100	10
5	100	0
6	90	- 10

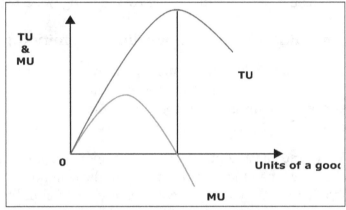

Total utility and Marginal utility.

The above table and the above figure clearly show that initially the total utility increases as we consume a good but as we consume more of a good it increases but at a diminishing rate as in we can see from the table and from the figure that initially the total utility increases to 40 and then to 70 to 90 to 100 but the marginal utility first increases by 40 and then by 30 ($TU_n - TU_{n-1}$; 70 - 40 = 30) then by 20 and then by just 10.

However, when the total utility reaches to its maximum i.e. at 100 then it started falling as the consumer increases his consumption; correspondingly the marginal utility becomes zero and then negative. Note that the point where the total utility reaches its maximum is the point where the marginal utility becomes zero and thereafter when the consumer increases his consumption of the goods again then total utility decreases and marginal utility goes negative.

Thus we can conclude that there exists the following relationship between the total utility and marginal utility:

- Total utility increases initially at an increasing rate first and marginal utility also increases.

- Thereafter total utility increases at a diminishing rate and marginal utility diminishes.

- When total utility reaches to its maximum, marginal utility becomes zero.

- When more of the units of the good is consumed even after achieving the highest level of total utility, then the total utility decreases and correspondingly marginal utility becomes negative.

Consumer Equilibrium Under Cardinal Approach

After talking about the assumptions and the total utility and marginal utility concept, we can now evaluate the consumer equilibrium according to the cardinal approach. As a general rule, a consumer is always in equilibrium at a point where he maximizes his Total Utility. This can be explained with the help of following two cases.

Case I: Consumer Equilibrium Under Single Commodity Case

Suppose that the consumer is having his money income and can consume only one commodity 'X'. In this case, he has only two choices; either spend his money income on the commodity or can retain his money income with himself where both of his money income and the commodity 'X' has a certain utility for him.

If he retains all of his income and purchase no commodity then the Marginal Utility of money would be lower than the marginal utility of the commodity because $MU_m = 1$(as per assumption). Thus the consumer can increase his total utility by exchanging his money income with the consumption of the commodity (as the marginal utility of the commodity is greater) as far as $MU_x > MU_m$. Moreover, as it has been stated in the assumptions above that X has a diminishing marginal utility and money has a constant marginal utility, therefore, the utility maximizing consumer will exchange his money income for commodity X as long as $MU_x > MU_m$ and will reach to his equilibrium level of consumption when $MU_x = MU_m$. However the prices of the commodities are generally greater than Rs.1, therefore, in this case the consumer equilibrium can be expressed as: $MU_x = P_x(MU_m)$, where $MU_m = 1$.

Hence, consumer equilibrium in case of single commodity occurs at a point where the consumer's $MU_x = P_x$. This can be represented graphically as follows:

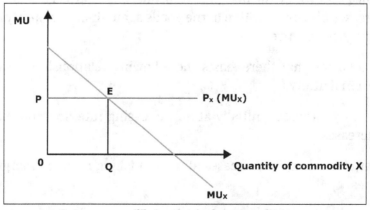

Consumer equilibrium in single commodity case.

Hence, the condition for the equilibrium is: $MU_x = P_x$

- If $MU_x > P_x$, the consumer can increase welfare by purchasing more of x commodities.

- If $MU_x < P_x$, the consumer can increase his total satisfaction by cutting down his purchase of x commodities.

- If $MU_x = P_x$, the consumer will be in equilibrium.

Case II: Consumer Equilibrium Under Multiple Commodity Case

In a real world, the consumer just does not spend on purchasing only one commodity. In order to make his living and fulfill his demand, a consumer always demands many commodities. We have earlier seen how he determines his equilibrium level of consumption when he just demands only one commodity. Let's now check out how the equilibrium of a utility maximizing consumer determined when he purchases several commodities.

As we know that different commodities are different so the utility derived by them would also be different. Some commodities would give the consumer the highest level of satisfaction or maximum utility where as some would give him second highest or even lesser utility. In such a condition the consumer keeps on switching his allocation of money income on different commodities as per their MU. He keeps on switching his consumption expenditure from one commodity to other till the MU of all the commodities becomes equals to each other. This is also known as the concept of equi marginal utility.

Let us now explain the law of equi marginal utility with the help of two commodities case.

In such a situation, suppose the consumer consumes only two commodities 'X' and 'Y' by spending his finite money income. The prices of the commodity 'X' is given as "P_x" and that of commodity 'Y' is given as "P_y". If we just apply the same concept which we have applied in Case I above, then as per that $MU_x = P_x(MU_m)$ and $MU_y = P_y(MU_m)$.

Now, $MU_x = P_x(MU_m)$

Or, $MU_x/P_x(MU_m) = 1$

Similarly, $MU_y = P_y(MU_m)$

Or, $MU_y/P_y(MU_m) = 1$

Therefore, from previous two equations, we get:

$MU_x/P_x(MU_m) = MU_y/P_y(MU_m) = 1$

Or, $MU_x/MU_y = P_x(MU_m)/P_y(MU_m)$

Or, $MU_x/MU_y = P_x/P_y$

Or, $MU_x/P_x = MU_y/P_y$

Thus, according to the above discussion, a utility maximizing consumer is in equilibrium under two commodity case at the consumption level where his $MU_x/MU_y = P_x/P_y$ or $MU_x/P_x = MU_y/P_y$.

Hence, accordingly, a consumer consuming multiple commodities (in his given money income) would maximize his utility at a point where, his $MU_x/P_x = MU_y/P_y = MU_z/P_z$ = ... MU_n/P_n. In other words, a utility maximizing consumer would be in equilibrium where the MU derived from each commodity is equal to each other i.e. where he equalizes the MU of each unit of his money expenditure on various goods and services.

Derivation of Demand Curve

The main purpose of studying the theory of consumer behavior is to derive the demand curve of the consumers. In order to derive the demand curve by the cardinal approach, we have to consider the single commodity case, where the consumer reaches to his equilibrium at the point where $MU_x = P_x$.

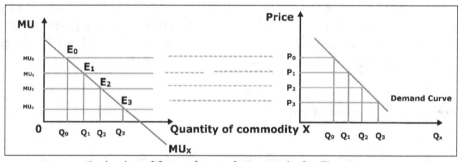

Derivation of demand curve from marginal utility curve.

The left hand panel shows the equilibrium of the consumer under cardinal approach. It shows that if the price of the commodity changes then the equilibrium quantity where the consumer maximizes his utility ($MU_x = P_x$) also changes. Suppose that the consumer is in equilibrium at point E_0, where given the price of X at P_0, $MU_x = P_0$. Here, the equilibrium quantity is OQ_0. Now, if the price of the commodity falls to P_1 the equilibrium condition will be disturbed making $MU_x > P_0$. Since MU_m is constant, the only way to attain the equilibrium again is to reduce MUx. This can be done only by buying more of commodity X. Thus, by consuming Q_0Q_1 additional units of X he reduces his MU_x to E_1Q_1 and, thereby, restores equilibrium condition, i.e., $MU_x = P_1$. Similarly, if the price falls further, he buys and consumes more to maximize his satisfaction.

As we can see from the left panel that as the price of the commodity falls, from P_0 to P_3, the equilibrium quantity where the consumer maximizes his utility increases (as each price line intersects with the MU_x curve at different equilibrium points which in turn gives the corresponding increasing equilibrium quantities).

However, when we stretch the equilibrium points derived at left panel to the right then we can see from the right panel that as the price is decreasing the quantity of the commodity consumed is increasing, which is depicting the law of demand. Hence joining all the equilibrium points, we get the demand curve at the right panel, which is downward sloping i.e. showing a negative relationship between the price and the quantity of the commodity.

Drawbacks of the Cardinal Approach

Although cardinal utility approach analyzes the consumer behavior in a easy and simple way but still the economists have drawn some of the drawbacks of this approach. Following are some of those drawbacks of the cardinal utility theory which were pointed out by the economists:

- First, the assumption of cardinal utility approach that utility is measurable in utils and in monetary terms is very dissatisfying. Utility is a subjective concept which cannot be measured quantifiably. It can always be measured by giving preferences for each level of utility.

- Secondly, cardinal utility approach assumes that marginal utility of money remains constant and it also serves as a measure of utility. This assumption is also unrealistic because the marginal utility of money can also change, like all other goods; thus it cannot serve as a measure of utility derived from goods and services.

- Thirdly, the psychological law of diminishing MU has been established from introspection. This law is accepted as an axiom/ proverb without any practical confirmation.

- Fourthly, cardinal utility approach and derivation of demand curve on the basis of this approach are based on the ceteris paribus assumption which is unrealistic. It is for this reason that this theory ignores the substitution and income effects which might operate simultaneously.

- Finally, cardinal approach considers that the effect of price changes on demand curve is exclusively price effect. This assumption is also unrealistic because price effect may include income and substitution effects also.

Indifference Curve Theory

The theory of consumer behavior based on the ordinal approach was propounded by J.R. Hicks and R.G.D. Allen in 1934. According to this approach, utility cannot be measured in any quantifiable number. It could only be measured by giving order, ranks or preferences. Hence the ordinal utility means consumers preferences or choice for one commodity or for a basket of goods over the other. Here, the preferences could be expressed in terms of 'more' or 'less' preferable. Moreover, since the consumers have a limited income which they can spend on their consumption, therefore, in this approach, a consumer will prefer a basket of goods over the other given the prices of the goods and the income of the consumer.

Assumptions of Ordinal Utility Theory

- Rationality: A consumer is always rational i.e. he always prefers more of goods and services to derive maximum utility. Thus he always buys the commodity which gives him maximum utility first and then he buys the least utility giving commodity at the end.

- Finite money income: The consumers have limited money income which they spend on the purchase of all the goods and services for their living. Thus they allocate this income as their consumption expenditure on all goods and services.

- Ordinal utility: The utility derived from the consumption of each good or a basket of goods could be measured ordinally by giving preferences for each good over the other.

- Transitivity and consistency of choice: Consumer's preferences are always transitive i.e., if a consumer prefers good X over good Y and the same consumer prefers good Y over good Z then according to this assumption of transitivity, he must prefer good X over good Z also.

    If, $X > Y$

    If, $Y > Z$

Therefore, $X > Z$.

Whereas as per consistency of choice, if a consumer prefers good X to good Y in one period then he must not prefer good Y to good X in another period or must not treat both the goods as equal. Symbolically,

    If, $X > Y$ in one period.

Then, $Y > X$ or $Y \neq X$ in other period.

- Non Satiety: According to this, a consumer always prefers more of a good or larger quantity of all the goods because he has not reached the saturation level nor he is oversupplied with all the goods.

- Diminishing marginal rate of substitution: Marginal rate of substitution refers to the rate at which a consumer substitute one good X for the other good Y so that the level of utility/satisfaction obtained from it remains the same to him. Symbolically, MRS = $\Delta X/\Delta Y$ or $\Delta Y/\Delta X$. According to this assumption, as a consumer continues to substitute X for Y or Y for X, his MRS diminishes/decreases.

Indifference Curve

Indifference curve is defined as the locus of the points of the different combinations of different goods which gives an equal level of satisfaction to the consumer. Therefore a consumer is indifferent between any of the combination which lies on the same indifference curve. This happens because the consumer has a power to substitute among various goods, given their prices and his income level.

For simplicity let's take the example of two goods x and y. Now given the income of the consumer and the prices of x and y, the consumer can choose different combinations of x and y to be consumed in order to maximize his satisfaction. All those combinations of x and y which gives an equal utility to the consumer forms an indifference curve (as in the following fig). Moreover the consumer can substitute between x and y and thus can either consume more of x or more of y but the main point is that the level of satisfaction arising from the different combination of x and y remains the same to him.

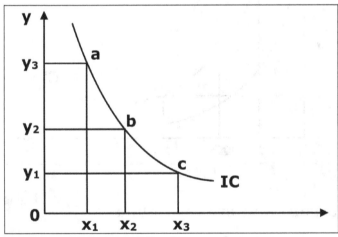

Indifference curve.

As has been depicted in the above figure, that at point 'a' the consumer consumes y_3 and x_1 combination of goods, whereas at point 'b' he substitute y with x and the combination at point 'b' becomes x_2 and y_2, similarly at point 'c' the consumer consumes x_3 and y_1 combination of both the goods, given his income and P_x and P_y. However all the points, a, b and c, gives the consumer equal level of satisfaction. Hence, he is indifferent among a, b and c. Therefore, the curve joining a, b and c is known as indifference curve, where the consumer is indifferent of the different choice which he has as they all gives him equal level of satisfaction. Here only the combinations of x and y are different at each point but the level of satisfaction which the consumer obtained from them is the same.

Now if the consumer either consumes more of a good or of both the goods then he would be able to increase his level of satisfaction and thus a new IC would be drawn above this IC which represents the different combinations of x and y (higher than the previous combinations) which gives him the same level of satisfaction (higher than the previous level of satisfaction).

Similarly a lower IC would represent the combinations of x and y (lesser than the previous combinations) which gives him equal satisfaction (lesser than the previous level of satisfaction).

Hence the higher an IC, the higher is the level of satisfaction and the lower the IC, the lesser is the level of satisfaction obtained by the consumer.

Representation of the different combinations of goods and different levels of satisfaction on a graph is known as an Indifference map.

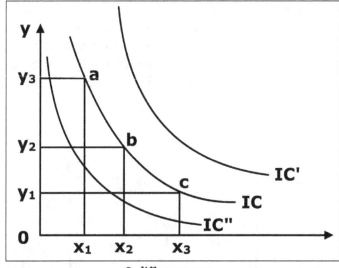

Indifference map.

Concept of Marginal Rate of Substitution

Marginal rate of substitution is defined as the rate at which a consumer substitutes one good for the other obtaining the same level of satisfaction. In this case, it is the rate at which a consumer substitute good y with good x in order to get the same level of satisfaction.

Symbolically, $MRS_{yx} = \Delta y/\Delta x$ or $MRS_{xy} = \Delta x/\Delta y$

MRS is also known as the slope of the IC.

As we can see from the diagram below, that as the consumer consumes more of x, he reduces the quantity of y from y_3 to y_2 in order to get the same level of satisfaction. Similarly, he further substitute y from y_2 to y_1 with good x in order to get more of x and the same level of satisfaction. This rate of change in y due to the increase in the quantity of x by one unit is known as Marginal rate of substitution (MRS).

As we can see, an IC has a diminishing MRS, means that the consumer substitute x for y at a diminishing rate. In other words, as the consumer increases the consumption of x by one unit, their consumption of y reduces at a decreasing rate. Hence we can say that an IC has a diminishing slope.

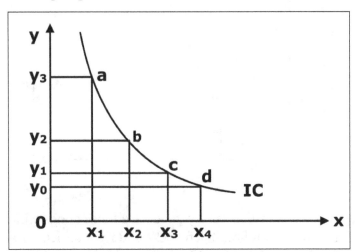

Diminishing marginal rate of substitution.

As we can see that $\Delta x_1 = \Delta x_2 = \Delta x_3 = \Delta x_4$ but $\Delta y_0 < \Delta y_1 < \Delta y_2 < \Delta y_3$.

This MRS falls because of the following reasons:

- Diminishing M.

- The decline in the ability of the consumer to sacrifice a commodity whose quantity goes on declining.

Properties of Indifference Curve

- IC's have a negative slope because of the diminishing MRS.

- IC's never intersect with each other else they will break the assumption of transitivity.

- IC is convex to origin for the imperfect substitute goods.

- A higher IC represents higher level of satisfaction.

Different Shapes of Indifference Curves

1. Substitute goods: Substitute goods are those goods which give the same utility to the consumers i.e. they can be substituted in place of their related good as they possess

almost same characteristics like their related good. In other words, two goods are considered as substitute goods for one another when the utility derived from both of them is same. For instance wheat and rice, coke and pepsi etc. Therefore the MRS between substitute goods is constant as $\Delta y = \Delta x$, so MRS = $\Delta y / \Delta x$. in this case we can write MRS = $\Delta x / \Delta x$ (because $\Delta y = \Delta x$), therefore, MRS = 1.

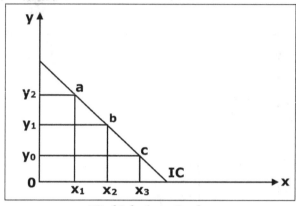

IC of Substitute Goods.

2. Complimentary goods: Complimentary goods are those goods which are consumed in fixed proportions like pen and refill, left socks and right socks, car and petrol etc. In such a case if we even increase the quantity of one good the quantity of other good does not increase, hence, MRS = 0.

Symbolically, MRS = $\Delta y = \Delta x$

But in such a case $\Delta y = 0$, $\Delta x = 1$

Thus, MRS = $0/1 = 0$.

Graphically,

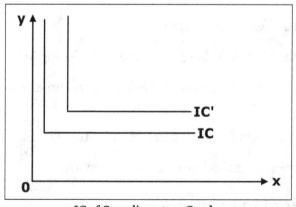

IC of Complimentary Goods.

3. One good is necessary: In case of one good is a necessary good without which we cannot survive like water, then in such a case the shape of the IC would be like follows:

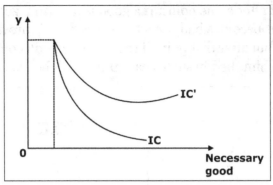

IC of Necessary Goods.

4. In case of a BAD good: A bad good is defined as a good whose excess is bad for the consumption i.e. if the consumer will consume more of it then his utility would decrease, for instance cigarette (for a mediocre or nonsmoker). In such a case the shape of the IC is as follows:

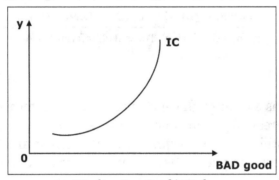

IC when One Good is Bad.

In order to draw an IC always find out the worst point of both the goods and then bend the IC towards that common worst point. As in, in this case, the worst of y is 0 however the worst of BAD is the excess, therefore the IC bend away from 0 towards x axis.

5. In case of a neutral good: Neutral goods are those goods which neither yield utility nor disutility to its consumers. Thus a consumer is indifferent to its consumption. In such a case the IC will be a straight line as shown below.

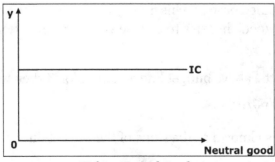

IC for a Neutral Goods.

6. A good turning bad after some point: If a good is a normal good till some point and then after that point it becomes bad for its consumer i.e. it provides utility to its consumer till some point but after that point if the consumer still consumes it then it starts providing disutility to him then in such a case the IC will be like:

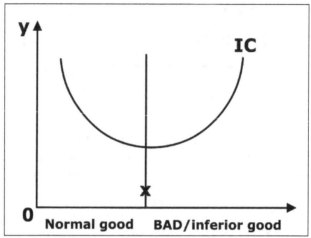

IC for a Good which Turns Bad/Inferior Good.

Concept of Budget Line

We have seen that IC is tool through which a consumer can measure his utility of consuming goods. But in real life, a consumer is always constrained with two things in order to maximize his utility. One is his limited money income and the other is the price of the commodities. Both limited money income and prices of the goods act as a constraint to the utility maximizing behavior of the consumer. This is known as budgetary constraint. Symbolically:

$$Px*X + Py*Y \leq M$$

This equation is known as budget line of a consumer, where Px and Py are the price of the two goods X and Y, X and Y are the respective quantities of X and Y which a consumer consumes given his money income M and prices of these goods.

Hence according to this budget line a consumer always decide about how much quantity of goods to be consumed based on his money income and the prices of the consumer. Then from this set of goods he tries to choose which combination would give him the maximum utility.

Now if we just adjust the above budget line equation for X then we get:

$$X = M/Px - Y*Py/PX$$

Here this −Py/Px is also known as the slope of the budget line.

Now if X=0, then Y= M/Py and if Y=0, then X= M/Px.

Plotting these points on a graph we get the following curve as the budget line:

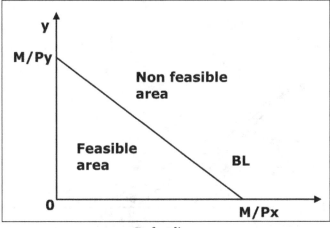

Budget line.

Hence as per the budget line all the points which come inside or on the budget line represents a feasible area as given the income of the consumer and prices of the goods the consumer can consume any combination. But if the combination costs more than his given income then that will fall outside the budget line, which is represented by infeasible area in the above graph.

Thus, the budget line is drawn based on the money income of the consumer and the prices of the goods, therefore, if any of these factors changes then the budget line will also change.

If the money income of the consumer changes then the budget line will shift either outside or inside as follows:

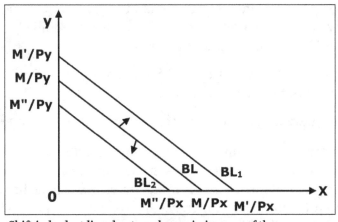

Shift in budget line due to a change in income of the consumer.

As it can be clearly seen from the above diagram, if the money income of the consumer changes from M to M', the budget line moves upward as now with more of his income he can consume more of both the goods and vice a versa.

Now if the prices of the goods changes then it will pivot the budget line as follows:

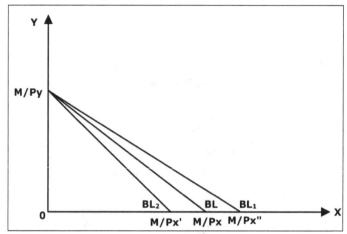

Change in the budget line due to a change in the price of the commodity X.

As it can be clearly seen from the above graph that if the price of X increases from Px to Px', then given his money income M, he will reduce the consumption of X as now X has become expensive. However he will continue consuming the same quantity of Y. Hence the budget line will pivot inward to B$_2$.

Similarly, if the price of X reduces from Px to Px" then he can increase his consumption of X as now given his money income M, X has become relatively cheaper. Hence the budget line will pivot outward to BL$_1$.

Consumer Equilibrium: Ordinal Approach

A consumer attains equilibrium at a point where he maximizes his utility from the consumption of goods, given his money income and the prices of the goods. According to the ordinal utility analysis two sets of conditions must be fulfilled for a consumer to attain equilibrium. These two conditions are as follows:

- Necessary condition: As per this MRS must be equal to Px/Py, i.e. the slope of budget line must be equal to the slope of the IC.

- Sufficient condition: The necessary condition must prevail on the highest IC.

As we can see that the equilibrium takes place on IC', it does not take place at IC nor on IC". The reason for this is that IC comes in the feasible area under the budget line but the consumer does not maximize his utility on IC because he has a higher income and thus using that income he can increase his consumption of both the goods and can move to IC'. So on IC' both the necessary as well as sufficient conditions apply. However, if he further moves from IC' to IC" then all those combinations lying on IC" are not feasible because his money income is less. All the points on IC" would definitely give the consumer a higher utility as compare to the combinations lying on

IC' but the combinations on IC" are not attainable. Hence the consumer equilibrium cannot take place on IC" too.

Hence, consumer equilibrium is attained where the above mentioned two conditions prevails. This is illustrated as follows:

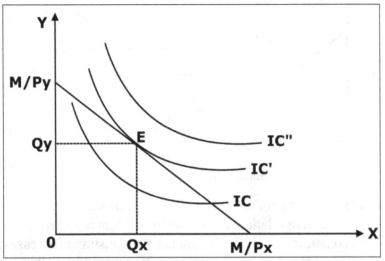

Consumer equilibrium: Ordinal approach.

As represented in the above diagram, 'E' is the equilibrium point where the slope of the budget line and that of the IC is the same. Thus, the consumer will consume Qx and Qy quantity of X and Y in order to maximize his utility, given his money income M and the prices of X and Y as Px and Py.

The Effect of Change in Income on Consumer Equilibrium

As we have seen that consumer equilibrium happens at the point where the IC is tangent on the budget line. But when the income of the consumer changes then the budget line also changes and correspondingly the IC also changes. For instance, if the income of the consumer increases then the budget line will shift upward. This represents that now the consumer can afford more of both the goods hence his IC will also shift and the tangency of the new IC with this new budget line gives new consumer equilibrium. Similarly if the process will go on then the equilibrium points will keep on changing. If we connect all these equilibrium point with a line, then this line joining all the equilibrium points is known as income consumption curve, which shows the changes in the consumer equilibrium due to a change in the income of the consumer. This is represented in the following diagram.

The above is the case of the normal goods. Here normal goods are the goods which show a positive relationship between the demand of the good and the income of the consumer, i.e. if the income of the consumer increases, his demand for normal good also increases and vice versa.

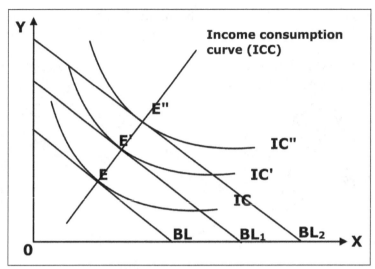

Income consumption curve.

However, in case of inferior goods, the ICC would not be upward sloping because inferior goods shows an inverse relationship between the demand of the inferior good and the income of the consumer, i.e. if the income of the consumer increases, his demand for the inferior good reduces. In such a case the ICC would be downward sloping, as given below:

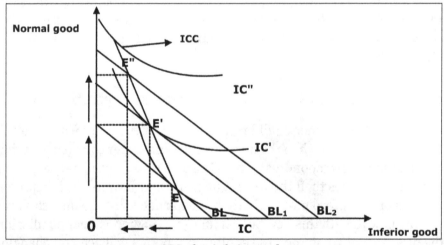

ICC of an inferior good.

As has been represented in the above diagram, as the income of the consumer increases his demand for the inferior good reduces and that of normal good increases. Hence based on this his budget line is shifting and IC is also increasing but the combination which he chooses for each increased income comprises of less of inferior good and more of normal good in order to maximize his utility.

ICC is also known as Engel curve. We can further derive the demand curve for a good based on his ICC.

Here we are only showing how to derive the demand curve of the normal good. You can derive the demand curve of the inferior good in the same way.

Let us now derive the demand curve from the ICC of a normal good:

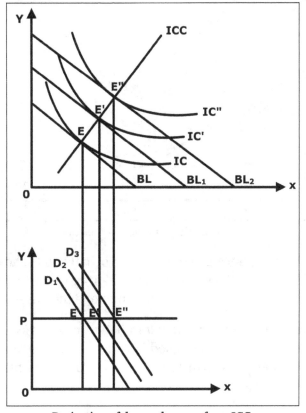

Derivation of demand curves form ICC.

Clearly, for a given price of a good, if the income of the consumer increases, he demands more of good X. This gives point E, E' and E" and three different demand curves emerges with ICC for good X.

Here we can see that the demand curve is downward sloping, representing an inverse relationship between the price and quantity of the good.

The Effect of Change in Prices of the Goods on Consumer Equilibrium

If the price of any of the good changes, then, this leads to a change in the consumer equilibrium too. For instance, if the price of X falls, then this will make X relatively cheaper and the consumer will demand more of X and same quantity of Y and thus this will pivot his budget line outward. But when budget line pivots then consumer will change his combination of goods which will maximize his consumption. Now his new basket of goods will comprise of more of X and less or same quantity of Y, hence his IC will shift upward too. The tangency of the new IC with the new budget line gives the new equilibrium point of the consumer. Joining all such points, gives the price consumption curve (PCC). This is depicted in the following diagram:

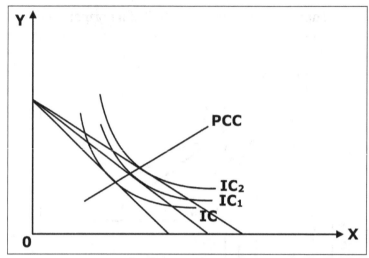

Price Consumption Curve.

The above is the case of the normal good, where normal goods shows the inverse relationship between the price of the good and the quantity of the good, i.e. if the price of the consumer falls it's quantity consumed or demanded increases.

However if there exists a positive relationship between the price of the good and the quantity of the good then that type of good is known as Giffen good. In such a case if the price of the Giffen good falls its quantity also falls. This is depicted in the following diagram:

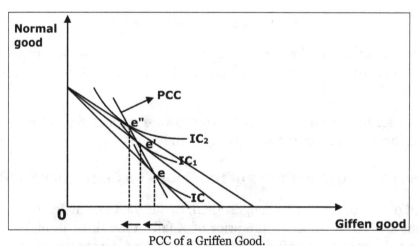

PCC of a Griffen Good.

In the above diagram we can see that if the price of the Giffen good falls the budget line pivots outward but the quantity demanded of the Giffen good reduces. And hence the points joining the consumer equilibrium i.e. e, e', e" gives a downward sloping PCC. We can also derive the demand curve with the help of PCC in the following way.

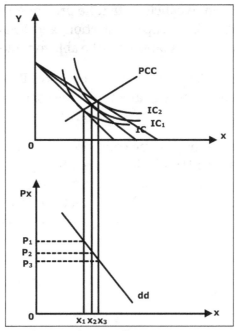

Derivation of Demand Curves Form PCC.

The above graph clearly shows that as the price of X reduces, budget line pivots outside and then the quantity of x increases, when these points drawn below then they form demand curve for X.

Revealed Preference Theory

Prof. Samuelson has invented an alternative approach to the theory of consumer behaviour which, in principle, does not require the consumer to supply any information about himself.

If his tastes do not change, this theory, known as the Revealed Preference Theory (RPT), permits us to find out all we need to know just by observing his market behaviour, by seeing what he buys at different prices, assuming that his acquisitions and buying experiences do not change his preference patterns or his purchase desires.

Given enough such information, it is even theoretically possible to reconstruct the consumer's indifference map.

Samuelson's RPT is based on a rather simple idea. A consumer will decide to buy some particular combination of items either because he likes it more than the other combinations that are available to him or because it happens to be cheap. Let us suppose, we observe that of two collections of goods offered for sale, the consumer chooses to buy A, but not B.

We are then not in a position to conclude that he prefers A to B, for it is also possible that he buys A, because A is the cheaper collection, and he actually would have been happier if he got B. But price information may be able to remove this uncertainty.

If their price tags tell us that A is not cheaper than B (or, B is no-more expensive than A), then there is only one plausible explanation of the consumer's choice—he bought A because he liked it better.

More generally, if a consumer buys some collection of goods, A, rather than any of the alternative collections B, C and D and if it turns out that none of the latter collections is more expensive than A, then we say that A has been revealed preferred to the combinations B, C and D or that B, C and D have been revealed inferior to A.

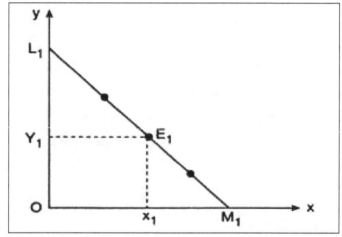

Revealed Preference.

Therefore, if the consumer buys the combination $E_1(x_1, y_1)$ of the goods X and Y and does not buy the combination $E_2(x_2, y_2)$ at the prices (p^1_x, p^1_y) of the goods, then we would be able to say that he prefers combination E_1 to combination E_2, if we obtain:

$$p^1_x x_1 + p^1_y y_1 \geq p^1_x x_2 + p^1_y y_2$$

The complete set of combinations of the goods X and Y to which a particular combination is revealed preferred can be found with the aid of the consumer's price line. Let us suppose that the consumer's budget line is $L_1 M_1$ in figure and he is observed to purchase the combination $E_1(x_1, y_1)$ that lies on this line.

Now, since the costs of all the combinations that lie on the budget line are the same as that of E_1 and since the costs of all the combinations that lie below and to the left of the budget line are lower than that of E_1 we may say that E_1 is revealed preferred to all the combinations lying on or below the consumer's budget line.

Again, since the costs of the combinations that lie above and to the right of the budget line are higher than that of E_1 we cannot say that the consumer prefers E_1 to these combinations when he is observed to buy E_1, because here E_1 is the cheaper combination.

We have to note here the difference between "preference" and "revealed preference". Combination A is "preferred" to B implies that the consumer ranks A ahead of B.

But A is "revealed preferred to B" means A is chosen when B is affordable (no-more-expensive). In our model of consumer behavior, we generally assume that people are choosing the best combination they can afford that the choices they make are preferred to the choices that they could have made. That is, if $(x_1 y_1)$ is directly revealed preferred to (x_2, y_2), then (x_1, y_1) is, in fact, preferred to (x_2, y_2).

Let us now state the RP principle more formally:

Let us suppose, the consumer is buying the combination (x_1, y_1) at the price set (p'_x, P'_y) let us also suppose that another combination is (x_2, y_2), such that $p'x_1 + p'_y y_1 \geq p'_x x_2 + p'_y y_2$. Now, if the consumer buys the most preferred combination subject to his budget constraint, then we will say the combination (x_1, y_1) is strictly preferred to combination (x_2, y_2).

The Assumptions:

With the help of the simple principle of RP, we may build up a powerful theory of consumer demand. The assumptions that we shall make here are:

1. The consumer buys and uses only two goods (X and Y). The quantities x and y of these goods are continuous variables.

2. Both these goods are of MIB (more-is-better) type. This assumption is also known as the assumption of monotonicity. This assumption implies that the ICs of the consumer are negatively sloped.

3. The consumer's preferences are strictly convex. This assumption implies that the ICs of the consumer would be convex to the origin, which again implies that there would be obtained only one point (the point of tangency) on the budget line of the consumer that would be chosen by him over all other affordable combinations.

This assumption is very important. On the basis of this assumption, we shall obtain a one- to-one relation between the consumer's price-income situation or budget line and his equilibrium choice—for any particular budget line of the consumer, there would be obtained one and only one equilibrium combination of goods and for any combination to be an equilibrium one, there would be obtained one and only one budget line.

4. The fourth assumption of the RP theory is known as the weak axiom of RP (WARP). Here we assume that if the consumer chooses the combination $E_1(x_1, y_1)$ over another affordable combination $E_2(x_2, y_2)$ in a particular price-income situation, then under no circumstances would he choose E_2 over E_1 if E_1 is affordable.

In other words, if a combination E_1 is revealed preferred to E_2, then, under no circumstances, E_2 can be revealed preferred to E_1.

5. The fifth assumption of the RP theory is known as the strong axiom of RP (SARP). According to this assumption, if the consumer, under different price-income situations, reveals the combination E_1 as preferred to E_2, E_2 to E_3,..., E_{k-1} to E_k, then E_1 would be revealed preferred to E_k and E_k would never (under no price-income situation) be revealed preferred to E_1.

Revealed Preference: Direct and Indirect

If RP is confined to only two combinations of goods, E_1 and E_2, and if, in a particular price- income situation, E_1 (x_1, y_1) is revealed preferred to combination E_2 (x_2, y_2), then it is said that E_1 is directly revealed preferred to E_2.

But if preferences are considered for more than two combinations and if preferences are established by way of transitivity of RP, then it is a case of indirectly revealed preference. For example, if E_1 is revealed preferred to E_2,..., E_{k-1} to E_k, then by SARP, we say E_1 is indirectly revealed preferred to E_k.

Violation of the WARP

Let us consider figure. Here let us suppose that, under the price income situation represented by the budget line $L_1 M_1$, the consumer purchases the combination E_1 (x_1, y_1) and he reveals combination E_1 $(x_1\, y_1)$ as preferred to E_2 (x_2, y_2).

For here he chooses E_1 over the affordable combination E_2. Again, let us suppose that when the budget line of the consumer changes from $L_1 M_1$ to $L_2 M_2$, the consumer buys the combination E_2 (x_2, y_2), although he could have obtained the affordable combination E_1 (x_1, y_1), i.e., under $L_2 M_2$, E_2 is revealed preferred to E_1.

What we have seen here is that under the budget line, $L_1 M_1$, the combination E_1 is revealed preferred to E_2 and under a different budget line $L_2 M_2$, E_2 is revealed preferred to E_1. Obviously, the consumer here violates the WARP.

The reason for this violation may be that the consumer here does not attempt to obtain the most preferred combination subject to his budget constraint; or, it may be that his taste or some other element in his economic environment has changed which should have remained unchanged by our assumptions.

Now, whatever may be the reason for the violation of WARP, this violation is not consistent with the model of consumer behaviour that we are discussing.

The model assumes that the consumer wants to maximise his level of satisfaction and, that is why, when he chooses a particular combination, say, E_1 subject to his budget, that must be the most 'preferred' to all other affordable combinations, and none of these 'other' combinations can be 'preferred' to E₁ under a different budget. WARP puts emphasis on this simple but important point. We may give the formal statement of WARP in the following way.

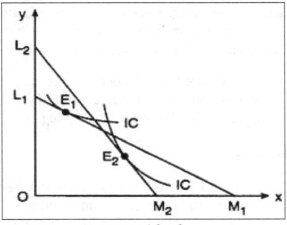

WARP Violated.

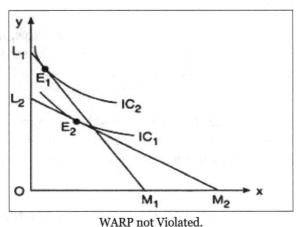

WARP not Violated.

If a particular combination $E_1 (x_1, y_1)$ is directly revealed by the consumer as preferred to a different combination $E_2 (x_2, y_2)$, then E_2 would never be revealed by the consumer as preferred to E_1.

In other words, if the consumer is observed to purchase $E_1 (x_1, y_1)$ at the price set $(p_x^{(1)}, p_y^{(1)})$ and $E_2 (x_2, y_2)$ at the price set $(p_x^{(1)}, p_y^{(2)})$, then if $(p_x^{(1)}x_1 + p_y^{(1)}y_1 \geq p_x^{(1)}x_2 + p_y^{(1)}y_2)$ below holds, then $(p_x^{(2)}x_2 + p_y^{(2)}y_2 \geq p_x^{(2)}x_1 + p_y^{(2)}y_1)$ must never hold:

$$p_x^{(1)}x_1 + p_y^{(1)}y_1 \geq p_x^{(1)}x_2 + p_y^{(1)}y_2$$
$$p_x^{(2)}x_2 + p_y^{(2)}y_2 \geq p_x^{(2)}x_1 + p_y^{(2)}y_1$$

As we have seen, WARP has been violated in figure, when the consumer buys combination E_1 on L_1M_1 and E_2 on L_2M_2. Here the preference ordering of the consumer breaks down. It may be verified in figure that the IC tangent to L_1M_1 at E_1 and the IC tangent to L_2M_2 at E_2 cannot be non-intersecting in this case.

In figure, on the other hand, let us suppose, the consumer buys the combination E_1 on L_1M_1 and the combination E_2 on L_2M_2. Here when he buys E_1 he chooses E_1 over the affordable combination E_2, i.e., E_1 is revealed preferred to E_2. But when he buys E_2, he chooses E_2 over an unaffordable E_1, i.e., E_2 is not revealed preferred to E_1.

Therefore, here, WARP is not violated, and so, here the preference ordering of the consumer does not break down. It may be seen in figure that the IC tangent to L_1M_1 at E_1 and the IC tangent to L_2M_2 at E_2 would be non- intersecting.

Significance of the SARP

Let us now discuss the significance of the strong axiom of revealed preference (SARP). According to this axiom, if the consumer reveals a combination E_1 (x_1, y_1) as preferred to another combination E_2 (x_2, y_2) and if E_2 (x_2, y_2) is revealed preferred to E_3 (x_3, y_3) then E, would always be revealed preferred to E_3.

This may be called the transitivity of revealed preferences. Now, if the consumer is a utility-maximising one, then the transitivity of revealed preferences would lead to transitivity of preferences—if E_1 is preferred to E_2 and E_2 to E_3, then E_1 would be preferred to E_3.

But this is necessary to ensure that the ICs are non-intersecting and the non-interesting ICs are necessary for arriving at the utility-maximising solution. It is evident that if any of the WARP and SARP is violated, then utility-maximisation cannot be achieved by the consumer.

Revealed Preference Theory and the Slutsky Theorem

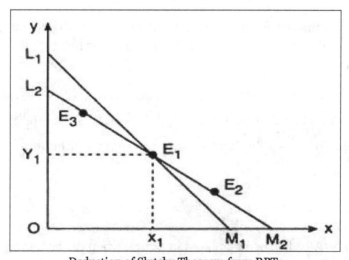

Deduction of Slutsky Theorem from RPT.

Let us now see how the RPT can be used to prove the Slutsky Theorem which states that if the income effect (IE) for a commodity is ignored, then its demand curve must have a negative slope. To explain this, we shall take the help of figure.

In this figure, let E_1 (x_1, y_1) represent the combination of goods that the consumer initially purchases when his budget line is L_1M_1. We want to show here that a ceteris paribus fall in the price of good X from L_1M_1 will increase the purchase of the good if we ignore the income effect, i.e., if we consider only the substitution effect (SE).

Let us suppose that the imaginary budget line for Slutsky-SE is L_2M_2. This line will be flatter than L_1M_1, since the price of X has fallen, ceteris paribus, and this line (L_2M_2) will pass through the combination E, so that, as per the Slutsky condition, the consumer might be able to buy the initial combination, if he liked, under the changed circumstances.

Let us now see, because of the SE, the point the consumer may select on the imaginary budget line L_2M_2 (if it is to be different from E), would be a point like E_2 to the right of the point E_1. To prove that this must be so, we have to note that selection of any point on L_2M_2 such as E_3 which lies to the left of E_1, is ruled out by WARP.

This is because, initially, E_1 has been revealed preferred to E_3, since E_3 lies below L_1M_1. But if E_3 were chosen when the price line was L_2M_2, it (E_3) is revealed preferred to E_1 since E_1 is no-more-expensive than E_3 (for they both lie on the same budget line L_2M_2). In that case, we obtain that E_1 is revealed preferred to E_3, and vice versa, which violates WARP.

Thus no point on L_2M_2 which, like E_3, lies to the left of E_1, can be chosen. On the other hand, if the consumer chooses a point like E_2 on L_2M_2 to the right of E_1, then there is no harm to the weak axiom, because when he purchases E_2, E_2 is revealed preferred to the no-more-expensive combination E_1 but, initially, when he purchased E_1 (on L_1M_1) and not a point like E_2, he did this, because E_1 was cheaper than these points.

From the analysis, it is clear that the SE of a fall in the price of X will generally increase the demand for the relatively cheaper commodity X at a point like E_2 to the right of E_1. Thus, the Slutsky theorem is deduced from the revealed preference approach.

We have seen that if the price of X falls, ceteris paribus, and if the income effect of this price fall is ignored, then the SE would increase the demand for X, i.e., the demand curve for X would be negatively sloped, and the law of demand is obtained.

From Revealed Preference to Preference

The principle of revealed preference (RP) is rather simple, but at the same time it is very powerful. Supported by the assumptions we have made, the RPT enables us to obtain the consumer's preference pattern or indifference curves (ICs) from his revealed preferences.

No introspective data are required from the consumer to achieve this task. If we know the price- income situation of the consumer as represented by his budget line and his point of revealed preference on the line, we would be able to derive his IC that passes through this point. The process of obtaining the IC is described below.

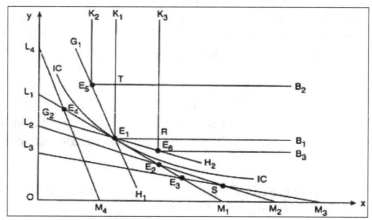

Derivation of the IC from the revalued preference system.

Let us suppose that the budget line of the consumer is L_1M_1 in figure and the combination of the goods that the consumer is observed to purchase, is E_1 (x_1, y_1). As we know, the consumer here prefers the point E, directly to all other points on the budget line or in the area OL_1M_1. For, in spite of all these points being within his budget, he purchases E_1. "All these points" are considered to be "worse" than E_1.

On the other hand, the costs of all the combinations lying to the right of the budget line L_1M_1 are more than that of the point E_1, or, E_1 is cheaper than these points. Apparently, the consumer chooses E_1 over these points because they are more expensive, and we cannot say anything about the 'revealed' preference of E_1 to any of these points.

That is why, the area in the commodity space to the right of L_1M_1 is known as the area of ignorance. We shall see, however, with the help of the assumptions of the RPT, that some of the points in the area of ignorance are directly or indirectly preferred or inferior to E_1 and some of the points are indifferent with E_1.

These latter points that are indifferent with E_1 give us the indifference curve (IC) passing through E_1, Let us now see how we can derive this curve.

At the very first, let us consider the area $K_1E_1B_1$. The commodity combinations (except E_1) belonging to this area are directly preferable to the consumer to E_1, since all these combinations have more of either one or both of the goods than the point E_1. These combinations may be called the "better" combinations.

So far we have obtained that the consumer directly prefers E_1 to the points to the left of the budget line L_1M_1, i.e., those lying in the area OL_1M_1 and he directly prefers the points lying in the area $K_1E_1B_1$ to E_1. Therefore, his IC through the point E_1 if it is obtained would be spread in the space between these two areas, and it would touch the line L_1M_1 and the area $K_1E_1B_1$ at the point E_1.

Let us now consider the points in the area of ignorance lying above the line L_1M_1 and outside the area $K_1E_1B_1$. At first, we shall try to identify the points that the consumer prefers less to E_1—these points may be called the "worse" points. In order to do this, let us consider any point E_2 lying on L_1M_1 to the right of E_1.

Let us suppose that the consumer is observed to purchase E_2 when his budget line is L_2M_2. He, therefore, reveals the point E_2 as preferred to the points to the left of the budget line L_2M_2. Since E_1 has already been revealed preferred to E_2, the consumer prefers E_1 to all these points lying in the area OL_2M_2.

Since a portion of this area, viz., $\square OL_2E_2M_1$ belongs to the area OL_1M_1, here the net increase in the area of "worse" points is obtained to be $\square E_2M_1M_2$. The consumer prefers E_1 indirectly to the points of this area through the combination E_2—he prefers E_1 to E_2 and E_2 to these points.

We may again increase the area of "worse" points to the right of E_1 by considering any other point E_3 lying on the line L_1M_1 to the right of E_2. Let as suppose that the consumer purchases E_3 when the budget line is L_3M_3. That is, he reveals the point E_3 as preferred to the points lying in the area OL_3M_3.

Again, since E_1 has already been revealed preferred to E_3, he may be said to prefer E_1 to these points in the area OL_3M_3. Here the net increase in the area of points worse than E_1 has been $\square SM_2M_3$. The consumer prefers E_1 indirectly (through the point E_3) to the points in $\square SM_2M_3$.

So far we have seen how we may lessen the area of ignorance by considering the points on the budget line L_1M_1 to the right of E_1. We may also do this job by considering points on L_1M_1 to the left of E_1. Let us suppose, E_4 is any point on L_1M_1 to the left of E_1 and the consumer is observed to purchase E_4 when his budget line is L_4M_4.

The point E_4, therefore, is revealed preferred to the points lying in the area OL_4M_4. But the point E_1 has already been revealed preferred to point E_4 and so the consumer prefers E_1 to these points. Here, if we leave out the common portion of areas OL_4M_1 and OL_4M_4, we obtain that the consumer indirectly prefers E_1 to the points of $\square E_4L_1L_4$.

Therefore, now we have been able to reduce the area of ignorance by $\square E_4L_1L_4$. We may, in this way, go on reducing the area of ignorance by considering more points on L_1M_1 lying to the left of the point E_1.

So far we have reduced the area of ignorance by increasing the area of "worse" combinations. We may now see how we may increase the area of "better" combinations outside the area $K_1E_1B_1$ and thereby reduce further the area of ignorance. Let us suppose that the consumer is observed to purchases the point E_5 when his budget line is $G_1E_1H_1$.

Here the consumer will prefer all the points in the area $K_2E_5B_2$ to the point E_5, since these points have more of either one or both the goods. Also it is now revealed that the consumer prefers E_5 to E_1, for he chooses E_5 over the affordable E_1. Therefore, what we obtain here is that the points lying in the area $K_2E_5B_2$ are "better" than the point E_1.

Here, if we leave out the portion of $\square K_2E_5B_2$ which is in common with $\square K_1E_1B_1$, we find that there has been a net increase in the area of "better" points and net decrease in the area of ignorance—this net increase is represented by the area lying in between the lines K_2E_5, K_1T and E_5T.

Again, because of our assumptions of convex preference and MIB, the consumer will prefer the points in $\square E_1E_5T$ to E_1. Therefore, this area is also added to the area of "better" combinations and the area of ignorance is reduced accordingly. We may go on increasing the area of "better" combinations in this way. For example, the consumer is observed to purchase the point E_6 on the budget line $G_2 E_1 H_2$.

Here we would find that the area of the "better" points gets an increase by the area in between the lines RB_1 RE_6 and E_6B_3 plus the area E_1E_6R. Therefore, these areas are also added to the area of "better" combinations and the area of ignorance is reduced accordingly.

In figure, we have seen that on the basis of the idea of revealed preference and with the help of the assumptions made, we may go on increasing the area of the combinations that are "worse" than a particular combination E_1 from below and we may also go on increasing the area of the combinations that are "better" than E_1 from above.

In the limit, the area between these two areas would get reduced to a border line curve of indifference. By applying the advanced methods of calculus and also intuitively, we may obtain that this indifference curve of the consumer would pass through the point E_1, would lie in between the two paths like $K_2E_5E_1E_6B_3$ and $L_4E_4E_1E_2SM_3$ and would be convex to the origin.

We have seen how we may obtain a consumer's IC through any particular combination E_1. Applying the same process, we may obtain his IC through any other point in the commodity space, i.e., we would obtain his indifference map.

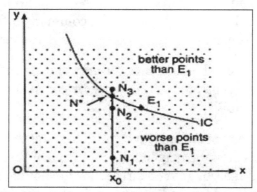

Intuitive deduction of an IC from the areas of "better" and "worse" combinations.

Let us now see with the help of figure, how we may conclude intuitively that the border-line between the areas of "better" and "worse" combinations than any point E_1 is an IC through that point.

In figure, we have represented that the areas of better and worse combinations than E_1 have been made to advance towards each other and in the limit the gap between them looks like an IC, and actually, it would be an IC, passing through E_1 We can understand this in the following way.

Let us move vertically from one point to another in the commodity space of figure starting from any point like N, (x^o, y_1) of the area of worse combinations. As we move upwards vertically, the quantity of good X remains the same at x_0 and that of good Y increases, and ultimately, very near the border of the "worse" area we shall arrive at a point like N_2 (x^o, y_2).

Let us suppose, if we still move upwards slightly beyond N_2, we shall arrive at a point N_3 (x^o, y_3) in the area of "better" combinations. Now we may easily understand intuitively that there lies a point N^* (x_0, y^*), $y_2 < y^* < y_3$, in the infinitesimally small vertical gap between the points N_2 and N_3 which is neither worse nor better than E_1 but which is indifferent with E_1.

Therefore, if we join the points E_1 and the points like N^* by a curve we would obtain the required IC through E_1.

Indifference Curve, Revealed Preference and Cost of Living Index

Let us first consider two price index formulas. One is Laspeyre's formula and the other is Paasche's formula. Laspeyre's price index number is the ratio of two aggregates—aggregate of current year prices at base year quantities and that of base year prices at base year quantities. Let us suppose that an individual purchases two goods.

The base year and current year prices of the goods are p_{o1}, p_{o2} and p_{t1}, p_{t2}. Also the base year and current year quantities of the goods purchased by the consumer are q_{o1}, q_{o2} and q_{t1}, q_{t2}. Then Laspeyre's price index would be:

$$L = \frac{p_{t1}q_{o1} + p_{t2}q_{o2}}{p_{o1}q_{o1} + p_{o2}q_{o2}}$$

Here the base year quantities of the goods have been taken as weights of their prices. L gives us the price index in the current year if the base year price index is 1. For example, if L = 1.5, then we obtain that current year price index is 1.5 when the base year price index is 1, i.e., the prices in the current year are 50 per cent more than those in the base year.

Laspeyer's price index may be interpreted in another way. The numerator of the right hand side of (previous equation) gives us the cost of the base year basket of goods (q_{o1},

q_{o2}) at the current year prices (p_{t1}, p_{t2}), and the denominator gives us the cost of buying the same basket of goods at the base year prices (p_{o1}, p_{o2}).

Looking in this way, L = 1.5 gives us that the cost of buying the base year basket of goods has increased by 50 per cent in the current year over the base year. That is, the Laspeyre's price index number L may also be considered as the Laspeyre's cost of living index number.

Let us now come to Paasche's price index number which is the ratio of the aggregate of current year prices at current year quantities and that of the base year prices at current year quantities. Therefore, we obtain Paasche's price index number as:

$$L = \frac{p_{t1}q_{t1} + p_{t2}q_{t2}}{p_{o1}q_{t1} + p_{o2}q_{t2}}$$

Here the current year quantities of the goods have been taken as the weights of their prices. Just like the Laspeyre's price index number, Paasche's price index number may also be considered as the Paasche's cost of living index number. It gives us the percentage increase in the cost of buying the current year basket of goods in the current year over the base year.

Let us now come to the total expenditure of the consumer in the base year and in the current year. In the base year his total expenditure is, say, E_o, and he purchases the quantities q_{o1} and q_{o2} at prices p_{o1} and p_{o2}. Therefore, his budget line in the base year is:

$$E_o = p_{o1}q_{o1} + p_{o2}q_{o2}$$

Similarly, in the current year his total expenditure is, say, E_t, and he purchases the quantities q_{t1} and q_{t2} at the prices p_{t1} and p_{t2}. Therefore, his budget line in the current year is:

$$E_t = p_{t1}q_{t1} + p_{t2}q_{t2}$$

Since it is assumed that expenditure equals income, E_t/E_o gives us the index of change in the consumer's income in the current year over the base year. That is, the index of money income change is:

$$E = \frac{E_1}{E} = \frac{p_{t1}q_{t1} + p_{t2}q_{t2}}{p_{o1}q_{o1} + p_{o2}q_{o2}}$$

Let us now suppose that:

$$p_{t1}q_{o1} + p_{t2}q_{o2} < E_t$$

This means that the cost of the base year basket at current year prices is less than the current year expenditure. In other words, in the current year, the consumer might purchase the base year basket, if he so desired, but he chose not to buy this basket. This means that he prefers the current year basket to the base year basket, i.e., he is better off in the current year than in the base year.

Dividing both sides of inequality (previous equation) by E_o, we get:

$$\left.\frac{p_{o1}q_{t1} + p_{o2}q_{t2}}{p_{o1}q_{o1} + p_{o2}q_{o2}} < \frac{E_t}{E_o} = E \quad \begin{array}{l} \text{or,} L < E \\ \text{i.e.,} E > L \end{array}\right\}$$

Therefore, $(p_{t1}q_{o1} + p_{t2}q_{o2} < E_t)$ implying (previous equation) gives us the condition for the consumer to be better off in the current period over the base period. Let us now consider the following case:

$$p_{t1}q_{o1} + p_{t2}q_{o2} < E$$

This means that the cost of the current year bundle at the base year prices is less than the base year expenditure. This implies that the consumer might have bought the current year basket in the base year, but he chose not to buy this basket.

Thus, he preferred the base year basket and was better off in the base period over the current period. In other words, he is worse off in the current year than in the base year. Dividing both sides of $p_{t1}q_{o1} + p_{t2}q_{o2} < E$ by E_t we have:

$$\frac{p_{o1}q_{t1} + p_{o2}q_{t2}}{p_{t1}q_{t1} + p_{t2}q_{t2}} < \frac{E_o}{E_t} = \frac{1}{E}$$

$$\Rightarrow \frac{1}{P} < \frac{1}{E} \Rightarrow P > E \Rightarrow E < P$$

Therefore, $(p_{t1}q_{o1} + p_{t2}q_{o2} < E)$ implying (previous equation) gives us the condition for the consumer to be better off in the base period or, worse off in the current period.

Next, let us suppose:

$$p_{t1}q_{o1} + p_{t2}q_{o2} < E_t$$

Dividing both the sides of inequality (previous equation) by E_o, we get:

$$\frac{p_{t1}q_{o1} + p_{t2}q_{o2}}{p_{o1}q_{o1} + p_{o2}q_{o2}} < \frac{E_t}{E_o} = E$$

$$\Rightarrow L > E, \Rightarrow E < L$$

From $(p_{t1}q_{o1} + p_{t2}q_{o2} < E_t)$ implying (previous equation), we obtain that the cost of the base year basket at current year prices is greater than the current year expenditure. Therefore, the base year basket is not available to the consumer in the current year.

That is, he purchases the current year basket not because he prefers it to the base year basket, but because it is cheaper. Therefore, we cannot say that the consumer is better off in the current year over the base year.

Similarly, if we suppose:

$$p_{o1}q_{t1} + p_{o2}q_{t2} < E_o$$

And divide (previous equation) by E_t to obtain:

$$\frac{p_{o1}q_{t1} + p_{o2}q_{t2}}{p_{t1}q_{t1} + p_{t2}q_{t2}} < \frac{E_o}{E_t}$$

$$\Rightarrow \frac{1}{P} > \frac{1}{E}$$

$$\Rightarrow E < P$$

From ($p_{o1}q_{t1} + p_{o2}q_{t2} < E_o$) implying (previous equation), we obtain that the cost of current year basket in the base year is greater than the base year income. Therefore, the consumer buys the base year basket in the base year not because he prefers it, but because it is cheaper than the current year basket. Therefore, here we cannot say that he is better off in the base year over the current year, or, worse off in the current year over the base year.

What we have obtained above is that if E > L as given by condition ($\frac{p_{o1}q_{t1} + p_{o2}q_{t2}}{p_{o1}q_{o1} + p_{o2}q_{o2}} < \frac{E_t}{E_o} = E \quad \left.\begin{matrix} or, L < E \\ i.e., E > L \end{matrix}\right\}$), the consumer is better off in the current year over the base year. On the other hand, if E < P as given by ($\frac{p_{o1}q_{t1} + p_{o2}q_{t2}}{p_{t1}q_{t1} + p_{t2}q_{t2}} < \frac{E_o}{E_t} = \frac{1}{E} \Rightarrow \frac{1}{P} < \frac{1}{E} \Rightarrow P > E \Rightarrow E < P$), the consumer is better off in the base year than in the current year.

We may use the indifference curves of the consumer to illustrate these points. Figure illustrates the first case, i.e., the consumer is better off in the current year than in the base year.

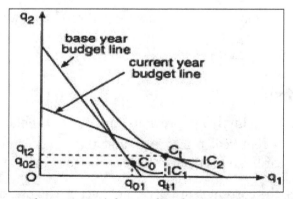

The consumer is better off in the current year.

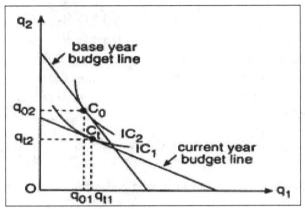

The consumer is better off in the base year.

Here, in the current year, the consumer buys at the point C_t on the current year budget line and he buys in the base year at the point C_o on the base year budget line. It is seen in figure that C_t lies on the higher IC, viz., IC_2, and C_o lies on the lower IC, viz., IC_1.

Similarly, figure illustrates the second case, i.e., the consumer is better off in the base year than in the current year. It is seen in this figure that C_o lying on the base year budget line, is placed on a higher IC, viz., IC_2, and C_t lying on the current year budget line, is placed on a lower IC, viz., IC_1.

From the above analysis, especially from the inequalities ($\dfrac{P_{o1}q_{t1} + P_{o2}q_{t2}}{P_{o1}q_{o1} + P_{o2}q_{o2}} < \dfrac{E_t}{E_o} = E$

$\left. \begin{array}{l} \text{or,} L < E \\ \text{i.e.,} E > L \end{array} \right\}$), ($\dfrac{P_{o1}q_{t1} + P_{o2}q_{t2}}{P_{t1}q_{t1} + P_{t2}q_{t2}} < \dfrac{E_o}{E_t} = \dfrac{1}{E} \Rightarrow \dfrac{1}{P} < \dfrac{1}{E} \Rightarrow P > E \Rightarrow E < P$), ($\dfrac{P_{t1}q_{o1} + P_{t2}q_{o2}}{P_{o1}q_{o1} + P_{o2}q_{o2}} < \dfrac{E_t}{E_o}$

$= E \Rightarrow L > E, \Rightarrow E < L$) and ($\dfrac{P_{o1}q_{t1} + P_{o2}q_{t2}}{P_{t1}q_{t1} + P_{t2}q_{t2}} < \dfrac{E_o}{E_t} \Rightarrow \dfrac{1}{P} > \dfrac{1}{E} \Rightarrow E < P$), we may distinguish

between four cases:

(i) E is greater than both L and P (E > L, E > P).

Here by ($\dfrac{P_{o1}q_{t1} + P_{o2}q_{t2}}{P_{o1}q_{o1} + P_{o2}q_{o2}} < \dfrac{E_t}{E_o} = E$ $\left. \begin{array}{l} \text{or,} L < E \\ \text{i.e.,} E > L \end{array} \right\}$), i.e., E > L, the consum-

er is better off in the current year over the base year. On the other hand, by

($\dfrac{P_{o1}q_{t1} + P_{o2}q_{t2}}{P_{t1}q_{t1} + P_{t2}q_{t2}} < \dfrac{E_o}{E_t} \Rightarrow \dfrac{1}{P} > \dfrac{1}{E} \Rightarrow E < P$), i.e., E > P, the standard of living does not fall

in the current year. Hence, the individual is definitely better off in the current period.

(ii) E is less than both P and L (E < P, E < L). Here it follows from

($\dfrac{P_{o1}q_{t1}}{P_{t1}q_{t1}} \quad \dfrac{P_{o2}q_{t2}}{P_{t2}q_{t2}} < \dfrac{E_o}{E_t} = \dfrac{1}{E} \Rightarrow \dfrac{1}{P} < \dfrac{1}{E} \Rightarrow P > E \Rightarrow E < P$) that if E < P, the consumer would be better off in the base year, and it follows from $(\dfrac{P_{t1}q_{01}+P_{t2}q_{02}}{P_{01}q_{01}+P_{02}q_{02}}<\dfrac{E_t}{E_o}=E\Rightarrow L>E,\Rightarrow E<L)$

that if $E < L$, the consumer would not be better off in the current period. Again, we obtain an unequivocal answer that if $E < P$ and $E < L$, then the consumer would be better off in the base period, i.e., his standard of living falls in the current period from what it was in the base period.

(iii) $L > E > P$. If $L > E$, or, $E < L$, then by $(\dfrac{P_{t1}q_{01}+P_{t2}q_{02}}{P_{01}q_{01}+P_{02}q_{02}}<\dfrac{E_t}{E_o}=E\Rightarrow L>E,\Rightarrow E<L)$,

it cannot be said whether the consumer would be better off or worse off in the current

period over the base period, and if $E > P$, then by $(\dfrac{P_{01}q_{t1}+P_{02}q_{t2}}{P_{t1}q_{t1}+P_{t2}q_{t2}}<\dfrac{E_o}{E_t}\Rightarrow\dfrac{1}{P}>\dfrac{1}{E}\Rightarrow E<P)$,

we cannot say that he would be better off in the base year. Consequently, in this case, no definite conclusion can be drawn in respect of improvement or deterioration in the standard of living of the consumer between the two periods.

(iv) $P > E > L$. If $P > E$, or, $E < P$, then by $(\dfrac{P_{01}q_{t1}+P_{02}q_{t2}}{P_{t1}q_{t1}+P_{t2}q_{t2}}<\dfrac{E_o}{E_t}=\dfrac{1}{E}\Rightarrow\dfrac{1}{P}<\dfrac{1}{E}\Rightarrow P>E\Rightarrow E<P)$

the consumer's standard of living falls in the current period, since he prefers the base year basket to the current year one, and if $E > L$, then by

$(\dfrac{P_{01}q_{t1}+P_{02}q_{t2}}{P_{01}q_{01}+P_{02}q_{02}}<\dfrac{E_t}{E_o}=E\quad\left.\begin{array}{l}\text{or, }L<E\\\text{i.e., }E>L\end{array}\right\})$, the consumer's standard of living increases in

the current year, since he prefers the current year basket to that of the base year.

Therefore, in this case also we cannot draw any definite conclusion regarding a change in the consumer's welfare, and this is the situation where the weak axiom of the revealed preference theory has been violated.

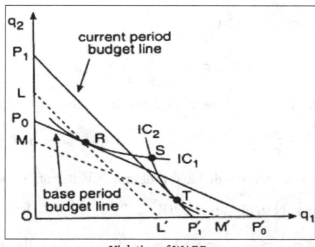

Violation of WARP.

This situation is illustrated in figure. Here the base period budget line is $P_oP'_o$ and the current period budget line is $P_1P'_1$. Let us suppose that the consumer chose R (q_{o1}, q_{o2}) on IC_1 when the budget line was P_oP_o' and T (q_{t1}, q_{t2}) on IC_2 when the budget line was P_1P_1'. Since LL' lies below P_1P_1' and is parallel to it and since R is on LL' and T is on P_1P_1', it must be true that expenditure at R at (p_{t1}, p_{t2}) must be less than that at T at (p_{t1}, p_{t2}), i.e., we would have:

$$p_{t1}q_{o1} + p_{t2}q_{o2} < p_{t1}q_{t1} + p_{t2}q_{t2}$$

So that:

$$\frac{p_{t1}q_{o1} + p_{t2}q_{o2}}{p_{o1}q_{o1} + p_{o2}q_{o2}} < \frac{p_{t1}q_{t1} + p_{t2}q_{t2}}{p_{o1}q_{o1} + p_{o2}q_{o2}}$$
$$\Rightarrow L < E$$

Also, since the point T (q_{t1}, q_{t2}) is on MM' which is parallel to p_op_o but lies below it, T has the same prices as p_op_o' but has less expenditure than the point R (q_{o1}, q_{o2}) which lies on P_oP_o', i.e., we have:

$$p_{o1}q_{o1} + p_{o2}q_{o2} < p_{o1}q_{t1} + p_{o2}q_{t2}$$
$$\Rightarrow \frac{p_{o1}q_{o1} + p_{o2}q_{o2}}{p_{t1}q_{t1} + p_{t2}q_{t2}} < \frac{p_{o1}q_{t1} + p_{o2}q_{t2}}{p_{t1}q_{t1} + p_{t2}q_{t2}}$$
$$\Rightarrow \frac{1}{E} > \frac{1}{P}$$
$$\Rightarrow E < P$$

Thus, we have $P > E > L$.

Thus, we have $P > E > L$. But in this case, there is inconsistency. This is also obvious from figure. The consumer could have purchased T in the base period, since T lies below the base period budget line p_op_o', but he actually chose R, implying that he prefers R to T.

But in the current period, he could have had R, since R lies below the current period budget line P_1P_1', but he chose T, implying that he prefers T to R.

This is inconsistent if his tastes remain unchanged between the base period and the current period, and the weak axiom of revealed preference is not complied with. This inconsistency is also reflected in the fact that the ICs through R and T, viz., IC_1 and IC_2, have not been obtained to be non-intersecting—they have intersected at the point S.

We have seen, therefore, that it is sometimes possible to determine whether the consumer's standard of living has increased or decreased by means of index number comparisons. However, there may be situations where we cannot arrive at any definite conclusions or where the results may be contradictory.

Examples of Slutsky Theorem

1. When two commodity baskets are purchased by the consumer at two different points in time, explain how price weighted quantity indices may be used to verify the weak axiom of revealed preference.

Solution: We have to explain how price-weighted quantity indices may be used to verify the weak axiom of revealed preference. Let us suppose that in the base period 'o', a consumer is observed to purchase the combination q_0 (q_{o1}, q_{o2}) of two goods Q_1 and Q_2 at the price set p_0 (p_{o1}, p_{o2}) and in the current period 't' he is observed to purchase the combination q_t (q_{t1}, q_{t2}) of the goods at the price set p_t (p_{t1}, p_{t2}).

Therefore, the costs of purchasing the combination q_0 at the price set p_0 and p_t are:

$$q_0 p_0 = q_{o1} p_{o1} + q_{o2} p_{o2}$$

And

$$q_0 p_t = q_{o1} p_{t1} + q_{o2} p_{t2}$$

Again, the costs of purchasing the combination q_t at the price set p_0 and p_t are:

$$q_t p_0 = q_{t1} p_{o1} + q_{t2} p_{o2}$$

And

$$q_t p_t = q_{t1} p_{t1} + q_{t2} p_{t2}$$

In the base period, the consumer purchases the quantity set q_0 at the price set p_0. If he happens to prefer q_0 to q_t, then by definition, the cost of the quantity set q_{o2} must be less than, or, (at most) equal to that of purchasing q_0 at p_0, i.e.,

$$q_t p_0 \leq q_0 p_0$$
$$\Rightarrow q_{t1} p_{o1} + q_{t2} p_{o2} \leq q_{o1} p_{o1} + q_{o2} p_{o2}$$
$$\Rightarrow \frac{q_{t1} p_{o1} + q_{t2} p_{o2}}{q_{o1} p_{o1} + q_{o2} p_{o2}} \times 100 \leq 100$$

Since the left-hand side of (previous equation) is, by definition, the Laspeyre's base year price weighted quantity index (L), we obtain the condition for q_0 at p_0 to be preferred by the consumer to q_0 at p_0 as:

$$L \leq 100$$

Again, in the current period, the consumer is observed to purchase the combination q_t

at price p_t. However, if the weak axiom of revealed preference is to be satisfied then he must not prefer q_t at p_t to q_o at p_t. Therefore, we may conclude that he purchases q in the current period because it is cheaper than q_o, i.e.,

$$q_t p_t \le q_o p_t$$
$$\Rightarrow q_{t1} p_{t1} + q_{t2} p_{t2} \le q_{o1} p_{t1} + q_{o2} p_{t2}$$
$$\Rightarrow \frac{q_{t1} p_{t1} + q_{t2} p_{t2}}{q_{o1} p_{t1} + q_{o2} p_{t2}} \times 100 < 100$$

Since the left-hand side of (previous equation) is by definition the Paasche's current year price weighted quantity index (P), we obtain the condition for p_t at q_t to be cheaper than p_o at q_t as:

$$P < 100$$

(L ≤100) and (P < 100) give us that the weak axiom of revealed preference would be satisfied if the Laspeyre's and Passche's quantity indices both are less than 100. Of course, L may be at most 100. Here 100 is the base period index numbers for both the formulas.

2. A consumer is observed to purchase $x_1 = 20$, $x_2 = 10$ at the prices $p_1 = 2$ and $p_2 = 6$. He is also observed to purchase $x_1 = 18$ and $x_2 = 4$ at the prices $p_1 = 3$ and $p_2 = 5$. Is his behaviour consistent with the weak axiom of revealed preference?

Solution: From the given data, we obtain:

- The cost of the combination ($x_1= 20$, $x_2 = 10$) at the prices ($p_1 = 2$, $p_2 = 6$) is $E_1 = 20 \times 2 + 10 \times 6 = 100$.

- The cost of ($x_1 = 18$, $x_2 = 4$) at the prices ($p_1 = 2$, $p_2 = 6$) is $E_2 = 18 \times 2 + 4 \times 6 = 60$.

- The cost of ($x_1 = 18$, $x_2 = 4$) at the prices ($p_1 = 3$, $p_2 = 5$) is $E_3 = 18 \times 3 + 4 \times 5 = 74$.

- The cost of ($x_1 = 20$, $x_2 = 10$) at the prices ($p_1 = 3$, $p_2 = 5$) is $E_4 = 20 \times 3 + 10 \times 5 = 110$.

From above, it is obtained that the consumer buys the first set of goods, (20, 10), not because it is cheaper than the second set but because he prefers it to the second set, since the cost of the former, $E_1 = 100$, is greater than the cost of the latter, i.e., $E_2 = 60$.

However, when he purchases the second set, not the first one, at the prices ($p_1 = 3$, $p_2 = 5$), he does this because it is cheaper than the first set, not because he prefers this set to the first set, since the cost of the second set, i.e., $E_3 = 74$, is less than that of the first set, i.e., $E_4 = 110$.

Therefore, the consumer's behavior is consistent with the weak axiom of revealed preference.

Convexity and Concavity

Convex and Concave Functions

Let us refer to figure. A function f (x) represented by the curve ABCDE, is convex over the interval (a, b) if we have:

$$f\left[\lambda x_1 +(1-\lambda)x_2\right]\le \lambda f\left(x_1\right)+(1-\lambda)f\left(x_2\right)$$

For all a ≤ x_1, x_1 ≤ b, and all 0 ≤ λ ≤ 1.

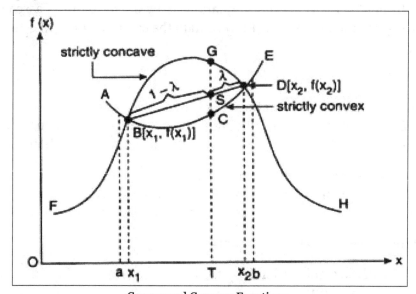

Convex and Concave Functions.

In figure, point S has divided the line segment BD in the ratio 1 − λ: λ. Therefore, the x and y coordinates of point S are:

$$OT = \lambda x_1, +(1 -\lambda)x_2$$

And

$$ST = \lambda f(x_1) + (1 -\lambda)f(x_2)$$

The function f(x) is said to be strictly convex over the interval (a, b) if strict inequality holds in ($f\left[\lambda x_1 +(1-\lambda)x_2\right]\le \lambda f\left(x_1\right)+(1-\lambda)f\left(x_2\right)$) for all 0 < λ < 1.

Let us again refer to figure. A function f(x), now represented by the curve FBGDH is concave over the interval (a, b) if we have:

$$f\left[\lambda x_1 + (1 -\lambda)x_2\right] \ge \lambda f(x_1) + (1 - \lambda)f(x_2)$$

And the function is strictly concave if strict inequality holds in (previous equation) for 0 < λ < 1.

Quasi-Convex and Quasi-Concave Functions

By definition, a function f(x) is quasi-convex over the interval (a, b) if we have:

$$f[\lambda x_1 + (1-\lambda)x_2] \leq \max[f(x_1), f(x_2)]$$

For all x_1 and x_2 in the interval and all $0 \leq \lambda \leq 1$. The function f(x) is strictly quasi-convex if strict inequality holds in (previous equation) for $0 < \lambda < 1$.

In figure, the curve A'BC'DE' represents, by definition, a quasi-convex function over the interval (a, b).

Let us now come to quasi-concavity. A function f(x) is quasi-concave over an interval (a, b) if we have:

$$f[\lambda x_1 + (1 - {}_1)x_2] \geq \min[f(x_1), f(x_2)]$$

For all x_1 and x_2 in the interval (a, b) and for all $0 \leq \lambda \leq 1$. The function is strictly quasi-concave if strict inequality holds in (previous equation) for $0 < \lambda < 1$. In figure, the curve F'BG'DH' represents, by definition, a quasi-concave function over the interval (a, b).

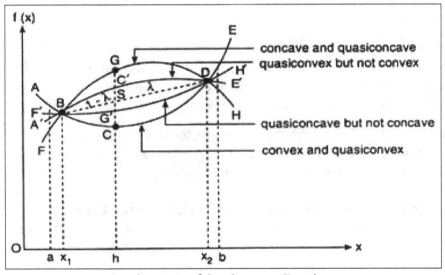

Quasi-convex and Quasi-concave Functions.

At the end of our discussion of convex and concave curves, let us note that, as per the definitions, a convex function is also quasi-convex for the former also satisfies (f [λx_1 + (1 -λ)x_2] $\leq$ max [f(x_1), f(x_2)]), but a quasi-convex function cannot be a convex function for it does not satisfy (f$[\lambda x_1 + (1-\lambda)x_2] \leq \lambda f(x_1) + (1-\lambda)f(x_2)$). Similarly, a concave function is also quasi-concave for it satisfies also (f[λx_1 + (1 - $_1$)x_2] $\geq$ min [f(x_1), f(x_2)]), but a quasi-concave function cannot be concave for it does not satisfy (f [λx_1 + (1 -λ)x_2] $\geq \lambda$f(x_1) + (1 - λ)f(x_2)).

From our discussions above we obtain the following with illustrations in figure:

(i) The curve, ABCDE, representing a function, f (x), is convex over a certain interval (a, b) if the line segment, BD, joining any two points, B and D, on the function in the said interval lies on or above the curve; and if the line segment lies throughout above the curve, it is said that the function is strictly convex.

(ii) On the other hand, a function f(x), viz., FGDH, is concave over a certain interval (a, b) if the line segment joining any two points, B and D, on the function in the said interval lies on or below the curve; and if the line segment lies throughout below the curve, it is said that the function is strictly concave.

We also obtain the following with illustrations in figure.

(iii) A function f(x), viz., A'BC'DE', is quasi-convex over a certain range between x = a and x = b, if at any x = h in the range, we have f(h) ≤ max [f(a), f(b)], and if the strict inequality holds, the function is said to be strictly quasi-convex.

It may be noted that a convex function is also quasi-convex, but a quasi-convex function cannot be convex, for some quasi-convex functions, like A'BC'DE', may lie above the line segment joining the points on the function at $x = x_1$ and $x = x_2$, which a convex function cannot.

(iv) Lastly, a function f(x), like F'BG'DH', is quasi-concave over a certain range between $x = x_1$ and $x = x_2$, if at any x = h in the range, we have f(h) ≥ min [$f(x_1)$, $f(x_2)$]; and if the strict inequality holds, the function is said to be strictly quasi-concave. It may be noted here that a concave function is also quasi-concave.

But a quasi-concave function cannot be concave, for some quasi-concave functions, like F'BG'DH', may lie below the line segment joining the points on the function at $x = x_1$ and $x = x_2$, which a concave function cannot.

Utility Function for Strictly Convex Indifference Curves

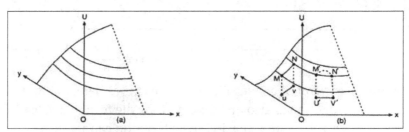

Utility functions for strictly convex indifference curves.

Our question here is what types of utility function will produce strictly convex indifference curves (ICs) and thus satisfy the second-order condition. Two functions that may be accepted as such utility functions have been shown in figure. Part (a) of the figure gives us a smooth strictly concave function.

Because of the assumption of positive marginal utilities, we have only shown the ascending portion of the dome-shaped surface. When this surface is cut with a plane parallel to the xy-plane, we obtain for each such cut a curve which will become a strictly convex downward sloping IC with respect to the xy-plane.

Strict concavity in a smooth utility function is, therefore, sufficient to fulfill the second-order condition (SOC) for utility-maximisation. However, if we examine part (b) of figure, it would be evident that strict concavity is not necessary for the SOC. This is because the strictly convex ICs can also be obtained from the utility function given in part (b) of the figure, which is not strictly concave—in fact, not even concave.

The function in figure is generally shaped like a bell. Of course, we have shown here only the ascending portion of the bell. The surface of this function is called strictly quasi-concave.

The geometric property of this function is that, for any pair of distinct points u and v in its domain, if the line segment uv (which is assumed to lie entirely in the domain) gives rise to the arc MN on the surface, and if M is lower than or equal in height to N, then all the points on arc MN other than M and N must be higher than M.

Algebraically, a function f is said to be strictly quasi-concave if, for any two distinct points in its domain like u and v, and for all values of λ, 0 < λ < 1, we would have:

$$f(u) < f(v) \Rightarrow f\left[\lambda u + (1-\lambda)v\right] > f(u)$$
$$\text{i.e., } f\left[\lambda u + (1-\lambda)v\right] > \min\{f(u).f(v)\}$$

The quasi-concavity of the function in figure may be verified by examining such arcs as MN (N higher than M) and M'N' (M' and N' being of equal height). We have to note here that in the case of arc M'N', it is the dotted arch that lies directly above the line segment u V, not the solid curve, which possesses the property of a quasi-concave function.

The interesting thing, however, is that the strictly concave function in figure (a) is also strictly quasi-concave.

From what we have obtained, we may conclude that only a smooth, increasing, strictly quasi-concave utility function would generate strictly convex ICs. Such a function may have convex as well as concave portions, as shown in figure (b) so that the marginal utilities may be either increasing or diminishing.

Intertemporal Choice

Intertemporal choice is an economic term describing how current decisions affect what options become available in the future. Theoretically, by not consuming today, consumption levels could increase significantly in the future, and vice versa.

Many of the choices we make have consequences for the future. For instance, deciding how much money to spend in the present and how much to squirrel away can greatly impact our quality of life both now and in the years ahead.

For companies, various investment decisions involve intertemporal choice. For individuals, on the other hand, decisions made in the near-term that can affect future financial opportunities relate mostly to saving and retirement.

An individual who saves today consumes less, causing their current utility to decline. Over time, the savings grow, increasing the number of goods the individual can consume and, therefore, the person's future utility.

Most individuals tend to be limited by budget constraints that prevent them from consuming to the extent of their desires. Nevertheless, behavioral finance theorists generally find that present bias is common, suggesting that people prefer to spend now, regardless of the impact it might have in later years.

It is common for people to make intertemporal choices that accommodate near-term needs and wants over long-term objectives.

Intertemporal Choice Example

If an individual makes an exorbitant purchase, such as paying for an around-the-world vacation that exceeds their usual budget and requires additional financing to cover, this could have a substantial impact on the person's long-term wealth. The individual might take out a personal loan, max out credit cards, or, when possible, even withdraw funds from retirement accounts in order to cover the expense.

Making such a choice would reduce the assets the individual has available to continue to save for retirement. The person may have to fund supplemental forms of income to augment their salary to compensate for the decline in assets.

This could be further exacerbated if unforeseen events affect current income. A sudden loss of employment, for example, would make it difficult to recoup recent expenses and set aside funds for retirement. If a consumer made a sizable purchase and then was laid off, their intertemporal choices combined with those external factors stand to change their future opportunities.

Perhaps the individual planned to retire by a certain age or was on track to finish paying off a mortgage. The shortfall in assets could mean postponing retirement or taking out a second mortgage to help deal with the more immediate issues.

Other Types of Intertemporal Choice

Decisions on employment can also factor into intertemporal choices. A professional might be presented with two job opportunities with salaries that vary depending on the intensity and demands of the role.

One position may be high-stress with long hours required. The compensation might also be higher than what is standard for such a position.

As an intertemporal choice, taking such a job might allow for more options on later pension plans. Conversely, taking the job that offers a lower salary but a better work-life balance may mean having fewer retirement options with less funding available.

References

- Basic-problems-of-an-economy, commerce: vedantu.com, Retrieved 29, June 2020
- Revealed-preference-theory-rpt-with-diagram, consumers-behavior-23081: economicsdiscussion.net, Retrieved 14, March 2020

Theories of Costs

Theory of costs states that the costs of a business are responsible for determining its supply and spending. Some of the major theories of cost are traditional theory of costs and modern theory of costs. This chapter has been carefully written to provide an easy understanding of these varied theories of cost.

Traditional Theory of Costs

The process of production involves a number of factors of production. The factors may be fixed and variable. The producers make payments to these factors for their services. These expenses are known as the costs of production.

The cost function shows the relationship between the firms cost and its output. $C = f(Q, P, T....)$ where C is the cost, Q is the level of output, P is the prices of inputs, T is technology.

Since the cost function combines the information given by the production function with the input prices, the cost functions are called as 'derived functions'. Depending upon the requirements of the firm and upon the time element, cost function can also be 'short run or long run'.

Concepts of Costs

The theory of costs revolves around different concepts of cost functions. Since cost functions are derived functions, therefore any change in production function has an impact on the cost.

Private Costs

The process of production involves two types of costs- private and social. Private costs refer to costs incurred on the purchase of inputs or the factors of production and also the implicit costs borne by the producers include the following:

- The costs incurred on the factors of production.

- Implicit/imputed costs on the resources provided by the producer/entrepreneur.

- Normal profits.

Social Costs

Besides private costs there are some costs which the producer does not include in his cost of production. Welfare economics takes account of such costs in addition to the explicit and implicit cost borne by the producer, though such costs are external to the firm. For example, a chemical factory is a great cause of pollution and ill health of the population. The producer is imposing a social cost on the society. From the society point of view, this cost is very important as society needs to be compensated.

Explicit Costs

Explicit cost is the most widely used concept of costs. It refers to the costs incurred by a firm on the purchase of factors of production. It refers to the expenditure on raw materials, wages, rent, interest payments and so on. It is also known as 'Money costs' or 'Accounting costs'.

Implicit Costs

The costs that are related with the factor inputs owned by the firm. These costs are also known as 'Economic costs'. The Economist has a wider view of costs in comparison to an accountant. Since such costs do not involve any monetary payments, therefore the Accountant does not take them into account. But if such resources are employed elsewhere, they could have earned returns for themselves. So such resources have an imputed or implicit cost. An entrepreneur who runs his factory on his own land is forgoing the returns he could have got if he had rented it out at market rate. The entrepreneur can work as a manager or a consultant and earn wages.

Opportunity Costs

As we all know that resources are not only scarce but have alternate uses, thus the concept of 'Opportunity costs' arises. Opportunity costs form the basis of the concept of cost. Also known as the Alternative costs. It is the cost linked with the prospects that have been foregone by not putting the firm's resources to the best possible uses. For example, a given amount of resources can produce 1000 kg of rice or 500 kg of sugar and the producer decides to produce one of the options and foregoes the other option. The decision of the producer depends upon many factors like the prices of factors of production, the price of the goods and so on.

Traditional Theory of Costs

Short-run Costs of Production

These broadly comprise of the total, average and marginal costs.

Total Costs

It is the sum of total fixed cost and total variable cost:

TC = TFC + TVC

Total Cost (TC) is the actual cost incurred to produce a given quantity of output.

Total Fixed Costs

Total Fixed Costs refer to the sum of all the expenditures by the firm on fixed inputs like land, depreciation of machinery, insurance etc. The payments for such factors are fixed in the short run and independent of the level of output. Even at zero level of production, the firm has to incur fixed costs which remain unchanged at all levels of output. The TFC curve runs parallel to the X-axis. For e.g. the cost incurred by a firm on fixed machinery, building blocks, remain fixed over a given span of time.

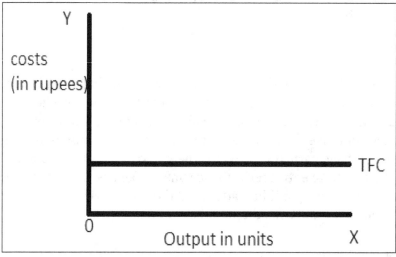

Total Fixed Costs.

Fixed Cost and Sunk Costs

Sunk costs are costs that have been incurred but cannot be retrieved if the firm goes out of business. Fixed costs can be escaped by going out of business. An example of Sunk costs is the expenditure incurred in purchasing a machine which does not have an alternative use when the firm decides to go out of business.

Total Variable Costs

Total Variable Costs refers to the firm's total expenditure on variable factors. Variable costs vary directly with the change in the level of output. Examples of such costs are costs of labour, raw materials, transportation etc. TVC is zero when output is zero. TVC has an inverse 'S '– shape reflecting the law of variable proportions.

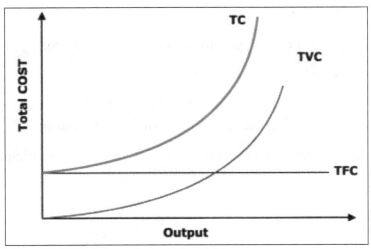

Total Cost and Total Variable Cost Curve.

Short Run Average Costs

In order to find out the per unit profit, the firm has to make a comparison between the per unit cost or the average costs and the per unit price or simply the price. The Average Cost is the sum of the Average fixed costs (AFC) and the Average variable cost (AVC).

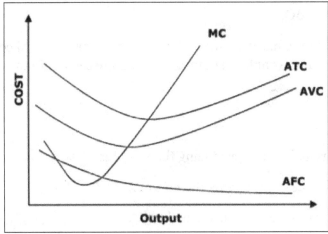

Marginal Cost Curve, Average Cost Curve, Average
Variable Cost Curve and Average Fixed Cost Curve.

Average Fixed Costs

AFC is per unit cost of the fixed factors of production. AFC= TFC/Q .The AFC is a rectangular hyperbola because multiplication of AFC with the quantity of output produced always yields a fixed value. The AFC will never touch the x-axis as the AFC cannot be zero, however large the level of output. Also, AFC curve never touches the Y- axis as TFC is a positive value at zero output and any positive value divided by zero will give an infinite value.

Average Variable Cost

AVC refers to the per unit cost of the variable factors of production.

AVC= TVC/Q, where Q is the level of output.

Since the total variable costs (TVC) are determined by the law of variable proportions, the AVC falls initially and rises later. The AVC is a dish –shaped curve.

Average costs are the sum of the Average fixed costs and Average variable costs.

$$AC= TC/Q$$

$$AC=TFC/Q + TVC /Q$$

$$AC=AFC + AVC$$

Marginal Cost

Marginal Cost refers to the incremental cost and is the addition to the total cost as a result of a unit increase in the output.

$$MC = \Delta TC/\Delta Q$$

$$MC = \Delta TVC/\Delta Q$$

Since the fixed cost remains constant in the short-run, the marginal cost is also defined as the increase in total variable cost due to a unit increase in output.

Mathematically, $MC_n = TC_n - TC_{n-1}$

Where,

- MC_n = marginal cost of producing the nth unit.

- TC_n = total costs of producing the n units.

- TC_{n-1} = total costs of producing 'n-1' units.

Marginal costs are the first derivative of the total cost function. $MC = \Delta TC/\Delta Q$. Graphically, the marginal cost is the slope of the total cost curve. With an inverse S-shaped of the total cost curve, the MC curve is U-shaped. In the short-run, the AC, AVC and MC curves are U-shaped and AFC is a rectangular hyperbola.

The relationship between AC and MC is as follows:

- When MC curve is below the AC curve, the AC falls.

- When MC curve is above the AC curve, the AC rises.

- The MC curve intersects the AC curve at its minimum point.

The MC curve intersects AVC curve and AC curve at their minimum points.

Relationship between AC and AVC

The U-shape of AVC and AC curves is due to the law of variable proportions. The behavior of the AC curve depends on the behavior of the AVC and AFC curves. Initially both AFC and AVC are falling leading to the fall in AC. The minimum point of AC occurs to the right of the minimum point of AVC. After reaching its minimum point, it starts rising. However, the AFC continues to fall. The AC reaches its minimum point when the rate of fall of AFC is equal to the rate of rise of AVC. When the rate of rise in AVC becomes greater than the rate of fall in AFC, the AC starts rising. The vertical distance between AC and AVC is the AFC, which continues to decline as the output increases.

Long-run Costs of Production

In the long-run, all factors of production are variable. All costs are variable costs. The firm can alter the size and scale of the plant to meet the changed market conditions. Therefore, there is LAC curve and LMC curve. Long- run costs are known as PLANNING COSTS as the firm has to plan its future expansion of output. The long-run cost curves are subject to the law of returns to scale as the scale of production may undergo change.

Derivation of the Long-run Cost Curve

The Long—run Average cost curve or the LAC curve is the locus of points denoting the least cost of producing different levels of output in the long run. It shows the minimum average costs of producing the corresponding output in the long-run. The LAC curve is thus a planning curve that guides the firm in deciding on the most optimal size of the plant for producing a given level of output. An optimal sized plant is one which enables the production of the output at the minimum costs per unit of output. Given the technology, the firm is free to choose the plant size which entails the least cost. For example, if the firm decides to produce OQ_1 level of output, then it will choose the plant size SAC_2 and not SAC_1.If the demand for the firm's output increases to OQ_3, then the average costs starts increasing along the plant SAC_2 and the firm decides to set up a larger plant size SAC_3 to minimize its average costs of production in the long-run.

The long-run average curve does not touch the short-run average cost curves on their minimum points. Graphically it can touch the minimum points of SACs only under constant returns to scale. In the phase of increasing returns to scale and decreasing cost, the LAC curve touches the SAC curves to the left of the minimum points of the SAC curves and in the phase of diminishing returns it touches the SAC curves to the right of their lowest point. The LAC is therefore, not the locus of lowest points of SAC curves. The downward sloping portion of LAC comprises of only increasing returns and diminishing cost portions of SAC curves.

The LAC curve is also known as the 'Envelope curve' as it envelops the short run cost curves.

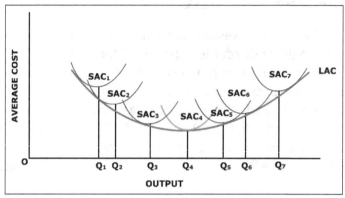

Long-Run Average Cost Curve.

Long-run Marginal Cost Curve

It is the additional cost of producing an additional unit of output in the long-run. Both short run MC curve and long run MC curve refer to the change in total cost due to a unit change in output. The key difference is that LRMC is not attributable to just one or two variable/factor but to all inputs/factors.

In the short run, the firm maximizes its profit by equating short run MR= MC. And in the long run, the firm maximizes profit by equating long run MR=MC.

Long run marginal cost shows the change in total cost consequent upon a small change in total output when the firm has adequate time to achieve the output changes by making the appropriate changes in the inputs/factors. The only difference between SMC and LRMC is that while in the short run the existing plant size is continued but in the long run the plant itself is changed due change in output.

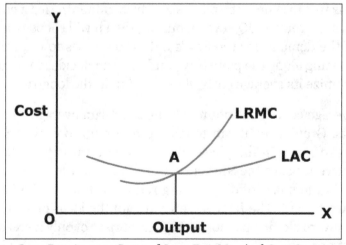

Long Run Average Cost and Long Run Marginal Coat Curve.

Since there is no fixed factor in the long-run, the law of diminishing marginal returns is irrelevant to the LRMC. In the long –run, marginal cost is affected by returns to scale- economies and diseconomies of scale.

Derivation of Long-run Marginal Cost Curve

Given the SAC and SMC curves and the LAC curves, we can derive the LRMC curve with the following steps:

- By drawing perpendiculars from the tangency points, A, B and C which inter-sects the SMC curves at M_1, M_2 and M_3.

- Join the points M_1, M_2, M_3, to obtain the LRMC curve.

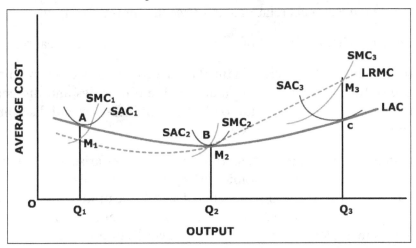

Derivation of Long Run Marginal Cost Curve.

Relationship between LAC and LRMC

The relationship between LAC and LRMC is the same as it exists between the short run average cost SAC and the SMC. LRMC lies below the LAC when LAC is falling and above it when LAC is rising. Thus LAC and LRMC intersect when LAC is the minimum.

Why is the LAC Curve 'U' Shaped?

In the short run, the shape of the average cost curves essentially reflects the returns to a variable factor as determined by the law of variable proportions. According to this law, as increasing amounts of variable factor are added to the fixed factor, then in the initial stages of production they yield increasing returns but eventually they yield diminishing returns. This explains why per unit costs of production tends to fall initially and ultimately rises up when diminishing returns to the variable factor sets in. Thus, the shape of SRAC curve is 'U' shaped.

The shape of the LAC is however explained by the 'returns to scale'. Returns to scale refer to the change in "optimum cost of production" when the scale of the plant is changed and comprises of:

- Constant returns to scale: When the successive plants have the same optimum cost.

- Diminishing returns to scale: When the optimum cost increases with an increase in scale.

- Increasing returns to scale: When the optimum cost decreases with an increase in scale.

The term 'a return to scale signifies two things:

- It reflects the technical relationship between inputs and output.

- It shows the changes in cost of production due to non-technical reasons also.

These two traits manifest themselves in the form of economies & diseconomies of scale. The 'U' shape of the LAC curve is explained by the economies and diseconomies of scale. Economies means lower per unit cost as output increases and diseconomies are higher per unit cost as output increases.

Economies can be internal and external. Internal economies arise on account of expansion of the firm itself. Internal economies arises due to specialization, choice of more suitable inputs, choice of technology, benefits of large scale production, managerial and supervisory economies and so on. Internal diseconomies arise from exhaustion, difficulties in management, lack of accountability and work culture and so on.

An external economy arises from external factors and the firm has no role in it. An external economy arises due to expansion of technical knowledge, growth of ancillary industry, development of transport facilities, and availability of banking system and so on. External diseconomies arise due to rise in wages, rise in input prices, pollution and so on.

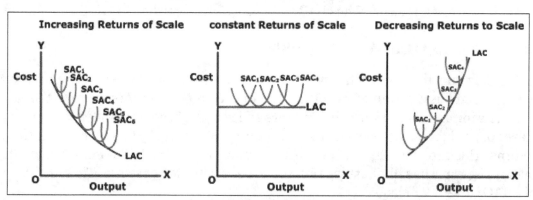

Different Phases of Returns to Scale.

In case of constant returns to scale, the LAC curve is parallel to the X- axis. The LAC curve is upward sloping in case of diminishing returns to scale and downward sloping in case of increasing returns to scale.

Thus, LAC curve is initially downward sloping, parallel to the X-axis up to a point and then upward sloping. The returns to scale determine the shape of the LAC, given the external economies.

Limitations

The traditional theory of costs assumes that each plant is designed to produce optimally a single level of output. Additional production will come at increasing costs. Further, according to the traditional theory, the firm can switch over to a larger plant size only in the long-run and meet the demand at lower costs.

Modern Theory of Costs

The modern theory of cost differs from the traditional theory of costs with regards to the shapes of the cost curves. The U-shaped cost curves of the traditional theory have been questioned by various writers both on theoretical, a priori, and on empirical grounds.

As early as 1939, George Stigler suggested that the short-run average variable cost has a flat stretch over a range of output which reflects the fact that firms build plant with some flexibility in their productive capacity. The reasons for this reserve capacity have been discussed in detail by various economists. The shape of the long run cost curve has attracted greater attention in economic literature, due to the serious policy implication of the economies of large scale production. Several reasons have been put forward to explain why the long-run cost curve is L-shaped rather than U-shaped. It has been argued that managerial diseconomies can be avoided by the improved methods of modern management science, and when they appear (at a very large scale of output) they are insignificant relative to the technical (production) economies of large plants, so that the total costs per unit of output falls, at least over the scales which have been operated in the real industrial world. Like the traditional theory, modern microeconomics distinguishes between short run and long run costs.

Short-run Costs Curves

As in the traditional theory, short-run costs in the modern theory of costs are distinguished into short-run average fixed cost (AFC), short-run average variable cost (SAVC), short-run average cost (SAC), and short-run marginal cost curves (SMC). As usual, they are derived from the total cost which is divided into fixed cost and total variable cost. But in the modern theory, the SAVC and SMC curves have a saucer-type shape or bowl-shape rather than a U-shape. As the AFC curve is a rectangular hyperbola, the SAC curve has a U-shape even in the modern theory.

The Average Fixed Cost

This is the cost of indirect factors; it is the cost of the physical and personal organizations of the firm. The fixed cost includes cost for (a) salaries and other expenses of administrative staff (b) salaries of staff involved directly in production but paid on a fixed term basis (c.) the wear and tear of machinery (standard depreciation allowance (d.) the expenses for maintenance of buildings (e.) the expenses for the maintenance of land on which the plant is installed and operated.

The planning of the plant (or the firm) consists of deciding the size of the fixed and indirect factors which determine the size of the plant, because they set limits to its production capacity. Direct factors such as labour and raw materials are assumed not to set limit on size; the firm can acquire them easily from the market without any time lag. The business man will start his planning with a figure for the level of output which he anticipates selling, and he will choose the size of plant which allows him to produce this level of output more efficiently, and with the maximum flexibility, the business man will want to be able to meet seasonal and cyclical fluctuations in his demand.

Reserve capacity will give the business man greater flexibility for repairs of broken down machinery without disrupting the smooth flow of the production process. The entrepreneur will want to have more freedom to increase his output if demand increases. All businessmen hope for growth. In view of anticipated increase in demand, the entrepreneur builds some reserve capacity because he would not like to let all new demand go to his rivals as this may endanger his future hold in the market. It also gives him some flexibility for minor alterations of his product, in view of changing tastes of customers.

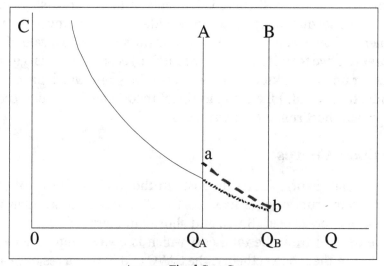

Average Fixed Cost Curve.

Technology usually makes it necessary to build into the plant some reserve capacity. Some basic types of machinery (e.g. a turbine) may not be technically fully employed when combined with other small types of machines in certain numbers. More of which may not be required, given the specific size of the chosen plant. Furthermore, some machinery may be so specialized as to be available only on order, which takes time. In this case, such machinery will be bought in excess of the minimum requirement at present numbers, as a reserve. Some reserve capacity will always be allowed in the land and buildings, since expansion of operations may be seriously limited if new land or new buildings have to be acquired. Finally, there will be some reserve capacity on the organizational and administrative level. The administrative staff will be hired at such numbers as to allow some increase in the operations of the firm.

In summary, the businessman will not necessarily choose the plant which will give him the lowest cost, but rather, that equipment which will allow him the greatest possible flexibility for minor alterations of his product or his technique of production.

Under these conditions, the AFC curve will be as in figure. The firm has some "largest capacity" units of machinery which set an absolute limit to the short-run expansion of output (boundary B). The firm also has small-unit machinery, which sets a limit to expansion (boundary A). This, however, is not an absolute boundary because the firm can increase its output in the short-run (until the absolute limit B is reached), either by paying overtime to direct labour for working longer hours (here the AFC is shown by the dotted line), or by buying some additional small unit type of machinery here the AFC curve shifts upwards, and starts falling again, as shown on line ab).

The Average Variable Cost

As in the traditional theory, the average variable cost of modern microeconomics includes the cost of: a.) direct labour which varies with output; b.) raw materials; c.) running expenses of machinery.

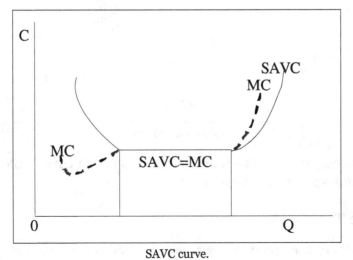

SAVC curve.

The short-run average cost curve (SAVC) in modern theory has a saucer-type shape, that is, it is broadly U-shaped but has a flat stretch over a range of output. The flat stretch corresponds to the built-in plant reserve capacity. Over this stretch, the SAVC is equal to the MC both being constant per unit of output. To the left of the flat stretch, MC lies below the SAVC, while to the right of the flat stretch the MC rises above the SAVC. The falling part of the SAVC shows the reduction in cost due to the better utilization of the fixed factor and the consequent increase in skills and productivity of the variable factor (labour). With better skills, the wastes in raw materials are also being reduced and a better utilization of the whole plant is reached.

The increasing part of the SAVC reflects reduction in labour productivity due to the longer hours of work, the increase in cost of labour due to overtime payment (which is higher than the current wage), the wastes in material and the more frequent break-down of machinery as the firm operates with overtime or with more shifts. The innovation of modern microeconomics in this field is the theoretical establishment of a short-run SAVC curve with a flat stretch over a certain range of output. The reserve capacity makes it possible to have constant SAVC within a certain range of output as shown in figure. It should be clear that this reserve capacity is planned in order to give the maximum flexibility in the operation of the firm. It is completely different from the excess capacity which arises with the U-shaped average cost curve of the traditional theory of the firm. The traditional theory assumes that each plant is designed without any flexibility, as such; if the firm produces an output Q, smaller than Qm, there is excess (unplanned) capacity, equal to the difference Qm-Q. This excess capacity is obviously undesirable because it leads to higher unit costs.

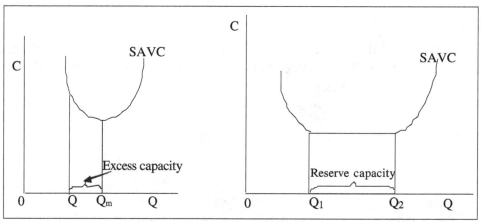

(a) Excess Capacity and (b) Reserve Capacity.

In the modern theory of costs, the range of output Q_1Q_2 in figure b reflects the planned capacity which does not lead to increased costs.

The Average Total Cost

The average total cost is obtained by fixed (inclusive of the normal profit) and the average variable cost at each level of output. The ATC curves fall continuously up to the level of output (Q_2) at which the reserve capacity is exhausted. Beyond that level, ATC will start rising. The MC will intersect the ATC Curve at its minimum point (which occurs to the right of the level of output Q_A, at which the flat stretch of the AVC ends).

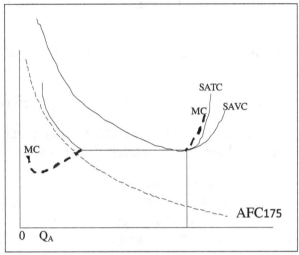

Short-run Cost Curves.

Long-run Costs in Modern Microeconomic Theory

All costs are variable in the long run and they give rise to a long run cost curve which is roughly L-shaped. Empirical evidence about the long run average cost curve reveals that the LAC curve is L-shaped rather than U-shaped. In the beginning, the LAC curve rapidly falls but after a point, "the curve remains flat, or may slope gently downwards, at its right-hand end". Production cost fall continuously with increases in output. At very large scales of output, managerial costs may rise. But the fall in production costs more than offsets the increase in the managerial costs, so that the total LAC falls with increases in scale. Economists have assigned the following reasons for the L-shape of the LAC curve.

Production and Managerial Costs

In the long-run, all costs being variable, production costs and managerial costs of a firm are taken into account when considering the effect of expansion of output on average costs. As output increases, production costs fall continuously while managerial cost may rise at very large scales of output. But the fall in production costs outweighs the increase in managerial costs so that the LAC curve falls with increases in output. We analyze the behaviour of production and managerial costs in explaining the L-Shaped of the LAC Curve.

- Production Costs: As a firm increases its scale of production, costs fell steeply in the beginning and then gradually. This is due to the technical economies of large scale production enjoyed by the firm. Initially, these economies are substantial, but after a certain level of output, when all or most of these economies have been achieved, the firm reaches the minimal optimal scale or minimum efficient scale (MES). Given the technology of the industry, the firm can continue to enjoy some technical economies at outputs larger than the MES for the following reasons:

- From further decentralization and improvement in skills and productivity of labour.

- From lower repair costs after the firm reaches a certain size.

- By itself producing some of the materials and equipment cheaply which the firm needs instead have buying them from other firms.

- Managerial Costs: In modern firms, for each plant there is a corresponding managerial set-up for its smooth operation. There are various levels of management, each having a separate management technique applicable to a certain range of output. Thus, given a managerial setup for a plant, its managerial costs first fall with the expansion of output and it is only at a very large scale of output, they rise very slowly. In summary, production costs fall smoothly at very large scales, while managerial costs may rise slowly at very large scales of output. But the fall in production costs more than offsets the rise in managerial costs so that the LAC curve falls smoothly or becomes flat at very large scales of output, thereby giving rise to the L-shape of the LAC curve. In order to draw such an LAC curve, we take three short-run average cost curves SAC_1, SAC_2, and SAC_3 representing three plants with the same technology.

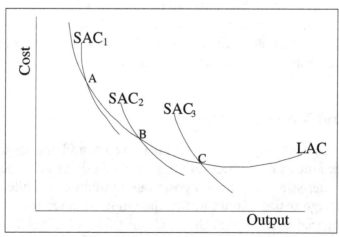

The LAC Curve.

Each SAC curve includes production costs, managerial costs, other fixed costs and a margin for normal profits. Each scale of plant (SAC) is subject to a typical load factor capacity so that points A, B and C represent the minimal optimal scale of output of each plant. By joining all such points as A, B and C of a large number of SACs, we trace out a smooth and continuous LAC curve, as shown in figure.

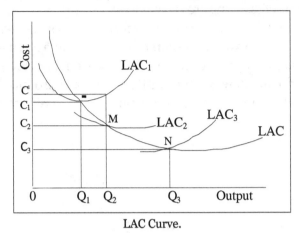

LAC Curve.

This curve does not turn up at very large scales of output. It does not envelope the SAC curves but intersects them at the optimal level of output of each plant.

Technical Progress

Another reason for the existence of the L-shaped LAC curve in the modern theory of costs is technical progress. The traditional theory of costs assumes no technical progress while explaining the U-shaped LAC curve. The empirical results on long-run costs confirm the widespread existence of economies of scale due to technical progress in firms. The period, between which technical progress has taken place, the long-run average costs show a falling trend. The evidence on diseconomies is much less certain. So an upturn of the LAC at the top end of the size scale has not been observed. The L-shape of the LAC curve due to technical progress is explained in figure.

Suppose the firm is producing OQ_1 output on LAC_1 curve at per unit cost of OC_1 output on LAC_1 curve at a per unit cost of OC_1. If there is an increase in demand for the firm's product to OQ_2, with no change in technology, the firm will produce OQ_2 output along the LAC_1 curve at per unit cost of OC'. If, however, there is technical progress in the firm, it will install a new plant having LAC_2 as the long-run average cost curve. On this plant, it produces OQ_2 output at a lower cost oC_2 per unit. Similarly, if the firm decides to increase its output to OQ_3 to meet further rise in demand, technical progress may have advanced to such a level that it installs the plant with the LAC_3 curve. Now it produces OQ_3 output at a still lower cost OC_3 per unit. If the minimum points, L, M and N of these U-shaped long-run average cost curves LAC_1, LAC_2 and LAC_3 are joined by a line, it forms an L-shaped gently sloping downward curve LAC.

Learning

Yet another reason for the L-shaped long-run average cost curve is the learning process.

Learning is the product of experience. If experience in this context can be measured by the amount of a commodity produced, then higher the production is, the lower it is per unit cost. The consequences of learning are similar to increasing returns. First, the knowledge gained from working on a large scale cannot be forgotten. Second, learning increases the rate of productivity. Third, experience is measured by the aggregate output produced since the firm first started to produce the product. Learning by doing has been observed when firm starts producing new products. After they have produced the first unit, they are able to reduce the time required for production and thus reduce per unit cost.

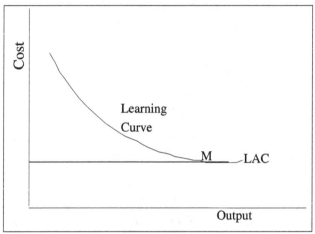

The Learning Curve.

Figure shows a learning curve (LAC) which relates the cost of producing a given output to the total output over the entire time period. Growing experience with making the product leads to falling costs as more and more of it is produced. When the firm has exploited all learning possibilities, costs reach a minimum level, M in the figure. Thus the LAC curve is L-shaped due to learning by doing.

Relationship Between LAC and LMC Curves

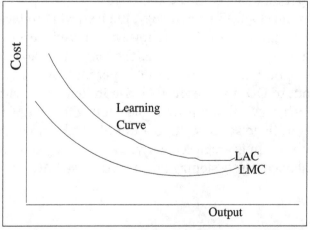

LAC and LMC Curves.

In the modern theory of costs, if the LAC curve falls smoothly and continuously even at very large scales of output, the LMC curve will lie below the LAC curve throughout its length, as shown in the figure.

If the LAC curve is downward sloping up to the point of a minimum optimal scale of plant or a minimum efficient scale (MES) of plant beyond which no further scale economies exist, the LAC curve becomes horizontal. In this case, the LMC curve lies below the LAC curve until the MES point M is reached, and beyond this point the LMC curve coincides with the LAC curve, as shown in figure.

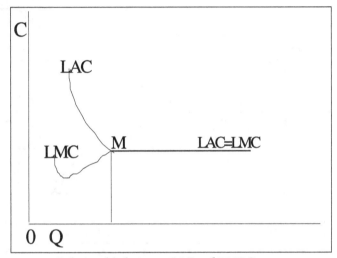

Relationship between LAC and LMC Curves.

Cost Functions' Derivation

Whether it is production or cost, there are three categories of concepts – total, average and marginal. In the short run, there are three types of total cost curves: total fixed cost curve, total variable cost curve and total cost curve whereas in the long run, there is no fixed cost, only variable and total cost. The average and marginal cost curves can be geometrically derived from a total cost curve.

Derivation of Cost Functions

The Total fixed cost (TFC) curve is parallel to the X-axis since the costs remain the same irrespective of the level of output. In the table, we find TFC is $ 240 at all levels of output. The Average Fixed cost (AFC) equals TFC divided by output. Geometrically, at the output level of one unit, AFC is equal to the slope of ray OA and refers to point 'a' on the AFC curve. At output level of two units, AFC is equal to the slope of ray OB and refers to point 'b' on the AFC curve .Similarly; we can plot for other levels of output and get the corresponding points on the AFC curve, as shown in figure.

The AFC curve is a rectangular hyperbola – it is asymptotic to the axes, which means that as the AFC curve moves further away from the origin along the axis, it gets closer to the axis but never touches it.

Output	TFC	TVC	TC	AFC	AVC	ATC	MC
0	240	0	240	240	-	240	-
1	240	120	360	240	120	360	120
2	240	160	400	120	80	200	40
3	240	180	420	80	60	140	20
4	240	212	452	60	53	113	32
5	240	280	520	48	56	104	68
6	240	420	660	40	70	110	140
7	240	640	880	30.43	90.14	120.57	220

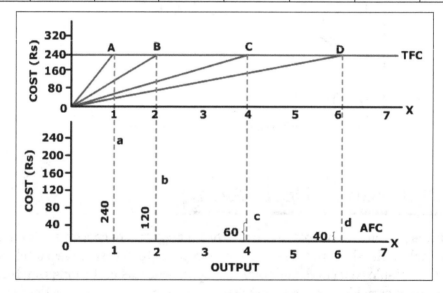

Derivation of Average Variable Cost Curve from Total Variable Cost Curve

The Average Variable cost (AVC) is equal to the TVC divided by output. The AVC is equal to $ 120 at output level of one unit (TVC is $ 120). It is represented by the slope of the ray OA and is plotted as point 'a' on the AVC curve. At output level of three units, AVC is $ 60, and is plotted as point 'c' on the AVC curve. Similarly, we can plot other points on the AVC curve. The AVC curve is downward sloping till point 'd' and then slopes upward. The slope of the ray OC from the origin to the TVC curve is the lowest at point 'C' on the TVC curve which implies that AVC at the output level of 4 units is the lowest at d.

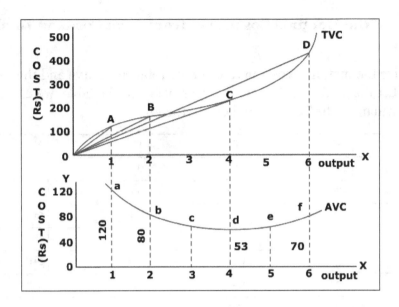

Derivation of Average Total Cost Curve from Total Cost Curve

When the level of output is 0, there is no variable cost. Therefore, the TFC = TC=AFC. When the output level is one, TC is \$ 360 and ATC is also \$ 360. When the output level is 2, TC is \$ 400 and ATC is 400 ÷ 2 = \$ 200. The ATC at different level of output is indicated by the slope of the ray from the origin to the TC curve. Thus, OA, OB, OC and OD are rays whose slope indicates the ATC at the corresponding level of output. These points are plotted to obtain points 'a', 'b', 'c', 'd' and so on to get the AVC curve. The slope of a ray from the origin falls up to point 'C' on TC curve and rises afterwards. The ray from the origin (OC) is tangent to the TC curve at point 'C'. Thus, ATC curve falls up to point 'C' (point 'c' is the lowest point on the ATC curve)and then rises , giving it a 'U'shape.

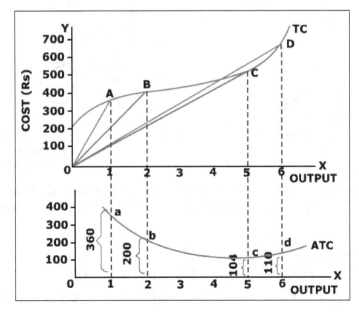

Derivation of the Marginal Cost Curve from Total Cost and Total Variable Cost Curve

We can derive the marginal cost curve from the total cost curve and the total variable cost curve. Let the TFC and TVC are given as below in the table, we can find the MC from it. We can draw the TC, TVC and derive the MC.

Output	TC	TFC	TVC	MC
0	120	120	0	-
1	180	120	60	60
2	200	120	80	20
3	210	120	90	10
4	230	120	110	20
5	270	120	150	40
6	360	120	240	90

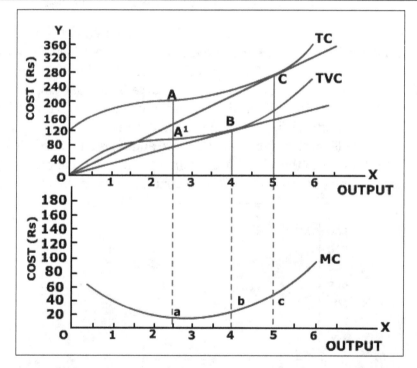

From the figure, we find that the slopes of the TVC curve and the TC curve are the same at every level of output. Point A and A¹ are the points of inflexion respectively on TC and TVC.

The MC falls up to 2.5 units of output and refers to point 'a 'on the MC curve and then rises. The MC is given by the slope of the TVC curve at point B. At 5 units of output, MC is equal to the slope of the TC curve at point C. Thus, point 'b' refers to the lowest AVC and point 'c' refers to the lowest AC. Marginal cost is sometimes known as 'incremental cost' – as it is the increase in TC consequent upon a small increase in output.

$$MC = \Delta TC/\Delta Q \text{ or } \Delta TVC/\Delta Q$$

- ΔTC is the change in total cost due to a small change in output.

- ΔTVC is the change in total variable cost due to a small change in output.

- ΔQ is the small change in output.

For example, the total cost of producing 4 units of output is $ 1000 and the total cost of producing 5 units of output is $ 1200, therefore marginal cost of the fifth unit is $ 200($ 1200 – $ 1000).

Because, fixed cost remains unchanged in the short run, therefore, marginal cost is also the increase in total variable cost due to a small increase in output.

Cost Curves in the Long–run

Since in the long-run, all factors are variable, therefore there is only variable cost. In the long run, to increase the level of production, all factors have to be increased and this results in expansion of scale.

The relationship between Total, Average and marginal cost concepts is the same. In the long run, the relationship between LRMC and LRAC is the same as it exists in the short run .The derivation of TC, ATC and MC can be explained in the same manner as under short run. The Long –run Average cost curve or the LAC curve is the locus of points denoting the least cost of producing different levels of output in the long run. It shows the minimum average costs of producing the corresponding output in the long-run.

The LAC curve is thus a planning curve that guides the firm in deciding on the most optimal size of the industrial plant for producing a given level of output. An optimal sized plant is one which enables the production of the output at the minimum costs per unit of output. Given the technology, the firm is free to choose the plant size which entails the least cost. For example, if the firm decides to produce OQ_1 level of output, then it will choose the plant size SAC_2 and not SAC_1.If the demand for the firm's output increases to OQ_3, then the average costs starts increasing along the plant SAC_2 and the firm decides to set up a larger plant size SAC_3 to minimize its average costs of production in the long-run.

The long-run average curve does not touch the short-run average cost curves on their minimum points. Graphically it can touch the minimum points of SACs only under constant returns to scale. In the phase of increasing returns to scale and decreasing cost, the LAC curve touches the SAC curves to the left of the minimum points of the SAC curves and in the phase of diminishing returns it touches the SAC curves to their right. The LAC is therefore, not the locus of lowest points of SAC curves. The downward sloping portion of LAC comprises of only increasing returns and diminishing cost portions of SAC curves.

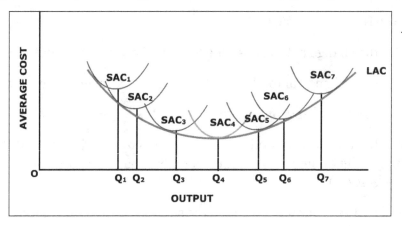

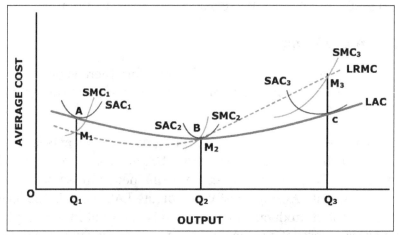

Given the SAC and SMC curves and the LAC curves, we can derive the LRMC curve with the following steps:

• By drawing perpendiculars from the tangency points, A, B and C which intersects the SMC curves at M_1, M_2 and M_3.

• Join the points M_1, M_2, M_3, to obtain the LRMC curve.

Relationship between LAC and LRMC

The relationship between LAC and LRMC is the same as it exists between the short run average cost SAC and the SMC. LRMC lies below the LAC when LAC is falling and above it when LAC is rising. Thus LAC and LRMC intersect when LAC is the minimum. In the long run, the plant size can be changed while in the short run, the existing plant will continue to be used for producing larger output. Since, in the long run all factors are variable, therefore, all cost of production are variable. There is no need to distinguish between fixed and variable cost.

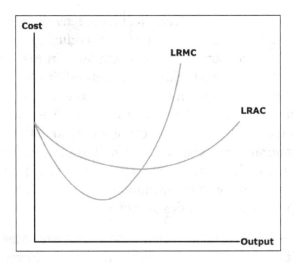

Economies of Scale

Scale economies may be defined initially (and traditionally) as those benefits that result when the increased size of a single operating unit (plant), producing a single product, reduces the unit cost of production. The minimum efficient scale (MES) is in theory the size of plant at which all economies of scale are exhausted and beyond which the long-term average cost curve either turns upward, or remains flat (reflecting constant returns to scale in production). The cost gradient is defined as the slope of the cost curve. The long-run average cost curve identifies minimum average costs for each production level, assuming given factor prices and quality, and state of technology.

In order to understand economies of scale, it is important to identify their different dimensions. Scale economies may be internal or external to the plant, internal or external to the firm, internal or external to the industry, static and/or dynamic. There are economies of scale in production and possibly in functions such as distribution, management, marketing and research.

Technical economies of scale for production are the theoretically best-known type and relate to estimates of the MES and cost gradients. There is the phenomenon of learning effects associated with increasing experience gained through the production of a product or a service. The learning curve postulates that the average cost for a product is a decreasing function of the total production of that product in the past, i.e. there is an average cost reduction over time due to production experience.

Technical economies of scale should not be confused with technical efficiency, which requires the minimization of costs for any given output (as distinct from average costs varying with output). However, when it comes to measurement issues, the two concepts are inevitably intertwined.

There are economies of scale arising from firm level activities which are distinct from those arising from large plants, large outputs for individual products and long production runs. Such firm level economies concern activities in management, advertising, research and development, and risk taking (e.g. possibilities for obtaining finance and innovation) and are sometimes known as dynamic economies of scale. There may also be economies of rapid firm (and market) growth. These arise from better scope for taking advantage of economies of scale, technical progress, and a relatively healthy working climate. Some economies may also result from the operation of multiple geographically-dispersed plants as an integrated system (multiplant economies). However, these may not be significant. Multi-product economies can result from the production of a diversified range of products (economies of scope).

External economies of scale usually refer to those that are external to the firm; the average costs of the firm depend on the size of the entire industry. A large industry in a country might generate a labour force with skills and habits useful for industrial life support an extensive infrastructure, allow many specialized crafts to develop, etc. An important reason for scale economies at the industry level is a greater division of labour. Scale economies are national if they depend on the size of the national industry. They are international if they depend on the world-wide (or possibly EU) size of the industry.

Economies external to the industry may also arise. They can also be national (external to the industries but internal to their home country) or international. Such economies result from cross-industry externalities. More particularly, they can arise from industrial inter-dependence such as that between buyers and suppliers of raw materials or intermediate products.

Potential economies of scale, as measured by rated capacity, are physical characteristics of the production facilities. Actual economies of scale, as determined by the actual amount of material processed within a specific time period, are organizational. Those economies would then depend on the organizational human capabilities essential to exploit the potential of technological processes such as knowledge, skill, experience and teamwork and/or the willingness of the firm (or industry) to reach them.

Potential economies of scale vary widely between different countries, industries and different time periods. It has been argued that those differences in economies of scale (and scope) result from differences in technologies of production and distribution, and differences in the sizes and location of markets. This is particularly relevant at a time of rapid technological change and changing market characteristics. Findings from research on economies of scale are debatable, requiring careful and sophisticated evaluation.

Economies of scale have been recognized as important determinants of the structure of an industry. Scale economies relate to the industrial organization literature in three main aspects. First, they are an important determinant of productive efficiency. Second, we wish to explain market concentration and to inquire whether industries are more concentrated than necessary to secure production efficiency. Third, we are concerned to know whether economies of scale represent a barrier to the entry for new firms (although it could be the presence of sunk costs rather than economies of scale that acts as a barrier to entry).

In the area of industrial structure, production has exogenous sunk costs, but some expenditure on advertising and on research and development are endogenous overheads (sunk costs) and can be used strategically by competing firms. Furthermore, learning-by-doing also involves a form of (exogenous) sunk cost that is the cost to produce.

The conventional theory of economic integration is largely associated with neo-classical and factor-endowment trade models, in which the measurement of the impact of economic integration is provided by the concepts of trade creation and trade diversion. This analysis is based on the assumptions that markets are characterized by perfect competition and production by constant returns to scale. It can be argued that the traditional theory is 'static' and that 'dynamic' effects also need to be considered because economic integration can yield significant growth-related gains.

These dynamic gains relate to enhanced economies of scale and scope linked to effective single market size as rates of capital formation; human resource development; technological change and entrepreneurial activity accelerate. A new literature has emerged in the study of economic integration, embracing dynamic effects and concentrating on imperfect competition, economies of scale and product diversity. In addition, when dynamic gains are considered, their locational distribution becomes an important issue.

Technical Economies of Scale

Methods of Measurement

There are three main techniques of estimation: statistical cost analysis, engineering estimates, and the survivor test.

The statistical approach relates costs to output volume of plants or firms of different sizes. A fairly large number of variables have to be taken into account to give significance to the results. Firms and plants classified in the same industry often have differences in product mix, differences in the age of the capital stock (and hence in the embodied technology), differences in input prices, cumulative output volume, and so forth. In practice, complete, reliable data are hard to come by. Moreover, this approach may reflect short-run rather than long-run average costs, especially as long-run costs often incorporate rents, and so reveal little about economies of scale.

The engineering approach looks directly for opinions from engineers and managers about the shape and position of the cost curves, and so tries to estimate the minimum efficient scale (MES) directly based on the use of the 'best current practice' techniques.

This approach is in principle the most promising. However, engineering estimates require a substantial, costly and time-consuming research process, so that they often give comparable estimates for only a small range of (manufacturing but not service) industries and deter researchers from employing them. Also, engineering data are necessarily hypothetical in the sense that they do not allow for managerial diseconomies, inelastic factor supplies, potentially greater strike activity in larger plants, transport costs, and heterogeneous products, etc. Nevertheless, they provide a useful benchmark.

The survivor technique attempts to identify the size class which is seen to be increasing its share of industry output over a period of time, and suggests that the average size of this class represents MES. The idea is that, taking all market considerations into account, the most successful size must be most efficient. There are limitations to this technique. It does not say anything about the level of costs and does not always clarify the shape of the cost curve. Survival patterns are not always stable over time and the criteria for distinguishing surviving from non-surviving size classes embody a certain amount of arbitrariness. Survivor estimates may be tainted by pecuniary conditions, when plants (and most certainly firms) may increase their market share not because they have lower costs but because of increased market power. The results of the 'survivor test' may also reflect differences between firms using different technologies and showing different innovative performances over a particular period of time. Lastly, the selected survival size class contains different plants over time as plants move in and out of their size class.

Measures of Typical Size

Faced with these problems, many analysts use existing size data, derived from census size distributions (say sales or employment) as a proxy variable for the minimum efficient scale. It is important to recognize that these are measures of 'typical' firm size, and not of MES. They have no theoretical foundation as direct measures of technical (or any other) economies of scale. However, because firm size and economies of scale are intimately related, they will be strongly correlated. For this reason, typical firm size is often used as a proxy for MES in empirical work. For some purposes, that may be reasonable, but on its own, a measure of typical size says nothing about the attainment of scale economies. Where these measures become truly revealing is when they are related to an independent measure of scale economies, such as engineering estimates.

Various proxy measures for MES figure in the empirical literature. The simplest measure is to take the arithmetic average. A more refined proxy is the average size of plants comprising the upper half of an industry's size distribution. Another example of typical size is the Florence median plant size, i.e. the size of plant of the midpoint of the size distribution in the sense that 50 per cent of industry size is accounted for by plants in excess of the midpoint. Formally, this is the median of the first moment distribution (MFMD).

Units of Measurement

Whatever measure of MES or typical size is chosen, we must also choose the units of measurement. Common units of measurement are total assets, net assets, sales, employment and value added. Empirical results are affected by the choice of size measure since the available measures are not perfectly correlated. In this case, studies which use different size variables are likely to reach broadly similar but different conclusions. This is a serious problem if, for example, the same firm is assigned to different size groups according to which size measure is used. In practice, gross value added, sales and employment are the variables most likely to be available for use in the measure of size.

Theoretically the most appropriate measure of a firm's activities is offered by value-added. However, this measure excludes contributions from all inputs other than labour and capital, and is affected by the degree of vertical integration of the firm. If the size measure is the turnover of the firm, it refers to the money values of its different products. Difficulties may arise in finding an appropriate deflation index when using data over time, or exchange rates when comparing data from different countries. Similar problems surround the valuation of fixed assets. In addition, firms may use different accounting procedures due to different depreciation methods, or differences in the lifetime of capital assets that is assumed for depreciation purposes. Firms also have different capital structure, e.g. representing a collection of capital of different vintages. The use of all these size measures may further be complicated by product mix variations between firms or plants.

Employment is the most common, often unique, measure used in size distributions of firms, contained in published national census of production data. Employment, i.e. the numbers of workers, is only an approximation of labour input for the firm which is better measured by man-hours. In the current period, this may be especially important as there is a large number of part-time workers. Bearing all the above points in mind, special care must be exercised in interpreting the results from size measurement.

Real and Pecuniary Economies of Scale

The measurement of economies of scale is primarily concerned with the 'real' economies of scale, i.e. those arising from the reduction of inputs consumed per unit of output at higher scales of output. Those technical economies of scale arise from the actual physical organization of production activities. They result in an increase in economic efficiency and a reduction of costs. Yet other economies and advantages of large scale may be obtained by individual firms or industries, such as pecuniary gains, but these do not reflect any improvement in real efficiency. Pecuniary gains may refer to bargaining power to obtain supplies at lower prices, privileged access to the capital market or effective lobbying. Both technical and pecuniary gains occur together, and no easy method has yet been designed in research to exclude all pecuniary elements from measures of scale economies. Only engineering estimates can explicitly exclude them.

Recent Empirical Studies

Technical economies of scale are the theoretically best known type of production economies. Apart from production economies of scale, economies achievable in other common functions at the level of the firm, such as promotion, research and development, management and financing, were often regarded as less significant and/or more difficult to quantify.

A feature of the existing analysis on economies of scale is that the information available forces a focus on manufacturing. For service industries it is not currently possible to provide a comprehensive assessment of scale economies similar to that in manufacturing industries. However, the manufacturing sector in Europe has, on the whole, been able to maintain its important role in the European Community despite the wild speculation on the 'deindustrialization' of Europe.

Currently, the main references concerning estimates of economies of scale have been published by the Commission of the European Community. He concluded that 'there are substantial scale effects for products and production runs to be obtained in a wide range of manufacturing industries'. Industries where economies of scale were found to be the largest included transport equipment, machinery and instrument manufacture, chemicals and paper and printing. Other industries such as textile and clothing, food, drink and tobacco were considered as generally having a limited scope for technical economies of scale.

Engineering estimates are believed to be reasonably reliable estimates of production scale economies. However, those estimates have been criticized elsewhere and it has been argued that the importance of economies of scale has been grossly exaggerated in much of the manufacturing sector as well as in other areas. Many studies have reported relatively small optimal plant size (MES), roughly constant costs at the firm level and relatively flat cost gradients. In addition, Estimates of cost gradients, especially at the firm level, probably contain a degree of bias as a result of pecuniary economies. It may also be that upward bias of estimates of internal economies of scale in Europe come from not taking into account the effects of other dynamic and external economies in those estimates.

Many studies have used the United States as a reference point for evaluating economic performance in Europe. In a comparative study of managerial enterprise in the United States, the United Kingdom and Germany from the 1880s through to the 1930s.

However, there cannot be universal generalization, and the success of American managers in the first years of the 20th century has to be placed in the context of the use of techniques of mass production and mass distribution. For many industries, especially those making differentiated products, new flexible manufacturing systems may have reduced the minimum optimal scale. But for other industries, especially mass production ones, there may be unexploited, even increasing, economies of scale in production. Technological innovations, often sponsored by changes in demand, generate a continually evolving process of change.

As far as services are concerned, estimates of economies of scale are scarce and difficult to construct empirically. Several attempts to measure technical economies of scale in services have produced different results. It would seem that those economies of scale are generally small and less than for manufacturing. Economies of scope, however, may play a more important role in services.

Learning Curve

Learning usually occurs when humans are involved; this is a basic consideration in the work/job design. It is important to be able to predict how learning will affect task times and costs.

The Concept of Learning Curves

Human performance of activities typically shows improvement when the activities are done on a repetitive basis: The time required to perform a task decreases with increasing repetitions. Learning curves display this phenomenon. The degree of improvement and the number of repetitions needed to realize the major portion of the improvement is a function of the task being done. If the task is short and somewhat routine, only a modest amount of improvement is likely to occur, and it generally occurs during the first few repetitions. If the task is fairly complex and has a longer duration, improvements will occur over a larger number of repetitions. Therefore, learning curves have little relevance for planning or scheduling of routine short activities, but they do have relevance for complex long repetitive activities.

Figure illustrates the basic relationship between units produced and time per unit: time per unit decreases as the number of units produced increases. In fact, the most common learning curve model, which is studied here, assumes that the rate of decrease in unit time remains constant as the number of units produced doubles. Also note that instead of time per unit, some applications use average time (up to and including the unit). The former is called Crawford's method (measures learning by the unit time) whereas the latter is called Wright's method (measures learning by the average time). In this supplement, we will exclusively focus on learning by unit time (i.e., Crawford's method).

The general relationship is also referred to as an improvement curve. When unit cost is used instead of unit time, the relationship is usually referred to as experience curve or progress function. Experts agree that the learning effect is also due to factors other than actual worker learning (which results in increased dexterity, reduced rework, etc.). Some of the improvement can be traced to changes in methods, layout, support services, tooling, design, and lot size increases. In addition, management input can be an important factor through improvements in planning, scheduling, motivation, and control.

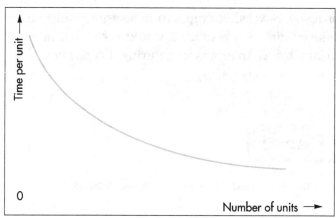

The learning effect: Time per unit decreases as the number of units produced increases.

Major changes that are made once production is underway, such as product redesign or new equipment, can actually cause a temporary increase in time per unit until workers adjust to the change. If a number of major changes are made during production, the learning curve would be more realistically described by a series of scallops instead of a smooth curve, as illustrated in figure. Nonetheless, it is convenient to work with a smooth curve, which can be interpreted as the average effect.

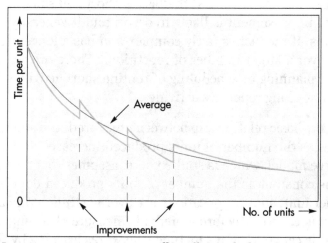

Improvements may create a scallop effect in the learning curve.

From an organizational standpoint, what makes the learning effect more than an interesting curiosity is its predictability, which becomes readily apparent if the relationship is plotted on a log-log scale. The straight line that results reflects a constant learning percentage, which is the basis of learning curve estimates: Every doubling of units produced results in a constant percentage decrease in the time per unit. Typical decreases range from 10 percent to 20 percent. By convention, learning curves are referred to in terms of the complements of their decrease rates. For example, an 80 percent learning curve denotes a 20 percent decrease in unit time with each doubling of units produced, and a 90 percent curve denotes a 10 percent decrease rate. The 80 or 90 percent learning percentage in the above examples is the "slope" of the learning curve. Note that a 100 percent curve would imply no decrease in unit time at all (i.e., no learning).

For some examples of learning curves in industry see figure, and for slopes of typical industrial activities see figure. Note the log-log scales and the fact that the unit time curves are approximately linear.

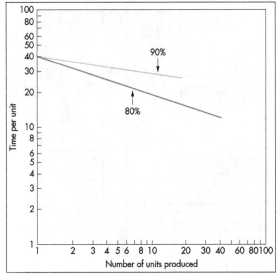

On a log-log graph, learning curves are straight lines.

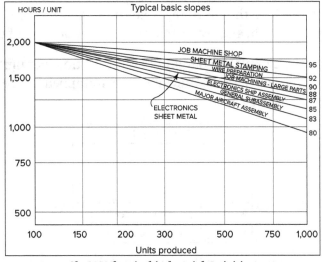

Slopes of typical industrial activities.

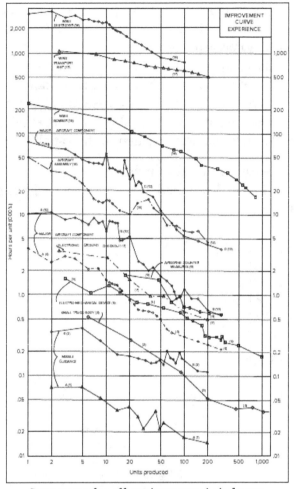

Some examples of learning curves in industry.

Example: An activity is known to have an 80 percent learning curve. It has taken a worker 10 hours to produce the first unit. Determine expected completion times for these units: the 2nd, 4th, 8th, and 16th (note successive doubling of units).

Solution: Each time the cumulative output doubles, the time per unit for that quantity should be approximately equal to the previous time multiplied by the learning percentage (80 percent in this case). Thus:

Unit	Unit Time (Hours)
1	= 10
2	0.8(10) = 8
4	0.8(8) = 6.4
8	0.8(6.4) = 5.12
16	0.8(5.12) = 4.096

Example illustrates an important point and also raises an interesting question. The point is that the time reduction per unit becomes smaller and smaller as the number of units produced increases. For example, the second unit required two hours less time than the first, but the decrease from the 8th to the 16th unit was only slightly more than one hour. The question raised is: How are times calculated for units such as three, five, six, seven, and other units that don't fall into the doubling pattern?

Determining Unit Times

There are two ways to obtain the unit times. One is to use a formula; the other is to use a table of values. First, consider the formula approach. The formula is based on the existence of a linear relationship between the time per unit and the number of units produced when these two variables are expressed in logarithms.

The unit time (i.e., the number of direct labour hours required) for the nth unit can be calculated using the formula:

$$T_n = T_1 \times n^b$$

Where,

- T_n = Time for the nth unit.

- T_1 = Time for the first unit.

- $b = \dfrac{\ln\left(\dfrac{\text{Learning Percentage}}{100}\right)}{\ln(2)}$

To use the formula, you need to know the time for the first unit T_1 and the learning percentage. For example, for an 80 percent learning curve with T_1 = 10 hours, the time for the third unit would be calculated as:

$$T_3 = 10(3^{\ln.8/\ln2}) = 10(3^{-.223/.693}) = 10(3^{-.322}) = 7.02$$

The second approach is to use a "learning factor" from table. The table shows two things for some selected learning percentages. One is the unit time factor for the unit number up to 30. The other is the total (cumulative) time factor. The calculation for both times is a relatively simple operation: Multiply the learning factor by the time required for the first unit.

To find the time for unit n (e.g., n = 10 → the 10th unit), use the formula:

$$T_n = T_1 \times \text{unit time factor}$$

Thus, for an 85 percent learning curve with T_1 = 4 hours, the time for the 10th unit would be 4 × .583 = 2.33 hours. To find the time for all units up to unit n (e.g., n = 10 → the first 10 units), use the formula:

$$\Sigma T_n = T_1 \times \text{total time factor}$$

Thus, for an 85 percent curve with $T_1 = 4$ hours, the total time for all first 10 units (including the time for unit 1) would be $4 \times 7.116 = 28.464$ hours.

Example: An airplane manufacturer is negotiating a contract for the production of 20 small jets. The initial jet required 400 days of direct labour. The learning percentage is 80 percent. Estimate the expected number of days of direct labour for:

- The 20th jet.

- All 20 jets.

- The average time for 20 jets.

Solution: Using Table with n = 20 and an 80 percent learning percentage, you find these factors: Unit time = .381. Total time = 10.485.

- Expected time for 20th jet: 400(.381) = 152.4 days.

- Expected total time for all 20 jets: 400(10.485) = 4,194 days.

- Average time for 20 jets: 4,194 ÷ 20 = 209.7 days.

Use of table requires a time for the first unit. If for some reason the completion time of the first unit is not available, or if the manager believes that the completion time for some later unit is more accurate, the table can also be used to obtain an estimate of the time for the first unit.

Table: Learning factors.

Unit Number	70% Unit	70% Total Time	75% Unit	75% Total Time	80% Unit	80% Total Time	85% Unit	85% Total Time	90% Unit	90% Total Time
1	1.000	1.000	1.000	1.000	1.000	1.000	1.000	1.000	1.000	1.000
2	.700	1.700	.750	1.750	.800	1.800	.850	1.850	.900	1.900
3	.568	2.268	.634	2.384	.702	2.502	.773	2.623	.846	2.746
4	.490	2.758	.562	2.946	.640	3.142	.723	3.345	.810	3.556
5	.437	3.195	.513	3.459	.596	3.738	.686	4.031	.783	4.339
6	.398	3.593	.475	3.934	.562	4.299	.657	4.688	.762	5.101
7	.367	3.960	.446	4.380	.534	4.834	.634	5.322	.744	5.845
8	.343	4.303	.422	4.802	.512	5.346	.614	5.936	.729	6.574
9	.323	4.626	.402	5.204	.493	5.839	.597	6.533	.716	7.290
10	.306	4.932	.385	5.589	.477	6.315	.583	7.116	.705	7.994
11	.291	5.223	.370	5.958	.462	6.777	.570	7.686	.695	8.689
12	.278	5.501	.357	6.315	.449	7.227	.558	8.244	.685	9.374
13	.267	5.769	.345	6.660	.438	7.665	.548	8.792	.677	10.052

14	.257	6.026	.334	6.994	.428	8.092	.539	9.331	.670	10.721
15	.248	6.274	.325	7.319	.418	8.511	.530	9.861	.663	11.384
16	.240	6.514	.316	7.635	.410	8.920	.522	10.383	.656	12.040
17	.233	6.747	.309	7.944	.402	9.322	.515	10.898	.650	12.690
18	.226	6.973	.301	8.245	.394	9.716	.508	11.405	.644	13.334
19	.220	7.192	.295	8.540	.388	10.104	.501	11.907	.639	13.974
20	.214	7.407	.288	8.828	.381	10.485	.495	12.402	.634	14.608
21	.209	7.615	.283	9.111	.375	10.860	.490	12.892	.630	15.237
22	.204	7.819	.277	9.388	.370	11.230	.484	13.376	.625	15.862
23	.199	8.018	.272	9.660	.364	11.594	.479	13.856	.621	16.483
24	.195	8.213	.267	9.928	.359	11.954	.475	14.331	.617	17.100
25	.191	8.404	.263	10.191	.355	12.309	.470	14.801	.613	17.713
26	.187	8.591	.259	10.449	.350	12.659	.466	15.267	.609	18.323
27	.183	8.774	.255	10.704	.346	13.005	.462	15.728	.606	18.929
28	.180	8.954	.251	10.955	.342	13.347	.458	16.186	.603	19.531
29	.177	9.131	.247	11.202	.338	13.685	.454	16.640	.599	20.131
30	.174	9.305	.244	11.446	.335	14.020	.450	17.091	.596	20.727

Example: The manager in previous example believes that some unusual problems were encountered in producing the first and second jets and would like to revise the time for the first unit based on the completion time of 276 days for the third jet.

Solution: The learning factor for n = 3 and an 80 percent curve is .702. Divide the actual time for S O L U T I O N unit 3 by the learning factor to obtain the revised estimate for the time of first unit: 276 days ÷ .702 = 393.2 days.

Determining the Learning Percentage

If the learning percentage of the activity cannot be estimated based on similar previous activities or the industry learning slope, given a few observations of unit times, one can estimate the learning percentage of the activity by fitting the power function of 7S-1 to the chart of the data. For simplicity, we will change notation to more familiar symbols: $y = T_n$, $a = T_1$, and $x = n$. The equation for the power function is $y = ax^b$. The fitted power function will provide the value for a = time of the first unit, and b = ln (learning percentage/100)/ ln 2. Solving the b equation gives:

$$\text{Learning percentage} = 100 \times 2^b$$

The power function can easily be obtained from Excel by charting the data as a Line chart and using "Trendline" under Add Chart Element of DESIGN menu. Make sure to specify the Power function under More Trendline Options and tick Display Equation on chart. If some data is missing, then a scatter chart should be used where the unit time or cost will be displayed on the y axis and cumulative quantity on the x axis.

Example: The cost per patient for heart transplant in a hospital 2 for the first 17 patients is displayed below.

Heart Transplant Patient	Cost (in $1,000)
1	133
2	97
3	250
4	120
5	115
6	125
7	98
8	94
9	57
10	201
11	52
12	86
13	93
14	89
15	70
16	64
17	75

Chart the line plot of the data, fit the power function to the chart, and estimate the learning percentage.

Solution: Note that in this case, the data given are unit costs instead of unit times, and cost is directly related to the times of surgeons and nurses. After charting the data in Excel as a line chart, the "Trendline" command under add chart element of design menu was used to fit the power function to the data.

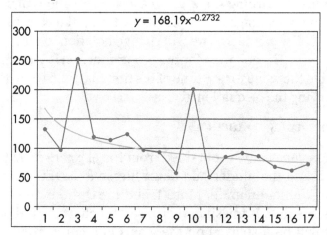

$$y = 168.19x^{-0.2732}$$

Substituting b = - 0.2732 into 100×2^b, the learning percentage = 82.75 percent.

Applications of Learning Curves

Learning curves have useful application in a number of management activities, including:

- Labour planning and scheduling.

- Negotiated selling/purchasing.

- Assessing labour training needs and performance.

Knowledge of output projections in learning situations can help managers make better decisions about how many workers they will need. Of course, managers recognize that improvement will occur; what the learning curve contributes is a method for quantifying expected future improvements.

Negotiated selling/purchasing often involves contracting for specialized items that may have a high degree of complexity. Examples include aircraft, ships, and special-purpose equipment. The direct labour cost per unit of such items can be expected to decrease as more units are produced. Hence, buyers should negotiate cost/price on that basis. For contracts that are terminated before delivery of all units, suppliers can use learning curve data to argue for an increase in the unit price for the smaller number of units. Conversely, the customer can use that information to negotiate a lower price per unit on follow-on orders on the basis of projected additional learning gains.

Learning curves can be used to determine the length of training for new workers doing complex-long-cycle jobs. The progress of each worker can be evaluated by measuring each worker's performance, graphing the results, and comparing the learning to an expected rate of learning. The comparison will reveal if a worker is underqualified , average, or overqualified for a given type of work. Also, learning curves can be used to determine the minimum number of repetitions to achieve a given standard.

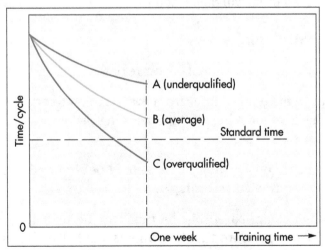

Worker learning curves can help guide personnel decisions.

Example: Use learning curves to predict the number of units that a trainee needs to produce to achieve a unit time of 6 minutes if the trainee took 10 minutes to produce the first unit and learning curve of 90 percent is expected. Use both:

1. Formula $T_n = T_1 \times$ unit time factor and table in reverse.

2. Logarithm version of Formula $T_n = T_1 \times n^b$:

$$\ln (T_n) = \ln (T_1) + b \ln (n)$$

Rewriting (where e = 2.71828):

$$n = e^{[\ln (T_n)-\ln (T_1)]/b}$$

1. Formula $T_n = T_1 \times$ unit time factor:

$$T_n = T_1 \times \text{unit time factor}$$

Setting T_n equal to the specified time of 6 minutes, T1 to 10 minutes, and solving for the unit time factor:

$$6 \text{ min} = 10 \text{ min} \times \text{unit time factor} \rightarrow \text{unit time factor} = 6 \text{ min} \div 10 \text{ min} = .600$$

Under 90 percent in the Unit Time column, we find .599 at 29 units is the closest to .600. Hence, approximately 29 units will be required to achieve the specified time.

2. Using the Formula $n = e^{[\ln (T_n)-\ln (T_1)]/b}$:

- Calculate b, b = ln(learning percentage/100) ÷ ln(2) = ln(.90) ÷ ln(2) = - 0.1054 ÷ 0.6931 = - 0.152

- $n = e^{[\ln(T_n)-\ln(T_1)]/b} = e^{[\ln(6)-\ln(10)]/-.152} = e^{[1.792-2.303)]/-.152} = e^{3.36} = 28.8$

Round to 29. Hence, 29 units will be needed to achieve a time of 6 minutes.

Cautions and Criticisms

Managers using learning curves should be aware of their limitations and pitfalls.

- Learning percentage may differ from organization to organization and by type of work. Therefore, it is best to base learning percentage on empirical studies rather than assumed percentage.

- Projections based on learning curves should be regarded as approximations of actual times and treated accordingly.

- If time estimates are based on the time for the first unit, considerable care should be taken to ensure that this time is valid. The first unit time (or even several units after that) may not be accurate due to time compression, design changes, equipment problems, etc. It may be desirable to revise the first unit time as later times become available. Since it is often necessary to estimate the time for the first unit prior to production, this caution is very important.

- Learning curves do not apply to mass production (which have short cycle times) because the decrease in time per unit is imperceptible.

- Users of learning curves sometimes fail to include carryover effects; previous experience with similar activities can reduce unit times. In this case, instead of Formula $T_n = T_1 \times$ unit time factor, the following model could be used: $T_n = T_1 \times (n + n_p)^b$ where n_p is the number of units produced previously.

References

- Thoery-of-cost: jiwaji.edu , Retrieved 25, July 2020

- Economies-of-scale-impact-on-competition-and-scale-effects: pitt.edu, Retrieved 12, January 2020

- Learning-Curves: mheducation.ca, Retrieved 03, August 2020

Understanding Supply and Demand

The quantity which the producers wish to sell is referred to as the supply and the quantity that the customers want to buy is termed as the demand. The aim of this chapter is to explore the various aspects of supply and demand such as supply curve, law of supply, demand curve and law of demand. These topics are crucial for a complete understanding of the subject.

Supply

Supply is a fundamental economic concept that describes the total amount of a specific good or service that is available to consumers. Supply can relate to the amount available at a specific price or the amount available across a range of prices if displayed on a graph. This relates closely to the demand for a good or service at a specific price; all else being equal, the supply provided by producers will rise if the price rises because all firms look to maximize profits.

Supply and demand trends form the basis of the modern economy. Each specific good or service will have its own supply and demand patterns based on price, utility and personal preference. If people demand a good and are willing to pay more for it, producers will add to the supply. As the supply increases, the price will fall given the same level of demand. Ideally, markets will reach a point of equilibrium where the supply equals the demand (no excess supply and no shortages) for a given price point; at this point, consumer utility and producer profits are maximized.

Supply Basics

The concept of supply in economics is complex with many mathematical formulas, practical applications and contributing factors. While supply can refer to anything in demand that is sold in a competitive marketplace, supply is most used to refer to goods, services, or labor. One of the most important factors that affects supply is the good's price. Generally, if a good's price increases so will the supply. The price of related goods and the price of inputs (energy, raw materials, labor) also affect supply as they contribute to increasing the overall price of the good sold.

The conditions of the production of the item in supply is also significant; for example, when a technological advancement increases the quality of a good being supplied, or if there is a disruptive innovation, such as when a technological advancement renders a good obsolete or less in demand. Government regulations can also affect supply, such as environmental laws, as well as the number of suppliers (which increases competition) and market expectations. An example of this is when environmental laws regarding the extraction of oil affect the supply of such oil.

Supply is represented in microeconomics by a number of mathematical formulas. The supply function and equation expresses the relationship between supply and the affecting factors, such as those mentioned above or even inflation rates and other market influences. A supply curve always describes the relationship between the price of the good and the quantity supplied. A wealth of information can be gleaned from a supply curve, such as movements (caused by a change in price), shifts (caused by a change that is not related to the price of the good) and price elasticity.

Related terms and concepts to supply in today's context include supply chain finance and money supply. Money supply refers specifically to the entire stock of currency and liquid assets in a country. Economists will analyze and monitor this supply, formulating policies and regulations based on its fluctuation through controlling interest rates and other such measures. Official data on a country's money supply must be accurately recorded and made public periodically. The European sovereign debt crisis, which began in 2007, is a good example of the role of a country's money supply and the global economic impact.

Global supply chain finance is another important concept related to supply in today's globalized world. Supply chain finance aims to effectively link all tenets of a transaction, including the buyer, seller, financing institution—and by proxy the supplier—to lower overall financing costs and speed up the process of business. Supply chain finance is often made possible through a technology-based platform, and is affecting industries such as the automobile and retail sectors.

Distinction between Supply and Stock

The terms 'supply' and 'stock' are often confused. A clear understanding of the difference between the two is essential. Stock is at the back of supply. It constitutes potential supply. Supply means the quantity actually offered for sale at a certain price, but stock means the total quantity which can be offered for sale if the conditions are favorable. At any time, the godowns in the 'mandi' may be full of wheat. This is the stock. If the price is low, very little wheat will come out of the godowns.

The quantity that actually comes out is the supply. The stock will change into supply and vice versa according as the market price raises or falls. In case of perishable articles, like fresh milk and vegetables, there is no difference between stock and supply. The entire stock is supply and has to be sold off for unless it is disposed of quickly, it will perish.

Supply Curve

The supply curve is a graphical representation of the correlation between the cost of a good or service and the quantity supplied for a given period. In a typical illustration, the price will appear on the left vertical axis, while the quantity supplied will appear on the horizontal axis.

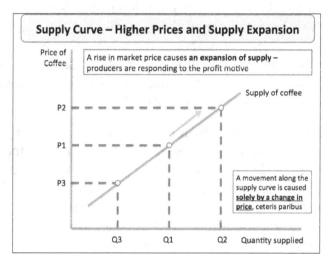

The supply curve will move upward from left to right, which expresses the law of supply: As the price of a given commodity increases, the quantity supplied increases, all else being equal.

Note that this formulation implies that price is the independent variable, and quantity the dependent variable. In most disciplines, the independent variable appears on the horizontal or x-axis, but economics is an exception to this rule.

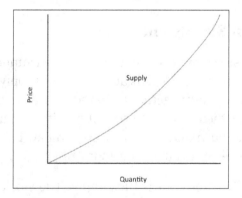

Example of Supply Curve

If the price of soybeans rises, farmers will have an incentive to plant less corn and more soybeans, and the total quantity of soybeans on the market will increase.

The degree to which rising price translates into rising quantity is called supply elasticity or price elasticity of supply. If a 50 percent rise in soybean prices causes the number of soybeans produced to rise by 50 percent, the supply elasticity of soybeans is 1. If a 50 percent rise in soybean prices only increases the quantity supplied by 10 percent, the supply elasticity is 0.2. The supply curve is shallower (closer to horizontal) for products with more elastic supply and steeper (closer to vertical) for products with less elastic supply.

The Supply Curve

Price usually is a major determinant in the quantity supplied. For a particular good with all other factors held constant, a table can be constructed of price and quantity supplied based on observed data. Such a table is called a supply schedule, as shown in the following example:

Supply Schedule

Price	Quantity Supplied
1	12
2	28
3	42
4	52
5	60

By graphing this data, one obtains the supply curve as shown below:

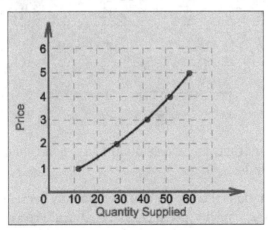

As with the demand curve, the convention of the supply curve is to display quantity supplied on the x-axis as the independent variable and price on the y-axis as the dependent variable.

The law of supply states that the higher the price, the larger the quantity supplied, all other things constant. The law of supply is demonstrated by the upward slope of the supply curve.

As with the demand curve, the supply curve often is approximated as a straight line to simplify analysis. A straight-line supply function would have the following structure:

Quantity = a + (b x Price)

where a and b are constant for each supply curve.

A change in price results in a change in quantity supplied and represents movement along the supply curve.

Shifts in the Supply Curve

While changes in price result in movement along the supply curve, changes in other relevant factors cause a shift in supply, that is, a shift of the supply curve to the left or right. Such a shift results in a change in quantity supplied for a given price level. If the change causes an increase in the quantity supplied at each price, the supply curve would shift to the right:

Supply Curve Shift

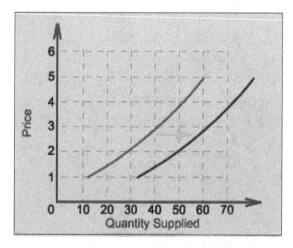

There are several factors that may cause a shift in a good's supply curve. Some supply-shifting factors include:

- Prices of other goods - the supply of one good may decrease if the price of another good increases, causing producers to reallocate resources to produce larger quantities of the more profitable good.

- Number of sellers - more sellers result in more supply, shifting the supply curve to the right.

- Prices of relevant inputs - if the cost of resources used to produce a good increases, sellers will be less inclined to supply the same quantity at a given price, and the supply curve will shift to the left.

- Technology - technological advances that increase production efficiency shift the supply curve to the right.

- Expectations - if sellers expect prices to increase, they may decrease the quantity currently supplied at a given price in order to be able to supply more when the price increases, resulting in a supply curve shift to the left.

Slope of Supply Curve

Since slope is defined as the change in the variable on the y-axis divided by the change in the variable on the x-axis, the slope of the supply curve equals the change in price divided by the change in quantity. Between the two points labeled above, the slope is (6-4)/(6-3), or 2/3. (Note again that the slope is positive because the curve slopes up and to the right).

Since this supply curve is a straight line, the slope of the curve is the same at all points.

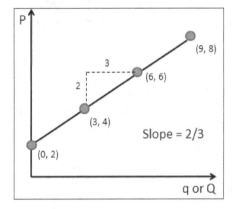

Change in Quantity Supplied

A movement from one point to another along the same supply curve, as illustrated above, is referred to as a "change in quantity supplied." Changes in quantity supplied are the result of changes in price.

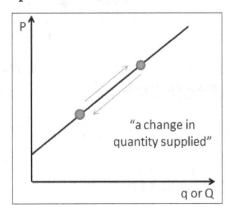

Supply Curve Equation:

$$Supply\ Curve:\ Q_S = -3 + \frac{3}{2}P$$

$$Inverse\ Supply\ Curve:\ P = 2 + \frac{2}{3}Q_S$$

The supply curve can also be written algebraically. The convention is for the supply curve to be written as quantity supplied as a function of price. The inverse supply curve, on the other hand, is price as a function of quantity supplied.

The equations above correspond to the supply curve shown earlier. When given an equation for a supply curve, the easiest way to plot it is to focus on the point that intersects the price axis. The point on the price axis is where the quantity demanded equals zero, or where 0=-3+(3/2)P. This occurs where P equals 2. Because this supply curve is a straight line, you can just plot one other random price/quantity pair and then connect the points.

You will most often work with the regular supply curve, but there are a few scenarios where the inverse supply curve is very helpful. Luckily, it is fairly straightforward to switch between the supply curve and the inverse supply curve by solving algebraically for the desired variable.

Law of Supply

Law of supply expresses a relationship between the supply and price of a product. It states a direct relationship between the price of a product and its supply, while other factors are kept constant.

For example, in case the price of a product increases, sellers would prefer to increase the production of the product to earn high profits, which would automatically lead to increase in supply.

Similarly, if the price of the product decreases, the supplier would decrease the supply of the product in market as he/she would wait for rise in the price of the product in future.

The statement given for the law of supply is as follows:

"Other things remaining unchanged, the supply of a commodity expands with a rise in its price and contracts with a fall in its price."

The law of supply can be better understood with the help of supply schedule, supply curve, and supply function. Let us discuss these concepts in detail in the next sections.

Supply Schedule

Supply schedule shows a tabular representation of law of supply. It presents the different quantities of a product that a seller is willing to sell at different price levels of that product.

A supply schedule can be of two types, which are as follows:

1. Individual Supply Schedule

Refers to a supply schedule that represents the different quantities of a product supplied by an individual seller at different prices.

Table- shows the supply schedule for the different quantities of milk supplied in the market at different prices:

Individual Supply Schedule	
Price of Milk (per liter in `)	Quantity Supplied(1000per day in liters)
10	10
12	13
14	20
16	25

2. Market Supply Schedule

Refers to a supply schedule that represents the different quantities of a product that all the suppliers in the market are willing to supply at different prices. Market supply schedule can be drawn by aggregating the individual supply schedules of all individual suppliers in the market.

Market Supply Schedule				
Price of Product (per unit in `)	Individual Supply (per day)			Market Supply (per day)
	A	B	C	
100	750	500	450	1700
200	800	650	500	1950
300	900	750	650	2300
400	1000	900	700	2600

shows the market supply schedule of a product supplied by three suppliers: A, B, and C.

Assumptions in Law of Supply

The law of supply expresses the change in supply with relation to change in price. In other words the main assumption of law of supply is that it studies the effect of price on supply of a product, while keeping other determinants of supply at constant.

Apart from this, there are certain assumptions that are necessary for the application of law of supply, which are as follows:

i.   Assumes that the price of a product changes, but the change in the cost of production is constant. This is because if the cost of production rises with increase in price, then sellers would not supply more due to the reduction in their profit margin. Therefore, law of supply would be applicable only when the cost of production remains constant.

ii.   Assumes that there is no change in the technique of production. This is because the advanced technique would reduce the cost of production and make the seller supply more at a lower price.

iii. Assumes that there is no change in the scale of production. This is because if the scale of production changes with a period of time, then it would affect the supply. In such a case, the law of supply would not be applicable.

iv.   Assumes that the policies of the government remain constant. If there is an increase in tax rates, then the supply of product would decrease even at the higher price. Therefore, for the application of law of supply, it is necessary that government policies should remain constant.

v.   Assumes that the transportation cost remain the same. In case the transportation cost reduces, then the supply would increase, which is invalid according to the law of supply.

vi.   Assumes that there is no speculation about prices in future, which otherwise can affect the supply of a product. If there is no speculation about products, then the economy is assumed to be at balance and people are satisfied with the available products and do not require any change.

Exception to Law of Supply

According to the law of supply, if the price of a product rises, then the supply of the product also rises and vice versa. However, there are certain conditions where the law of supply is not applicable. These conditions are known as exceptions to law of supply. In such cases, the supply of a product falls with the increase in price of a product at a particular point of time.

For example, there would be decrease in the supply of labor in an organization when the rate of wages is high. The exception of law of supply is represented on the regressive supply cure or backward sloping curve. It is also known as exceptional supply curve.

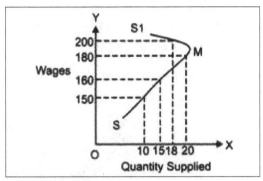

Exceptional Supply Curve.

In this case, wages are regarded as the price of labor. It can be interpreted from the graph that as the wages of a worker increases, its quantity supplied that is working hours decreases, which is an exception to the law of supply.

Some of the exceptions of law of supply are as follows:

a. Speculation

Refers to the fact that the supply of a product decreases instead of increasing in present when there is an expected increase in the price of the product. In such a case, sellers would not supply the whole quantity of the product and would wait for the increase in price in future to earn high profits. This case is an exception to law of demand.

b. Agricultural Products

Imply that law of supply is not valid in case of agricultural products as the supply of these products depends on particular seasons or climatic conditions. Thus, the supply of these products cannot be increased after a certain limit in spite of rise in their prices.

c. Changes in other Situations

Refers to the fact that law of supply ignores other factors (except price) that can influence the supply of a product. These factors can be natural factors, transportation conditions, and government policies.

Price Elasticity of Supply

The price elasticity of supply is the measure of the responsiveness in quantity supplied to a change in price for a specific good.

The price elasticity of supply (PES) is the measure of the responsiveness of the quantity supplied of a particular good to a change in price (PES = % Change in QS / % Change in Price). The intent of determining the price elasticity of supply is to show how a change in price impacts the amount of a good that is supplied to consumers. The price elasticity of supply is directly related to consumer demand.

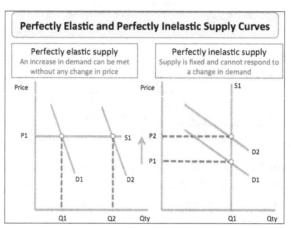

Elasticity

The elasticity of a good provides a measure of how sensitive one variable is to changes in another variable. In this case, the price elasticity of supply determines how sensitive the quantity supplied is to the price of the good.

Calculating the PES

When calculating the price elasticity of supply, economists determine whether the quantity supplied of a good is elastic or inelastic. The percentage of change in supply is divided by the percentage of change in price. The results are analyzed using the following range of values:

- PES > 1: Supply is elastic.

- PES < 1: Supply is inelastic.

- PES = 0: Supply is perfectly inelastic. There is no change in quantity if prices change.

- PES = infinity: Supply is perfectly elastic. An decrease in prices will lead to zero units produced.

Factors that Influence the PES

There are numerous factors that impact the price elasticity of supply including the number of producers, spare capacity, ease of switching, ease of storage, length of production period, time period of training, factor mobility, and how costs react.

Extreme Cases

There are three extreme cases of PES.

1. Perfectly elastic, where supply is infinite at any one price.

2. Perfectly inelastic, where only one quantity can be supplied.

3. Unit elasticity, which graphically is shown as a linear supply curve coming from the origin.

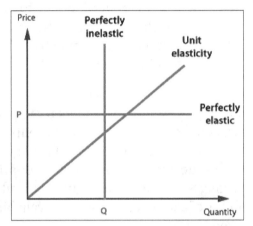

Improving PES

Because a high PES is desirable, it may be necessary for firms to undertake actions that improve their speed of response to changes in market conditions. Examples of these actions include:

1. Creating spare capacity;

2. Using the latest technology;

3. Keeping sufficient stocks;

4. Developing better storage systems;

5. Prolonging the shelf life of products;

6. Developing better distribution systems;

7. Providing training for workers;

8. Having flexible workers who can do a range of jobs;

9. Locating production near to the market;

10. Allowing inward migration of labour if there is a labour shortage.

Demand

Demand is an economic principle referring to a consumer's desire and willingness to pay a price for a specific good or service. Holding all other factors constant, an increase in the price of a good or service will decrease demand, and vice versa. Think of demand as your willingness to go out and buy a certain product. For example, market demand is the total of what everybody in the market wants.

Businesses often spend a considerable amount of money to determine the amount of demand the public has for their products and services. Incorrect estimations either result in money left on the table if demand is underestimated or losses if demand is overestimated. Demand is what helps fuel the economy, and without it, businesses would not produce anything.

Demand is closely related to supply. While consumers try to pay the lowest prices they can for goods and services, suppliers try to maximize profits. If suppliers charge too much, demand drops and suppliers do not sell enough product to earn sufficient profits. If suppliers charge too little, demand increases but lower prices may not cover suppliers' costs or allow for profits. Some factors affecting demand include the appeal of a good or service, the availability of competing goods, the availability of financing and the perceived availability of a good or service.

Economists use the term demand to refer to the amount of some good or service consumers are willing and able to purchase at each price. Demand is based on needs and wants—a consumer may be able to differentiate between a need and a want, but from an economist's perspective, they are the same thing. Demand is also based on ability to pay. If you can't pay for it, you have no effective demand.

What a buyer pays for a unit of the specific good or service is called the price. The total number of units purchased at that price is called the quantity demanded. A rise in the price of a good or service almost always decreases the quantity of that good or service demanded. Conversely, a fall in price will increase the quantity demanded. When the price of a gallon of gasoline goes up, for example, people look for ways to reduce their consumption by combining several errands, commuting by carpool or mass transit, or taking weekend or vacation trips closer to home. Economists call this inverse relationship between price and quantity demanded the law of demand. The law of demand assumes that all other variables that affect demand are held constant.

An example from the market for gasoline can be shown in the form of a table or a graph. (Refer back to "Reading: Creating and Interpreting Graphs" in module 0 if you need a refresher on graphs.) A table that shows the quantity demanded at each price, such as Table, is called a demand schedule. Price in this case is measured in dollars per gallon of gasoline. The quantity demanded is measured in millions of gallons over some time period (for example, per day or per year) and over some geographic area (like a state or a country).

Price (per gallon)	Quantity Demanded (millions of gallons)
$1.00	800
$1.20	700
$1.40	600
$1.60	550
$1.80	500
$2.00	460
$2.20	420

Table: Price and Quantity Demanded of Gasoline.

Aggregate Demand vs. Individual Demand

Every consumer faces a different set of circumstances. The factors she faces vary in type and degree. The extent to which these factors affect market demand overall is different from the way they affect the demand of a particular individual. Aggregate demand refers to the overall or average demand of many market participants. Individual demand refers to the demand of a particular consumer. For example, a particular consumer's demand for a product is strongly influenced by her personal income. However, her personal income does not significantly affect aggregate demand in a large economy.

Aggregate Demand

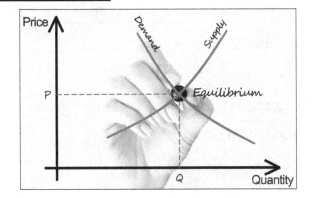

Aggregate demand refers to the total demand for final goods and services in the economy.

Since aggregate demand is measured by total expenditure of the community on goods and services, therefore, aggregate demand is also defined as 'total amount of money which all sectors (households, firms, government) of the economy are ready to spend on purchase of goods and services.

Alternatively, it is the total expenditure which the community intends to incur on purchase of goods and services. Thus, aggregate demand is synonymous with aggregate expenditure in the economy. If the total intended (i.e., ex-ante) expenditure on buying all the output is larger than before, this shows a higher aggregate demand.

On the contrary, if the community decides to spend less on the available output, it shows a fall in the aggregate demand. In simple words, aggregate demand is the total expenditure on consumption and investment. It should be noted that determination of output and employment in Keynesian framework depends mainly on the level of aggregate demand in short period.

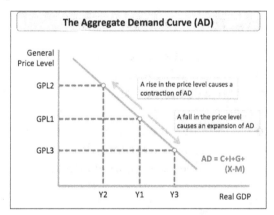

Components of AD

The main components of aggregate demand (aggregate expenditure) in a four sector economy are:

1. Household (or private) consumption demand(C);

2. Private investment demand(I);

3. Government demand for goods and services(G);

4. Net export demand(X-M).

Thus,

AD = C + I + G+(X-M)

Mind, all the variables represent planned (ex-ante) and not actual (ex-post).

Household Consumption Demand

It is defined as 'Value of goods and services that households are able and willing to buy.' Alternatively, it refers to ex-ante (planned) consumption expenditure to be incurred by all households on purchase of goods and services. For instance, households' demand for food, clothing, housing, books, furniture, cycles, radios, TV sets, educational and medical services will be called household consumption demand. Consumption (C) is a function (f) of disposable income (Y), i.e., C =J(Y).

As disposable income increases, consumption expenditure also increases but by how much? It depends upon propensity to consume. The relationship between income and consumption is called 'propensity to consume' or consumption function. Consumption function is represented by the equation.

Private Investment Demand

This refers to planned (ex-ante) expenditure on creation of new capital assets like machines, buildings and raw materials by private entrepreneurs. Remember, investment in Keynesian sense does not imply purchase of existing shares or securities but means expenditures on creation of new capital assets such as plants and equipment, inventories, construction works, etc. that help in production. Investment is made not only to maintain present level of production, but also to increase production capacity in future.

An economy grows through investment. Among three categories of investment, namely, purchase of new buildings, addition to stock and investment in fixed plant or machinery, the investment demand is focused on last category, i.e., machinery.

The relationship between investment demand and rate of interest is called investment demand function. There is inverse relationship between rate of interest and investment demand. Investment is of two types—Autonomous and Induced but all private investment expenditure is assumed as induced investment.

What determines investment in private enterprise economy? Just as household consumption demand depends on disposable income of households, investment demand in private enterprise economy depends mainly on two factors, namely, MEI {Marginal Efficiency of Investment) and Rate of Interest. In other words, the investors Judge whether the expected rate of return on new investment is equal to or greater than or less than the market rate of interest.

Suppose a businessman makes an additional investment by taking loan. He has to pay interest on it which is his expenditure on new investment. Before making investment, he would compare the interest he has to pay on loan and the profit he is expected to get on this investment. According to Keynes, the net return expected from a new unit of investment is called Marginal Efficiency of Investment (MEI).

Thus, three Elements which are Important in Understanding Investment are:

(i) Revenue (i.e., rate of return on new investment);

(ii) Cost (i.e., rate of interest);

(iii) Expectations (of profit).

Investment Demand Function

Of the three elements which affect investment, rate of interest is the most important. The relationship between investment demand and rate of interest is called investment demand function. There is inverse relationship between the rate of interest and investment demand, i.e., higher the rate of interest, the lower will be the investment demand.

Government Demand for Goods and Services

It refers to government planned (ex-ante) expenditure on purchase of consumer and capital goods to fulfill common needs of the society. The level of government expenditure is determined by government policy Present-day states are by and large welfare states wherein government participation in economic welfare of the people has increased manifold.

Government demand may be for satisfying public needs for roads, schools, hospitals, water works, railway transport or for infrastructure (like roads, bridges, airports), maintenance of law and order and defence from external aggression. Investment can be induced and autonomous.

It needs to be noted that whereas investment in private sector is made with profit motive and, therefore, called induced investment, government investment is guided by people's welfare motive and, therefore, called autonomous investment. Since investment expenditure is assumed to be autonomous, graphically investment curve is a horizontal line parallel to x-axis as shown as RI in.

Net Exports Demand

Net export is the difference between export of goods and services and import of goods and services during a given period. Net exports reflect the demand of foreign countries for our goods and services over our demand for foreign countries' goods and services. Thus, net exports show expected (ex-ante) net foreign demand.

This strengthens the income, output and employment process of our economy. As against it, imports from abroad drive out the earning of the economy and, therefore, they do not encourage domestic output and employment.

There are many factors which influence the volume of net foreign demand such as foreign exchange rates, terms of trade, trade policy of the importing and exporting countries, relative prices of goods, incomes of the nations, balance of payment position, types of exchange control, etc. Since net exports or foreign expenditure on our goods and services constitute a small proportion of the total expenditure (or aggregate demand), this constituent of net exports is usually ignored.

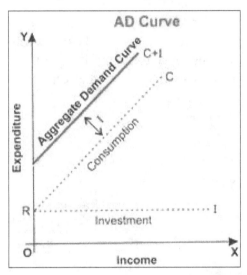

In sum, aggregate demand is the sum of the above- mentioned four types of demand (expenditure), i.e., AD = C + 1 + G + (X-M). Since determination of income (output) and employment is to be studied in the context of a two sector (Household and Firm) economy we shall, therefore, include in aggregate demand (AD) only two broad components of demand such as consumption demand (C) and investment demand (I). Put in symbols:

AD = C + I

This has been depicted in. Aggregate demand curve has been shown as sum of consumption (C) and investment (I).

Following are Noteworthy Points of the Diagram:

i.   AD curve has a positive slope which means when income increases, AD (expenditure) also increases.

ii. AD curve does not originate at point O which shows that even at zero level of income, some minimum level of consumption (equal to OR in the figure above) is essential.

iii. Investment curve is a straight line parallel to X-axis because according to Keynes, level of investment remains constant at all levels of income during short period.

Aggregate Demand and the Circular Flow

Aggregate demand can be illustrated by reference to the circular flow of income.

Aggregate demand is generated as income is transferred to spending as a result of the circular flow of income. Income is spent on consumer goods and services (C) plus spending on capital goods by firms (I). Spending is also generated by government when it allocates resources to public goods, merit goods and income transfers, such as pension benefits. Finally, there is 'net overseas spending', which is overseas spending on an economy's exports of goods and services, less what the economy spends on importing goods and services.

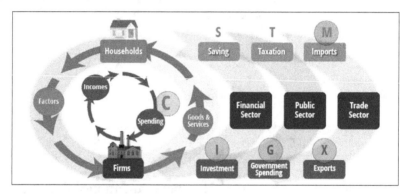

Prices and Output

The AD - AS model shows how changes in the level of AD and AS affect an economy's national output (income) and its price level.

Demand Curve

The Demand Curve is a line that shows how many units of a good or service will be purchased at each possible price. The price is plotted on the vertical (Y) axis while the quantity is plotted on the horizontal (X) axis.

Demand curves are used to determine the relationship between price and quantity and follows the law of demand, which states that the quantity demanded will decrease as the price increases. In addition, demand curves are commonly combined with supply curves to determine the equilibrium price and equilibrium quantity of the market.

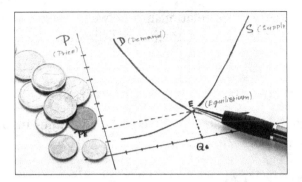

Drawing a Demand Curve

The demand curve is based on the demand schedule. The demand schedule shows exactly how many units of a good or service will be purchased at different price points.

For example, below is the demand schedule for high-quality organic bread:

Price	Quantity Demanded
$ 10.00	1000
$ 9.00	1200
$ 8.00	1400
$ 7.00	1700
$ 6.00	2000
$ 5.00	2400
$ 4.00	3000
$ 3.00	3700
$ 2.00	4500

It is important to note that as the price decreases, the quantity demanded increases. The relationship follows the law of demand. Intuitively, if the price for a good or service is lower, there would be a higher demand for it.

From the demand schedule above, the graph can be created:

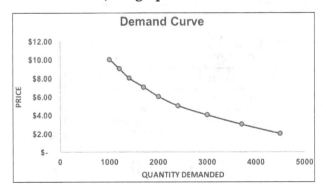

Through the demand curve, the relationship between price and quantity demanded is clearly illustrated. As the price for notebooks decreases, the demand for notebooks increases.

Shifts in Demand Curve

Shifts in the demand curve are strictly affected by consumer interest. Several factors can lead to a shift in the curve, for example:

1. Changes in Income Levels

If the good is a normal good, higher income levels would lead to an outward shift of the demand curve while lower income levels will lead to an inward shift. When income is increased, demand for normal goods or services will increase.

2. Changes in the Market's Size

A growing market results in an outward shift of the demand curve while a shrinking market results in an inward shift. A larger market size results from more consumers. Therefore, the demand (due to more consumers) will increase.

3. Changes in the Price of Related Goods and Services

When the price of complementary good decreases, the demand curve will shift outwards. Alternatively, if the price of complementary good increases, the curve will shift inwards. The opposite is true for substitute goods. For example, if the price for peanut butter goes down significantly, the demand for its complementary good – jelly – increases.

Example of a Shift in the Demand Curve

Recall the demand schedule for high-quality organic bread:

Price	Quantity Demanded
$ 10.00	1000
$ 9.00	1200
$ 8.00	1400
$ 7.00	1700
$ 6.00	2000
$ 5.00	2400
$ 4.00	3000
$ 3.00	3700
$ 2.00	4500

Assume that the price of a complementary good – peanut butter – decreases. How would this affect the demand curve for high-quality organic bread.

Since peanut butter is a complementary good to high-quality organic bread, a decrease in the price of peanut butter would increase the quantity demanded of high-quality organic bread. When consumers buy peanut butter, organic bread is also bought (hence, complementary). If the price of peanut butter decreases, more consumers would purchase peanut butter. Therefore, consumers would also purchase more high-quality organic bread as it is a complement to peanut butter.

Price	Quantity Demanded	New Quantity Demanded
$ 10.00	1000	1500
$ 9.00	1200	1700
$ 8.00	1400	1900
$ 7.00	1700	2300
$ 6.00	2000	2700
$ 5.00	2400	3300
$ 4.00	3000	4000
$ 3.00	3700	4800
$ 2.00	4500	5900

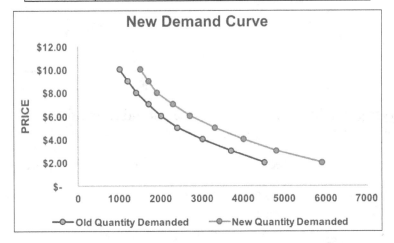

We can see from the chart above that a decrease in the price of a complementary good would increase the quantity demanded of high-quality organic bread.

Movements Along the Demand Curve

Changes in price cause movements along the demand curve. Following the original demand schedule for high-quality organic bread, assume the price is set at P = $6. At this price, the quantity demanded would be 2000.

Price	Quantity Demanded
$ 10.00	1000
$ 9.00	1200
$ 8.00	1400
$ 7.00	1700
$ 6.00	2000
$ 5.00	2400
$ 4.00	3000
$ 3.00	3700
$ 2.00	4500

If the price were to change from P = $6 to P = $4, it would cause a movement along the demand curve as the new quantity demanded would be 3000.

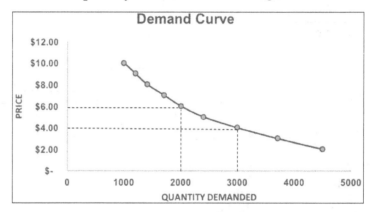

Demand curves generally have a negative gradient indicating the inverse relationship between quantity demanded and price.

There are at least three accepted explanations of why demand curves slope downwards:

1. The law of diminishing marginal utility.

2. The income effect.

3. The substitution effect.

Diminishing Marginal Utility

One of the earliest explanations of the inverse relationship between price and quantity demanded is the law of diminishing marginal utility. This law suggests that as more of a product is consumed the marginal (additional) benefit to the consumer falls, hence consumers are prepared to pay less. This can be explained as follows:

Most benefit is generated by the first unit of a good consumed because it satisfies all or a large part of the immediate need or desire.

A second unit consumed would generate less utility - perhaps even zero, given that the consumer now has less need or less desire.

With less benefit derived, the rational consumer is prepared to pay rather less for the second, and subsequent, units, because the marginal utility falls.

Consider the following figures for utility derived by an individual when consuming bars of chocolate. While total utility continues to rise from extra consumption, the additional (marginal) utility from each bar falls. If marginal utility is expressed in a monetary form, the greater the quantity consumed the less the marginal utility and the less value derived - hence the rational consumer would be prepared to pay less for that unit.

Utility

While total utility continues to rise from extra consumption, the additional (marginal) utility from each bar falls. If marginal utility is expressed in a monetary form, the greater the quantity consumed the lower the marginal utility and the less the rational consumer would be prepared to pay.

Bars	Total Utility	Marginal Utility
1	100	
2	190	90
3	270	80
4	340	70
5	400	60
6	450	50
7	490	40
8	520	30
9	540	20

The Income Effect

The *income* and *substitution* effect can also be used to explain why the demand curve slopes downwards. If we assume that money income is fixed, the income effect suggests that, as the price of a good falls, *real income* - that is, what consumers can buy with their *money income* - rises and consumers increase their demand.

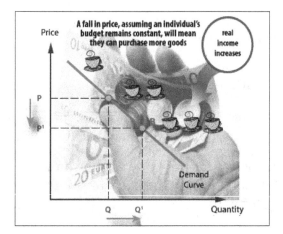

Therefore, at a lower price, consumers can buy more from the same money income, and, ceteris paribus, demand will rise. Conversely, a rise in price will reduce real income and force consumers to cut back on their demand.

The Substitution Effect

In addition, as the price of one good falls, it becomes relatively less expensive. Therefore, assuming other alternative products stay at the same price, at lower prices the good appears cheaper, and consumers will switch from the expensive alternative to the relatively cheaper one.

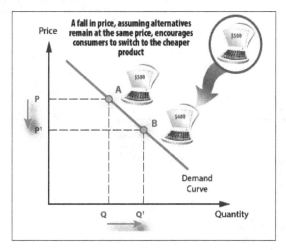

It is important to remember that whenever the price of any resource changes it will trigger both an income and a substitution effect.

Exceptions

It is possible to identify some exceptions to the normal rules regarding the relationship between price and current demand.

Giffen Goods

Giffen goods are those which are consumed in greater quantities when their price rises. These goods are named after the Scottish economist Sir Robert Giffen, who is credited with identifying them by Alfred Marshall in his highly influential Principles of Economics. In essence, a Giffen good is a staple food, such as bread or rice, which forms are large percentage of the diet of the poorest sections of a society, and for which there are no close substitutes. From time to time the poor may supplement their diet with higher quality foods, and they may even consume the odd luxury, although their income will be such that they will not be able to save. A rise in the price of such a staple food will not result in a typical substitution effect, given there are no close substitutes. If the real incomes of the poor increase they would tend to reallocate some of this income to luxuries, and if real incomes decrease they would buy more of the staple good, meaning it is an inferior good. Assuming that the money incomes of the poor are constant in the short run, a rise in price of the staple food will reduce real income and lead to an inverse income effect. However, most inferior goods will have substitutes, hence despite the inverse income effect, a rise in price will trigger a substitution effect, and demand will fall. In the case of a Giffen good, this typical response does not happen as there are no substitutes, and the price rise causes demand to increase.

Example

For example, a family living on the equivalent of just $150 a month, may purchase some bread (say 50 loaves at $2 each, which is the minimum they need to survive), and a luxury item at $50. If the price of bread rises by 25% to $2.50 per loaf, continuing to purchase 50 loaves would cost the individual $125, making the luxury unaffordable. They cannot reduce their consumption of bread, given that their current consumption is the minimum they require, and they cannot find a suitable substitute for their stable food. Not being able to afford the luxury would leave the family with an extra $25 to spend, and, given no alternatives to bread, they would purchase 10 more loaves each month. Hence the 25% price increase has resulted in a 20% increase in the demand for bread - from 50 to 60 loaves.

Veblen Goods

Veblen goods are a second possible exception to the general law of demand. These goods are named after the American sociologist, Thorsten Veblen, who, in the early 20th century, identified a 'new' high-spending leisure class. According to Veblen, a rise in the price of high status luxury goods might lead members of this leisure class to increase in their consumption, rather than reduce it. The purchase of such higher priced goods would confer status on the purchaser - a process which Veblen called conspicuous consumption.

Inverse Demand Function

The inverse demand curve is found by taking the inverse of the demand function. This changes demand from the independent to the dependent variable. Price changes from the dependent to the independent variable. This moves price from the Y (vertical) axis to the X (horizontal) axis and demand from the X axis to the Y axis. Here is an example inverse calculation:

$$P = 2Q$$

$$P/2 = Q$$

$$Q = P/2$$

This equation states that for every \$1 increase in the price of this good, the quantity demanded will fall by 1/2 of a unit.

Graph Structure

The primary change between a demand curve and an inverse demand curve is the shape of the graphs. The two functions are complete opposites of each other. The independent and dependent variables are reversed. Demand moves to the Y axis and price to the X axis on an inverse function. The slopes are opposite as well. A steep demand curve has a flat inverse demand curve and vice versa.

Inverse Demand Equation

The inverse demand equation can also be written as:

- $P = a - b(Q)$;
- a = intercept where price is 0;
- b = slope of demand curve;

Law of Demand

The law of demand states that all other things being equal, the quantity bought of a good or service is a function of price. As long as nothing else changes, people will buy less of something when its price rises. They'll buy more when its price falls.

The demand schedule tells you the exact quantity that will be purchased at any given price. A real-life example of how this works in the demand schedule for beef in 2014.

The demand curve plots those numbers on a chart. The quantity is on the horizontal or x-axis, and the price is on the vertical or y-axis.

If the amount bought changes a lot when the price does, then it's called elastic demand. An example of this is ice cream. You can easily get a different dessert if the price rises too high.

If the quantity doesn't change much when the price does, that's called inelastic demand. An example of this is gasoline. You need to buy enough to get to work regardless of the price.

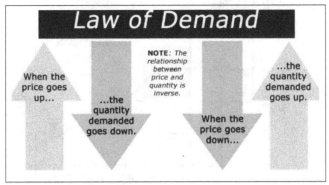

Assumptions of the Law of Demand

These Assumptions are Following:

(i)   There is no change in the tastes and preferences of the consumer;

(ii)   The income of the consumer remains constant;

(iii)   There is no change in customs;

(iv)   The commodity to be used should not confer distinction on the consumer;

(v)   There should not be any substitutes of the commodity;

(vi)   There should not be any change in the prices of other products;

(vii)   There should not be any possibility of change in the price of the product being used;

(viii) There should not be any change in the quality of the product;

(ix)   The habits of the consumers should remain unchanged. Given these conditions, the law of demand operates. If there is change even in one of these conditions, it will stop operating.

Table: Demand Schedule	
Price (Rs)	Quantity Demanded
5	100 Units
4	200 Units
3	300 Units
2	400 Units
1	600 Units

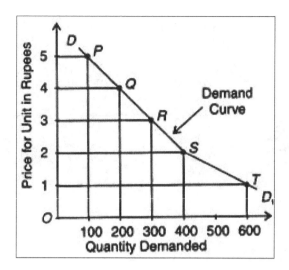

The above table shows that when the price of say, orange, is Rs.5 per unit, 100 units are demanded. If the price falls to Rs.4, the demand increases to 200 units. Similarly, when the price declines to Re.1, the demand increases to 600 units. On the contrary, as the price increases from Re. 1, the demand continues to decline from 600 units.

In the figure, point P of the demand curve DD_1 shows demand for 100 units at the Rs. 5. As the price falls to Rs. 4, Rs. 3, Rs. 2 and Re. 1, the demand rises to 200, 300, 400 and 600 units respectively. This is clear from points Q, R, S, and T. Thus, the demand curve DD_1 shows increase in demand of orange when its price falls. This indicates the inverse relation between price and demand.

Exceptions to the Law of Demand

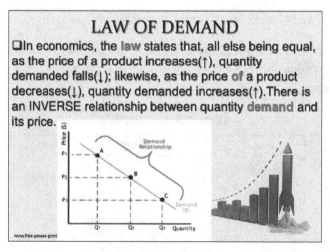

In certain cases, the demand curve slopes up from left to right, i.e., it has a positive slope. Under certain circumstances, consumers buy more when the price of a commodity rises, and less when price falls, as shown by the D curve in Figure. Many causes are attributed to an upward sloping demand curve.

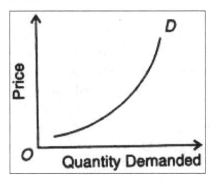

(i) War

If shortage is feared in anticipation of war, people may start buying for building stocks or for hoarding even when the price rises.

(ii) Depression

During a depression, the prices of commodities are very low and the demand for them is also less. This is because of the lack of purchasing power with consumers.

(iii) Giffen Paradox

If a commodity happens to be a necessity of life like wheat and its price goes up, consumers are forced to curtail the consumption of more expensive foods like meat and fish, and wheat being still the cheapest food they will consume more of it. The Marshallian example is applicable to developed economies.

In the case of an underdeveloped economy, with the fall in the price of an inferior commodity like maize, consumers will start consuming more of the superior commodity like wheat. As a result, the demand for maize will fall. This is what Marshall called the Giffen Paradox which makes the demand curve to have a positive slope.

(iv) Demonstration Effect

If consumers are affected by the principle of conspicuous consumption or demonstration effect, they will like to buy more of those commodities which confer distinction on the possessor, when their prices rise. On the other hand, with the fall in the prices of such articles, their demand falls, as is the case with diamonds.

(v) Ignorance Effect

Consumers buy more at a higher price under the influence of the "ignorance effect", where a commodity may be mistaken for some other commodity, due to deceptive packing, label, etc.

(vi) Speculation

Marshall mentions speculation as one of the important exceptions to the downward sloping demand curve. According to him, the law of demand does not apply to the demand in a campaign between groups of speculators. When a group unloads a great quantity of a thing on to the market, the price falls and the other group begins buying it. When it has raised the price of the thing, it arranges to sell a great deal quietly. Thus when price rises, demand also increases.

(vii) Necessities of Life

Normally, the law of demand does not apply on necessities of life such as food, cloth etc. Even the price of these goods increases, the consumer does not reduce their demand. Rather, he purchases them even the prices of these goods increase often by reducing the demand for comfortable goods. This is also a reason that the demand curve slopes upwards to the right.

The Law of Demand and the Business Cycle

Politicians and central bankers understand the law of demand very well. The Federal Reserve's mandate is to prevent inflation while reducing unemployment. During the expansion phase of the business cycle, the Fed tries to reduce demand for all goods and services by raising the price of everything. It does this with contractionary monetary policy. It raised the fed funds rate, which increases interest rates on loans and mortgages. That has the same effect as raising prices, first on loans, then on everything bought with loans, and finally everything else.

Of course, when prices go up, so does inflation. That's not always a bad thing. The Fed has a 2 percent inflation target for the core inflation rate. The nation's central bank wants that level of mild inflation. It sets an expectation that prices will increase 2 percent a year. Demand increases because people know that things will only cost more next year. They may as well buy it now ceteris paribus.

During a recession or the contraction phase of the business cycle, policymakers have a worse problem. They've got to stimulate demand when workers are losing jobs and homes and have less income and wealth. Expansionary monetary policy lowers interest rates, thereby reducing the price of everything. If the recession is bad enough, it doesn't reduce the price enough to offset the lower income.

In that case, fiscal policy is needed. The federal government starts spending to create public works jobs. It extends unemployment benefits and cuts taxes. As a result, the deficit increases because the government's tax revenue falls. Once confidence and demand are restored, the deficit should shrink as tax receipts increase.

Price Elasticity of Demand

Price elasticity of demand is a measure of the change in the quantity demanded or purchased of a product in relation to its price change. Expressed mathematically:

Price Elasticity of Demand = % Change in Quantity Demanded / % Change in Price

If the quantity demanded of a product exhibits a large change in response to its price change, it is termed "elastic," that is, quantity stretched far from its prior point. If the quantity purchased has a small change in response to its price, it is termed "inelastic"; quantity didn't stretch much from its prior point.

The more easily a shopper can substitute one product with a rising price for another, the more the price will fall – be "elastic."

The more discretionary a purchase, the more quantity will fall in response to price rises the higher the elasticity. The less discretionary, the less quantity will fall. Inelastic examples include luxuries where shoppers "pay for the privilege" of buying a brand name, addictive products and required add-on products. Addictive products include tobacco and alcohol. Sin taxes on these products are possible because the lost tax revenue from fewer units sold is exceeded by the higher taxes on units still sold. Examples of add-on products are ink-jet printer cartridges or college textbooks.

Time matters. Response is different for a one-day sale than for a price change over a season or year. Clarity in time sensitivity is vital to setting better online shopping prices.

For example, if the price of a daily newspaper increases from £1.00 to £1.20p, and the daily sales fall from 500,000 to 250,000, the PED will be:

$$\frac{-50}{+20} = (-)2.5$$

The negative sign indicates that P and Q are inversely related, which we would expect for most price/demand relationships. This is significant because the newspaper supplier can calculate or estimate how revenue will be affected by the change in price. In this case, revenue at £1.00 is £500,000 (£1 x 500,000) but falls to £300,000 after the price rise (£1.20 x 250,000).

Example of PED:

- If price increases by 10% and demand for CDs fell by 20%;

- Then PED = -20/10 = -2.0;

- If the price of petrol increased from 130p to 140p and demand fell from 10,000 units to 9,900;

- % change in Q.D = (-100/10,000) *100 = − 1%;

- % change in price 10/130) * 100= 7.7%;

- Therefore PED = − 1/7.7 = -0.13;

- If price increase from £50 to £55 and PED was 0.5 How much did quantity demanded fall;

- 0.5 = % change in QD;

- Therefore % QD = -5.

The Range of Responses

The degree of response of quantity demanded to a change in price can vary considerably. The key benchmark for measuring elasticity is whether the co-efficient is greater or less than proportionate. If quantity demanded changes proportionately, then the value of PED is 1, which is called 'unit elasticity'.

PED can also be:

- Less than one, which means PED is inelastic;

- Greater than one, which is elastic;

- Zero (0), which is perfectly inelastic;

- Infinite (∞), which is perfectly elastic.

Types of Price Elasticity of Demand

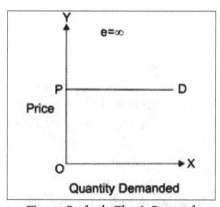

Figure: Perfectly Elastic Demand.

The demand curve is represented as a horizontal straight line, which is shown in above figure.

From figure it can be interpreted that at price OP, demand is infinite; however, a slight rise in price would result in fall in demand to zero. It can also be interpreted from figure above that at price P consumers are ready to buy as much quantity of the product as they want. However, a small rise in price would resist consumers to buy the product.

Though, perfectly elastic demand is a theoretical concept and cannot be applied in the real situation. However, it can be applied in cases, such as perfectly competitive market and homogeneity products. In such cases, the demand for a product of an organization is assumed to be perfectly elastic.

From an organization's point of view, in a perfectly elastic demand situation, the organization can sell as much as much as it wants as consumers are ready to purchase a large quantity of product. However, a slight increase in price would stop the demand.

Perfectly Inelastic Demand

A perfectly inelastic demand is one when there is no change produced in the demand of a product with change in its price. The numerical value for perfectly inelastic demand is zero ($e_p=0$).

In case of perfectly inelastic demand, demand curve is represented as a straight vertical line, which is shown in figure:

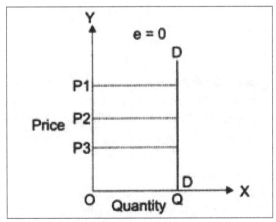

Figure: Perfectly Inelastic Demand.

It can be interpreted from above figure that the movement in price from OP_1 to OP_2 and OP_2 to OP_3 does not show any change in the demand of a product (OQ). The demand remains constant for any value of price. Perfectly inelastic demand is a theoretical concept and cannot be applied in a practical situation. However, in case of essential goods, such as salt, the demand does not change with change in price. Therefore, the demand for essential goods is perfectly inelastic.

Relatively Elastic Demand

Relatively elastic demand refers to the demand when the proportionate change produced in demand is greater than the proportionate change in price of a product. The numerical value of relatively elastic demand ranges between one to infinity.

Mathematically, relatively elastic demand is known as more than unit elastic demand ($e_p > 1$). For example, if the price of a product increases by 20% and the demand of the product decreases by 25%, then the demand would be relatively elastic.

The demand curve of relatively elastic demand is gradually sloping, as shown in figure:

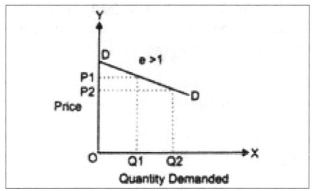

Figure: Relatively Elastic Demand.

It can be interpreted from above figure that the proportionate change in demand from OQ_1 to OQ_2 is relatively larger than the proportionate change in price from OP_1 to OP_2. Relatively elastic demand has a practical application as demand for many of products respond in the same manner with respect to change in their prices.

For example, the price of a particular brand of cold drink increases from Rs.15 to Rs.20. In such a case, consumers may switch to another brand of cold drink. However, some of the consumers still consume the same brand. Therefore, a small change in price produces a larger change in demand of the product.

Relatively Inelastic Demand

Relatively inelastic demand is one when the percentage change produced in demand is less than the percentage change in the price of a product. For example, if the price of a product increases by 30% and the demand for the product decreases only by 10%, then the demand would be called relatively inelastic. The numerical value of relatively elastic demand ranges between zero to one ($e_p < 1$). Marshall has termed relatively inelastic demand as elasticity being less than unity.

The demand curve of relatively inelastic demand is rapidly sloping, as shown in figure.

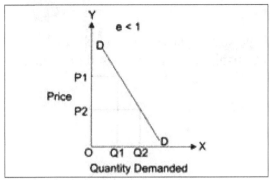

Figure: Relatively Inelastic Demand.

It can be interpreted from above figure that the proportionate change in demand from OQ_1 to OQ_2 is relatively smaller than the proportionate change in price from OP_1 to OP_2. Relatively inelastic demand has a practical application as demand for many of products respond in the same manner with respect to change in their prices. Let us understand the implication of relatively inelastic demand with the help of an example.

Example–The Demand Schedule for Milk is given in table:

Table-3 Demand Schedule for Milk	
Price of milk(per litre)	Quantity Demanded (litres)
15	100
20	90

Calculating the price elasticity of demand and determining the type of price elasticity:

P= 15

Q = 100

P_1 = 20

Q_1 = 90

Therefore, Change in the Price of Milk is:

$\Delta P = P_1 - P$

$\Delta P = 20 - 15$

$\Delta P = 5$

Similarly, Change in Quantity Demanded of Milk is:

$\Delta Q = Q_1 - Q$

$\Delta Q = 90 - 100$

$\Delta Q = -10$

The change in demand shows a negative sign, which can be ignored. This is because of the reason that the relationship between price and demand is inverse that can yield a negative value of price or demand.

Price Elasticity of Demand for Milk is:

$e_p = \Delta Q / \Delta P * P/Q$

$e_p = 10/5 * 15/100$

$e_p = 0.3$

The price elasticity of demand for milk is 0.3, which is less than one. Therefore, in such a case, the demand for milk is relatively inelastic.

Unitary Elastic Demand

When the proportionate change in demand produces the same change in the price of the product, the demand is referred as unitary elastic demand. The numerical value for unitary elastic demand is equal to one (e_p=1).

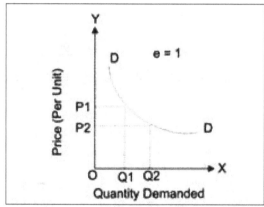

Figure: Unitary Elastic Demand.

The demand curve for unitary elastic demand is represented as a rectangular hyperbola,

From Figure, it can be interpreted that change in price OP_1 to OP_2 produces the same change in demand from OQ_1 to OQ_2. Therefore, the demand is unitary elastic.

PED along a Linear Demand Curve

PED on a linear demand curve will fall continuously as the curve slopes downwards, moving from left to right. PED = 1 at the midpoint of a linear demand curve.

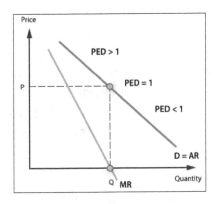

PED and Revenue

There is a precise mathematical connection between PED and a firm's revenue.

There are three 'types' of revenue:

1. Total revenue (TR), which is found by multiplying price by quantity sold (P x Q).

2. Average revenue (AR), which is found by dividing total revenue by quantity sold (TR/Q). Consider these figures and calculate Total, Marginal and Average Revenue.

3. Marginal revenue (MR), which is defined as the revenue from selling one extra unit. This is calculated by finding the change in TR from selling one more unit.

Observations

When TR is at a maximum, MR = zero, and PED = 1.

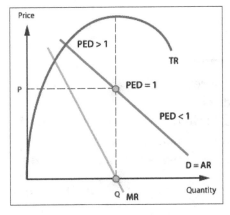

1. Price and AR are identical, because AR = TR/Q, which is P x Q/Q, and cancel out the Qs to get P.

2. A curve plotting AR (=P) against Q is also a firm's demand curve.

3. TR increases, reaches a peak and decreases.

A Firm PED

There are several reasons why firms gather information about the PED of its products. A firm will know much more about its internal operations and product costs than it will about its external environment. Therefore, gathering data on how consumers respond to changes in price can help reduce risk and uncertainly. More specifically, knowledge of PED can help the firm forecast its sales and set its price.

Sales Forecasting

The firm can forecast the impact of a change in price on its sales volume, and sales revenue (total revenue, TR). For example, if PED for a product is (-) 2, a 10% reduction in price (say, from £10 to £9) will lead to a 20% increase in sales (say from 1000 to 1200). In this case, revenue will rise from £10,000 to £10,800.

Pricing Policy

Knowing PED helps the firm decide whether to raise or lower price, or whether to price discriminate. Price discrimination is a policy of charging consumers different prices for the same product. If demand is elastic, revenue is gained by reducing price, but if demand is inelastic, revenue is gained by raising price.

Non-Pricing Policy

When PED is highly elastic, the firm can use advertising and other promotional techniques to reduce elasticity.

Hicksian Demand

The Hicksian welfare measures can be used for the evaluation of any change of state as long as the agent's indirect utility for income is well defined before and after the change. The set of optimal commodity vectors in the EMP is denoted as $h(p,u) \subset R^L_+$. It is known as the Hicksian or compensated demand corresponding or function if single valued. The figure shows the solution set $h(p, u)$ for two different price vectors p and p'.

The basic properties of the Hicksian demand function is explained as follows:

Suppose u (.) is a continuous utility function representing a locally non satiated preference relation $\geq$ defined on the consumption set $X = R^L_+$. Then for any $p \gg 0$, the Hicksian demand correspondence $h(p, u)$ possesses the following two properties. Homogeneity of degree zero in P follow because the optimal vector. The minimizing p.x is subject to $u(x) \geq u$. It is same as that for minimizing $\propto p.x$. It is subject to this constraint for any scalar $\propto > 0$.

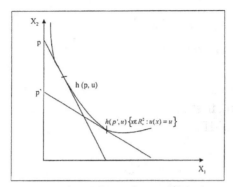

Figure: The Hicksian demand function.

We will explain properties and proof in the following paragraph:

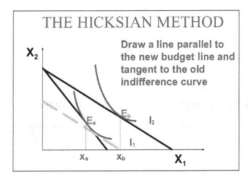

Property 1

No excess utility for any $x \in h$ (p, u), $u(x) = u$

Proof

This property follows from continuity of u (.). Suppose there exists an $x \in h$ (p, u), such that u(x) > u.

If we consider a bundle $x' = \epsilon x$, where $\propto \in$ *(0, 1)*. By continuity for $\propto$ close enough to 1.u *(x')* $\geq u$ and $p.x' < p.x_1$ contradicting x being optimal in the EMP with required utility level u.

Property 2

Convexity/Uniqueness

If $\geq$ is strictly convex, then u (.) is strictly quasi-concave. Then there is a unique element in h (P, u).

If there is utility function $u(x_1, x_2) = \propto In\ x_1 + (1 - \propto)\ ln x_2$. Then substituting x_1 *(p, w)* and x_2 *(p, w)* into u(x) we have,

$$V(p,w) = u\big(x(p,w)\big)$$
$$= \big[\alpha\, In\,\alpha + (1-\alpha)\, In\,(1-\alpha)\, In\, p_2\big]$$

As the UMP, when u (.) is differentiate, the optimal consumption bundle in the EMP can be characterizing using first order condition. The first order condition bears a close similarity to those of the UMP.

Proposition

If we assume that u (.) is differentiable and it shows that the first order condition for the EMP as follows:

$$p \geq \lambda \nabla u\big(x^*\big)$$

And

$$x^*\big[p - \lambda \nabla u\big(x^*\big)\big] = 0$$

For some λ ≥ o, compare this with the first order conditions for the UMP.

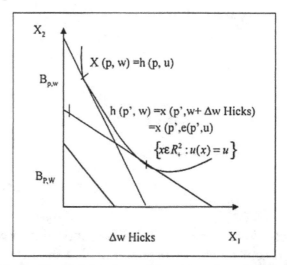

Figure: The Hicksian demand function and wealth effect.

Using above proposition, we can relate the Hicksian and Walrasian demand correspondence as follows:

$$H(p,u) = x\big(p,e(p,u)\big) \; and \; x(p,w) = h\big(p,v(p,w)\big)$$

The first of these relations explains the use of the term compensated demand correspondence to describe h (p, u). Suppose if the price change, h (p, u) gives the level of demand that would arise if the consumers wealth were simultaneously adjusted to keep his/her utility level at u. Government helps consumer through subsidized goods. In

India, it is done through public distribution system. This type of wealth compensation to consumer is depicted in above diagram. It is known as Hicksian wealth compensation.

Above diagram shows that consumers initial situation is the price wealth pair (p, w); prices then change to p', where $p'_1 = p_1$ and $p'_2 > p_2$.

The Hicksian Wealth Compensation is Defined Follows

$$\Delta w_{Hicks} = e(p',u) - w$$

Therefore the demand function h (p, u) keeps the consumer's utility level fixed as prices change. In contract with the Walrasian demand function it keeps money wealth fixed but allows utility to vary.

As with the value functions the EMP and UMP, the relations allow us to develop a tight linkage between the properties of the Hicksian demand correspondence $h\ (p,\ u)$ and the Walrasian demand correspondence $x\ (p,\ w)$.

Hicksian Demand and Compensated Law of Demand

The property of Hicksian demand is that it satisfies the compensated law of demand. The price and demand of commodities move in opposite directions. The price change is accompanied by Hicksian wealth compensation.

Proposition

If u (.) is a continuous utility function representing a locally no satiated preference relation $\geq$ and that h (p, u) consists of a single element for all p » o.

Then the Hicksian Demand Function h (p, u) Satisfies the Compensated Law of Demand:

For all p' and p",

$$(p''-p)\big[h(p'',u)-h(p',u)\big] \leq 0$$

Proof

For any pk"o, consumption bundle h (p, u) is optimal in the EMP and so it achieves a lower expenditure at prices p than any other bundle that offers a utility level of at least u.

Therefore

$$p''.h(p'',u) \leq p''.h(p',u)$$

And

$$p'.h(p'',u) \geq p'.h(p',u)$$

Subtracting these two inequalities yields the results.

Hicksian Demand and Expenditure Functions for the Cobb-Douglas Utility Function:

If we assume that the consumer has Cobb-Douglas utility function over the two goods. That is $u(x_1,x_2) = x_1^a x_1^{1-a}$. By deriving the first order conditions for the EMP and substituting from the constraints $u\ (h_1(p,\ u),\ h_2(p,\ u) = u,$, we obtain the Hicksian demand functions.

$$h_1(p,u) = \left[\frac{\alpha p_2}{(1-\alpha)_{p_1}} \right]^{1-\alpha} u$$

&

$$h_2(p,u) = \left[\frac{(1-\alpha)p_1}{\alpha p_2} \right]^{\alpha} u$$

If we Calculate it as Follows:

$E\ (p,\ u) = p.h\ (p,\ u)$ yields the following equation

$$e(p,u) = \left[\alpha^{-\alpha}(1-\alpha)^{1-\alpha} \right] p_1^{\alpha} p_2^{\frac{1}{2}-\alpha} u$$

Above function is Hicksian demand and expenditure functions for the Cobb-Douglas utility function.

References

- Supply-in-economics-meaning-law-and-elasticity-of-supply-with-diagram-1665: economicsdiscussion.net, Retrieved 18, April 2020

- Price-elasticity-of-supply, boundless-economics: lumenlearning.com, Retrieved 24, May 2020

- Reading-what-is-demand, microeconomics: lumenlearning.com, Retrieved 09, July 2020

- Aggregate-demand-its-meaning-and-components-economics-721: economicsdiscussion.net, Retrieved 22, March 2020

- Supply-curve: investopedia.com, Retrieved 21, May 2020

- Introduction-to-the-supply-curve-1147940: thoughtco.com, Retrieved 13, March 2020

- Law-of-supply-schedule-curve-function-assumptions-and-exception-3367: economicsdiscussion.net, Retrieved 14, July 2020

Forms of Competition in Economics

The situation wherein different economic firms contend for obtaining goods which are limited by varying the elements of the marketing mix is termed as competition. Some of the different types of competition are perfect competition, oligopoly and monopoly. The diverse applications of these types of competition have been thoroughly discussed in this chapter.

Perfect Competition

In order to analyse a firm's profit maximisation problem, we must first specify the market environment in which the firm functions. In this chapter, we study a market environment called perfect competition. A perfectly competitive market has the following defining features:

- The market consists of a large number of buyers and seller.

- Each firm produces and sells a homogenous product. i.e., the product of one firm cannot be differentiated from the product of any other firm.

- Entry into the market as well as exit from the market is free for firms.

- Information is perfect.

The existence of a large number of buyers and sellers means that each individual buyer and seller is very small compared to the size of the market. This means that no individual buyer or seller can influence the market by their size. Homogenous products further mean that the product of each firm is identical. So a buyer can choose to buy from any firm in the market, and she gets the same product. Free entry and exit mean that it is easy for firms to enter the market, as well as to leave it. This condition is essential for the large numbers of firms to exist. If entry was difficult, or restricted, then the number of firms in the market could be small. Perfect information implies that all buyers and all sellers are completely informed about the price, quality and other relevant details about the product, as well as the market.

These features result in the single most distinguishing characteristic of perfect competition: price taking behaviour. From the viewpoint of a firm, what does price-taking entail? A price-taking firm believes that if it sets a price above the market price, it will be unable to sell any quantity of the good that it produces. On the other hand, should the set price be less than or equal to the market price, the firm can sell as many units of the good as it wants to sell. From the viewpoint of a buyer, what does price-taking entail? A buyer would obviously like to buy the good at the lowest possible price. However, a price-taking buyer believes that if she asks for a price below the market price, no firm will be willing to sell to her. On the other hand, should the price asked be greater than or equal to the market price, the buyer can obtain as many units of the good as she desires to buy.

Price-taking is often thought to be a reasonable assumption when the market has many firms and buyers have perfect information about the price prevailing in the market. Why? Let us start with a situation where each firm in the market charges the same (market) price. Suppose, now, that a certain firm raises its price above the market price. Observe that since all firms produce the same good and all buyers are aware of the market price, the firm in question loses all its buyers. Furthermore, as these buyers switch their purchases to other firms, no "adjustment" problems arise; their demand is readily accommodated when there are so many other firms in the market. An individual firm's inability to sell any amount of the good at a price exceeding the market price is precisely what the price-taking assumption stipulates.

Revenue

We have indicated that in a perfectly competitive market, a firm believes that it can sell as many units of the good as it wants by setting a price less than or equal to the market price. But, if this is the case, surely there is no reason to set a price lower than the market price. In other words, should the firm desire to sell some amount of the good, the price that it sets is exactly equal to the market price.

A firm earns revenue by selling the good that it produces in the market. Let the market price of a unit of the good be p. Let q be the quantity of the good produced, and therefore sold, by the firm at price p. Then, total revenue (TR) of the firm is defined as the market price of the good (p) multiplied by the firm's output (q). Hence,

$$TR = p \times q$$

To make matters concrete, consider the following numerical example. Let the market for candles be perfectly competitive and let the market price of a box of candles be $ 10. For a candle manufacturer, Table shows how total revenue is related to output. Notice that when no box is sold, TR is equal to zero; if one box of candles is sold, TR is equal to 1×$ 10= $ 10; if two boxes of candles are produced, TR is equal to 2 × $ 10 = $ 20; and so on.

Boxes sold	TR (in $)
0	0
1	10
2	20

3	30
4	40
5	50

We can depict how the total revenue changes as the quantity sold changes through a Total Revenue Curve. A total revenue curve plots the quantity sold or output on the X-axis and the Revenue earned on the Y-axis. Figure shows the total revenue curve of a firm. Three observations are relevant here. First, when the output is zero, the total revenue of the firm is also zero. Therefore, the TR curve passes through point O. Second, the total revenue increases as the output goes up. Moreover, the equation 'TR = p × q' is that of a straight line because p is constant. This means that the TR curve is an upward rising straight line. Third, consider the slope of this straight line. When the output is one unit (horizontal distance Oq_1 in figure), the total revenue (vertical height Aq_1 in Figure) is p × 1 = p. Therefore, the slope of the straight line is Aq_1/Oq_1 = p.

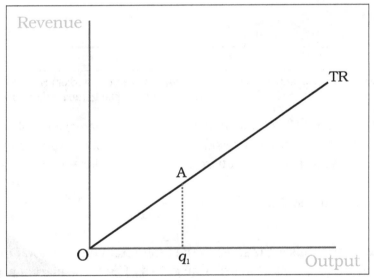

Total Revenue curve. The total revenue curve of a firm shows the relationship between the total revenue that the firm earns and the output level of the firm. The slope of the curve, Aq_1/Oq_1, is the market price.

The average revenue (AR) of a firm is defined as total revenue per unit of output. Recall that if a firm's output is q and the market price is p, then TR equals p × q. Hence,

$$AR = \frac{TR}{q} = \frac{p \times q}{q} = p$$

In other words, for a price-taking firm, average revenue equals the market price.

Now consider figure. Here, we plot the average revenue or market price (y-axis) for different values of a firm's output (x-axis). Since the market price is fixed at p, we obtain a horizontal straight line that cuts the y-axis at a height equal to p. This horizontal straight line is called the price line. It is also the firm's AR curve under perfect competition The price line also depicts the demand curve facing a firm. Observe that the demand curve is perfectly elastic. This means that a firm can sell as many units of the good as it wants to sell at price p.

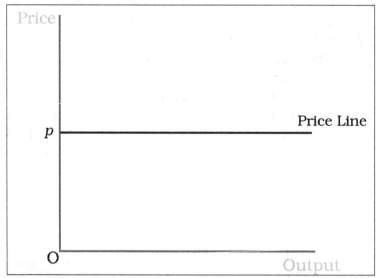

Price Line. The price line shows the relationship between the market price and a firm's output level. The vertical height of the price line is equal to the market price, p.

The marginal revenue (MR) of a firm is defined as the increase in total revenue for a unit increase in the firm's output. Consider table again. Total revenue from the sale of 2 boxes of candles is $20. Total revenue from the sale of 3 boxes of candles is $30.

$$\text{Marginal Revenue}\,(\text{MR}) = \frac{\text{Change in total revenue}}{\text{Change in quantity}} = \frac{30-20}{3-2} = 10$$

Is it a coincidence that this is the same as the price? Actually it is not. Consider the situation when the firm's output changes from q_1 to q_2. Given the market price p,

$$MR = (pq_2 - pq_1)/(q_2 - q_1) = [p\,(q_2 - q_1)]/(q_2 - q_1) = p$$

Thus, for the perfectly competitive firm, MR=AR=p In other words, for a price-taking firm, marginal revenue equals the market price.

Setting the algebra aside, the intuition for this result is quite simple. When a firm increases its output by one unit, this extra unit is sold at the market price. Hence, the firm's increase in total revenue from the one-unit output expansion – that is, MR – is precisely the market price.

Profit Maximisation

A firm produces and sells a certain amount of a good. The firm's profit, denoted by π, is defined to be the difference between its total revenue (TR) and its total cost of production (TC). In other words,

$$\pi = TR - TC$$

Clearly, the gap between TR and TC is the firm's earnings net of costs.

A firm wishes to maximise its profit. The firm would like to identify the quantity q_0 at which its profits are maximum. By definition, then, at any quantity other than q_0, the firm's profits are less than at q_0. The critical question is: how do we identify q_0?

For profits to be maximum, three conditions must hold at q_0:

- The price, p, must equal M.

- Marginal cost must be non-decreasing at q_0.

- For the firm to continue to produce, in the short run, price must be greater than the average variable cost (p > AVC); in the long run, price must be greater than the average cost (p > AC).

Condition 1: Profits are the difference between total revenue and total cost. Both total revenue and total cost increase as output increases. Notice that as long as the change in total revenue is greater than the change in total cost, profits will continue to increase. Recall that change in total revenue per unit increase in output is the marginal revenue; and the change in total cost per unit increase in output is the marginal cost. Therefore, we can conclude that as long as marginal revenue is greater than marginal cost, profits are increasing. By the same logic, as long as marginal revenue is less than marginal cost, profits will fall. It follows that for profits to be maximum, marginal revenue should equal marginal cost.

In other words, profits are maximum at the level of output (which we have called q_0) for which MR = MC.

For the perfectly competitive firm, we have established that the MR = P. So the firm's profit maximizing output becomes the level of output at which P=MC.

Condition 2: Consider the second condition that must hold when the profit-maximising output level is positive. Why is it the case that the marginal cost curve cannot slope downwards at the profitmaximising output level? To answer this question, refer once again to figure. Note that at output levels q_1 and q_4, the market price is equal to the marginal cost. However, at the output level q_1, the marginal cost curve is downward sloping. We claim that q_1 cannot be a profit-maximising output level. Why?

Observe that for all output levels slightly to the left of q_1, the market price is lower than the marginal cost.

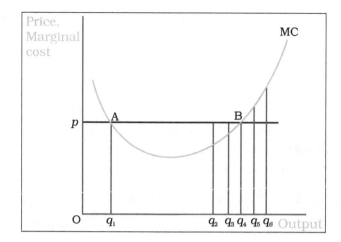

Conditions 1 and 2 for profit maximisation. The figure is used to demonstrate that when the market price is p, the output level of a profit maximising firm cannot be q_1 (marginal cost curve, MC, is downward sloping), q_2 and q_3 (market price exceeds marginal cost), or q_5 and q_6 (marginal cost exceeds market price).

Condition 3: Consider the third condition that must hold when the profit maximising output level is positive. Notice that the third condition has two parts: one part applies in the short run while the other applies in the long run.

Case 1: Price must be greater than or equal to AVC in the short run.

We will show that the statement of Case 1 is true by arguing that a profit maximising firm, in the short run, will not produce at an output level wherein the market price is lower than the AVC.

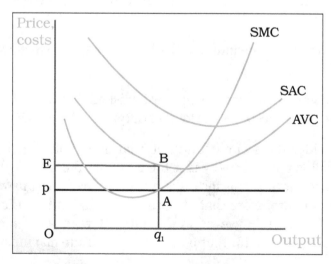

Price-AVC Relationship with Profit Maximisation (Short Run). The figure is used to demonstrate that a profit-maximising firm produces zero output in the short run when the market price, p, is less than the minimum of its average variable cost (AVC). If the firm's output level is q_1, the firm's total variable cost exceeds its revenue by an amount equal to the area of rectangle pEBA.

Let us turn to figure. Observe that at the output level q_1, the market price p is lower than the AVC. We claim that q_1 cannot be a profit-maximising output level. Why?

Notice that the firm's total revenue at q_1 is as follows:

TR = Price × Quantity

= Vertical height Op × width Oq_1

= The area of rectangle $OpAq_1$

Similarly, the firm's total variable cost at q_1 is as follows:

TVC = Average variable cost × Quantity

= Vertical height OE × Width Oq_1

= The area of rectangle $OEBq_1$

Now recall that the firm's profit at q_1 is TR − (TVC + TFC); that is, [the area of rectangle $OpAq_1$] − [the area of rectangle $OEBq_1$] − TFC. What happens if the firm produces zero output? Since output is zero, TR and TVC are zero as well. Hence, the firm's profit at zero output is equal to − TFC. But, the area of rectangle $OpAq_1$ is strictly less than the area of rectangle $OEBq_1$. Hence, the firm's profit at q_1 is [(area EBAp) - TFC], which is strictly less than what it obtains by not producing at all. So, the firm will choose not to produce at all, and exit from the market.

Case 2: Price must be greater than or equal to AC in the long run.

We will show that the statement of Case 2 is true by arguing that a profit-maximising firm, in the long run, will not produce at an output level wherein the market price is lower than the AC.

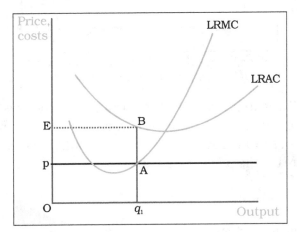

Price-AC Relationship with Profit Maximisation (Long Run). The figure is used to demonstrate that a profit-maximising firm produces zero output in the long run when the market price, p, is less than the minimum of its long run average cost (LRAC). If the firm's output level is q_1, the firm's total cost exceeds its revenue by an amount equal to the area of rectangle pEBA.

Let us turn to figure. Observe that at the output level q_1, the market price p is lower than the (long run) AC. We claim that q_1 cannot be a profit-maximising output level. Why?

Notice that the firm's total revenue, TR, at q_1 is the area of the rectangle $OpAq_1$ (the product of price and quantity) while the firm's total cost, TC, is the area of the rectangle $OEBq_1$ (the product of average cost and quantity). Since the area of rectangle $OEBq_1$ is larger than the area of rectangle $OpAq_1$, the firm incurs a loss at the output level q_1. But, in the long run set-up, a firm that shuts down production has a profit of zero. Again, the firm chooses to exit in this case.

The Profit Maximisation Problem: Graphical Representation

Let us graphically represent a firm's profit maximisation problem in the short run. Consider Figure. Notice that the market price is p. Equating the market price with the (short run) marginal cost, we obtain the output level q_0. At q_0, observe that SMC slopes upwards and p exceeds AVC. Since the three conditions are satisfied at q_0, we maintain that the profit-maximising output level of the firm is q_0.

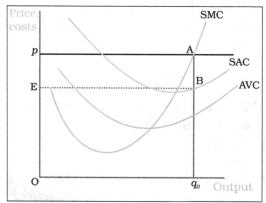

Geometric Representation of Profit Maximisation (Short Run). Given market price p, the output level of a profit-maximising firm is q_0. At q_0, the firm's profit is equal to the area of rectangle EpAB.

What happens at q_0? The total revenue of the firm at q_0 is the area of rectangle $OpAq_0$ (the product of price and quantity) while the total cost at q_0 is the area of rectangle $OEBq_0$ (the product of short runs average cost and quantity). So, at q_0, the firm earns a profit equal to the area of the rectangle EpAB.

Supply Curve of a Firm

A firm's 'supply' is the quantity that it chooses to sell at a given price, given technology, and given the prices of factors of production. A table describing the quantities sold by a firm at various prices, technology and prices of factors remaining unchanged is called a supply schedule. We may also represent the information as a graph, called a supply curve. The supply curve of a firm shows the levels of output (plotted on the x-axis) that the firm chooses to produce corresponding to different values of the market price (plotted on the y-axis), again keeping technology and prices of factors of production unchanged. We distinguish between the short run supply curve and the long run supply curve.

Short Run Supply Curve of a Firm

Let us turn to figure and derive a firm's short run supply curve. We shall split this derivation into two parts. We first determine a firm's profit-maximising output level when the market price is greater than or equal to the minimum AVC. This done, we determine the firm's profit-maximising output level when the market price is less than the minimum AVC.

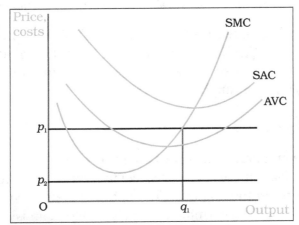

Market Price Values. The figure shows the output levels chosen by a profit-maximising firm in the short run for two values of the market price: p_1 and p_2. When the market price is p_1, the output level of the firm is q_1; when the market price is p_2, the firm produces zero output.

Case 1: Price is greater than or equal to the minimum AVC.

Suppose the market price is p_1, which exceeds the minimum AVC. We start out by equating p_1 with SMC on the rising part of the SMC curve; this leads to the output level q_1. Note also that the AVC at q_1 does not exceed the market price, p_1. Thus, all three conditions highlighted are satisfied at q_1. Hence, when the market price is p_1, the firm's output level in the short run is equal to q_1.

Case 2: Price is less than the minimum AVC.

Suppose the market price is p_2, which is less than the minimum AVC. We have argued that if a profit-maximising firm produces a positive output in the short run, then the market price, p_2, must be greater than or equal to the AVC at that output level. But notice from figure that for all positive output levels, AVC strictly exceeds p_2. In other words, it cannot be the case that the firm supplies a positive output. So, if the market price is p_2, the firm produces zero output.

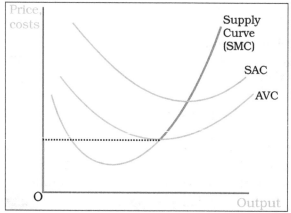

The Short Run Supply Curve of a Firm. The short run supply curve of a firm, which is based on its short run marginal cost curve (SMC) and average variable cost curve (AVC), is represented by the bold line.

Combining cases 1 and 2, we reach an important conclusion. A firm's short run supply curve is the rising part of the SMC curve from and above the minimum AVC together with zero output for all prices strictly less than the minimum AVC. In figure, the bold line represents the short run supply curve of the firm.

Long Run Supply Curve of a Firm

Let us turn to figure and derive the firm's long run supply curve. As in the short run case, we split the derivation into two parts. We first determine the firm's profit-maximising output level when the market price is greater than or equal to the minimum (long run) AC. This done, we determine the firm's profit maximising output level when the market price is less than the minimum (long run) AC.

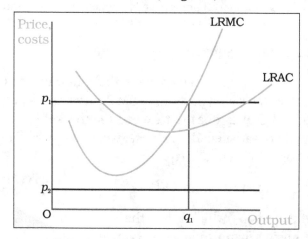

Profit maximisation in the Long Run for Different Market Price Values. The figure shows the output levels chosen by a profit maximising firm in the long run for two values of the market price: p_1 and p_2. When the market price is p_1, the output level of the firm is q_1; when the market price is p_2, the firm produces zero output.

Case 1: Price greater than or equal to the minimum LRAC.

Suppose the market price is p_1, which exceeds the minimum LRAC. Upon equating p_1 with LRMC on the rising part of the LRMC curve, we obtain output level q_1. Note also that the LRAC at q_1 does not exceed the market price, p_1. Thus, all three conditions highlighted are satisfied at q_1. Hence, when the market price is p_1, the firm's supplies in the long run become an output equal to q_1.

Case 2: Price less than the minimum LRAC.

Suppose the market price is p_2, which is less than the minimum LRAC. We have argued that if a profit-maximising firm produces a positive output in the long run, the market price, p_2, must be greater than or equal to the LRAC at that output level. But notice from figure that for all positive output levels, LRAC strictly exceeds p_2. In other words, it cannot be the case that the firm supplies a positive output. So, when the market price is p_2, the firm produces zero output. Combining cases 1 and 2, we reach an important conclusion. A firm's long run supply curve is the rising part of the LRMC curve from and above the minimum LRAC together with zero output for all prices less than the minimum LRAC. In figure, the bold line represents the long run supply curve of the firm.

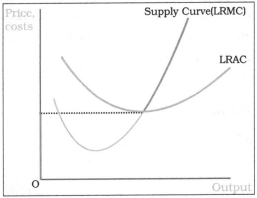

The Long Run Supply Curve of a Firm. The long run supply curve of a firm, which is based on its long run marginal cost curve (LRMC) and long run average cost curve (LRAC), is represented by the bold line.

The Shut Down Point

Previously, while deriving the supply curve, we have discussed that in the short run the firm continues to produce as long as the price remains greater than or equal to the minimum of AVC. Therefore, along the supply curve as we move down, the last price-output combination at which the firm produces positive output is the point of minimum AVC where the SMC curve cuts the AVC curve. Below this, there will be no production. This point is called the short run shut down point of the firm. In the long run, however, the shutdown point is the minimum of LRAC curve.

The Normal Profit and Break-even Point

The minimum level of profit that is needed to keep a firm in the existing business is defined as normal profit. A firm that does not make normal profits is not going to continue in business. Normal profits are therefore a part of the firm's total costs. It may be useful to think of them as an opportunity cost for entrepreneurship. Profit that a firm earns over and above the normal profit is called the super-normal profit. In the long run, a firm does not produce if it earns anything less than the normal profit. In the short run, however, it may produce even if the profit is less than this level. The point on the supply curve at which a firm earns only normal profit is called the break-even point of the firm. The point of minimum average cost at which the supply curve cuts the LRAC curve (in short run, SAC curve) is therefore the break-even point of a firm.

Opportunity Cost

In economics, one often encounters the concept of opportunity cost. Opportunity cost of some activity is the gain foregone from the second best activity. Suppose you have $ 1,000 which you decide to invest in your family business. What is the opportunity cost of your action? If you do not invest this money, you can either keep it in the house-safe which will give you zero return or you can deposit it in either bank-1 or bank-2 in which case you get an interest at the rate of 10 per cent or 5 per cent respectively. So the maximum benefit that you may get from other alternative activities is the interest from the bank-1. But this opportunity will no longer be there once you invest the money in your family business. The opportunity cost of investing the money in your family business is therefore the amount of forgone interest from the bank-1.

Determinants of a Firm's Supply Curve

We have seen that a firm's supply curve is a part of its marginal cost curve. Thus, any factor that affects a firm's marginal cost curve is of course a determinant of its supply curve.

Technological Progress

Suppose a firm uses two factors of production – say, capital and labour – to produce a certain good. Subsequent to an organisational innovation by the firm, the same levels of capital and labour now produce more units of output. Put differently, to produce a given level of output, the organisational innovation allows the firm to use fewer units of inputs. It is expected that this will lower the firm's marginal cost at any level of output; that is, there is a rightward (or downward) shift of the MC curve. As the firm's supply curve is essentially a segment of the MC curve, technological progress shifts the supply curve of the firm to the right. At any given market price, the firm now supplies more units of output.

Input Prices

A change in input prices also affects a firm's supply curve. If the price of an input (say, the wage rate of labour) increases, the cost of production rises. The consequent increase in the firm's average cost at any level of output is usually accompanied by an increase in the firm's marginal cost at any level of output; that is, there is a leftward (or upward) shift of the MC curve. This means that the firm's supply curve shifts to the left: at any given market price, the firm now supplies fewer units of output.

Impact of a Unit Tax on Supply

A unit tax is a tax that the government imposes per unit sale of output. For example, suppose that the unit tax imposed by the government is $ 2. Then, if the firm produces and sells 10 units of the good, the total tax that the firm must pay to the government is $10 \times \$ 2 = \$ 20$.

How does the long run supply curve of a firm change when a unit tax is imposed? Let us turn to figure. Before the unit tax is imposed, $LRMC^0$ and $LRAC^0$ are, respectively, the long run marginal cost curve and the long run average cost curve of the firm. Now, suppose the government puts in place a unit tax of $ t. Since the firm must pay an extra $ t for each unit of the good produced, the firm's long run average cost and long run marginal cost at any level of output increases by $ t. In figure, $LRMC^1$ and $LRAC^1$ are, respectively, the long run marginal cost curve and the long run average cost curve of the firm upon imposition of the unit tax.

Recall that the long run supply curve of a firm is the rising part of the LRMC curve from and above the minimum LRAC together with zero output for all prices less than the minimum LRAC. Using this observation in figure, it is immediate that S^0 and S^1 are, respectively, the long run supply curve of the firm before and after the imposition of the unit tax. Notice that the unit tax shifts the firm's long run supply curve to the left: at any given market price, the firm now supplies fewer units of output.

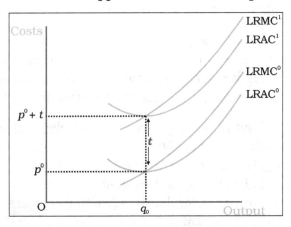

Cost Curves and the Unit Tax. LRACo and LRMCo are, respectively, the long run average cost curve and the long run marginal cost curve of a firm before a unit tax is imposed. LRAC^1 and LRMC^1 are, respectively, the long run average cost curve and the long run marginal cost curve of a firm after a unit tax of \$ t is imposed.

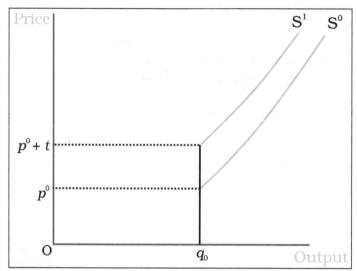

Supply Curves and Unit Tax. S^0 is the supply curve of a firm before a unit tax is imposed. After a unit tax of \$ t is imposed, S^1 represents the supply curve of the firm.

Market Supply Curve

The market supply curve shows the output levels (plotted on the x-axis) that firms in the market produce in aggregate corresponding to different values of the market price (plotted on the y-axis).

How is the market supply curve derived? Consider a market with n firms: firm 1, firm 2, firm 3, and so on. Suppose the market price is fixed at p. Then, the output produced by the n firms in aggregate is [supply of firm 1 at price p] + [supply of firm 2 at price p] + ... + [supply of firm n at price p]. In other words, the market supply at price p is the summation of the supplies of individual firms at that price.

Let us now construct the market supply curve geometrically with just two firms in the market: firm 1 and firm 2. The two firms have different cost structures. Firm 1 will not produce anything if the market price is less than $\bar{p}_1$ while firm 2 will not produce anything if the market price is less than $\bar{p}_2$. Assume also that $\bar{p}_2$ is greater than $\bar{p}_1$.

In panel (a) of figure we have the supply curve of firm 1, denoted by S_1; in panel (b), we have the supply curve of firm 2, denoted by S_2. Panel (c) of figure shows the market supply curve, denoted by S_m. When the market price is strictly below $\bar{p}_1$, both firms choose not to produce any amount of the good; hence, market supply will also be zero for all such prices. For a market price greater than or equal to $\bar{p}_1$ but strictly less than $\bar{p}_2$, only firm 1 will produce a positive amount of the good. Therefore, in this range, the market supply curve coincides with the supply curve of firm 1. For a market price greater than or equal to $\bar{p}_2$, both firms will have positive output levels. For example, consider a situation wherein the market price assumes the value p_3 (observe that p_3 exceeds $\bar{p}_1$). Given p_3, firm 1 supplies q_3 units of output while firm 2 supplies q_4 units of output. So, the market supply at price p_3 is q_5, where $q_5 = q_3 + q_4$. Notice how the market supply curve, S_m, in panel (c) is being constructed: we obtain S_m by taking a horizontal summation of the supply curves of the two firms in the market, S_1 and S_2.

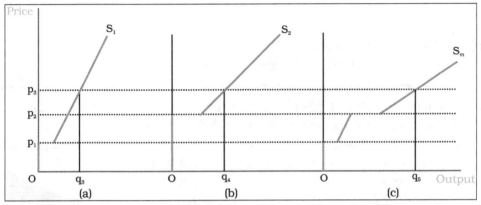

The Market Supply Curve Panel. (a) shows the supply curve of firm 1. Panel (b) shows the supply curve of firm 2. Panel (c) shows the market supply curve, which is obtained by taking a horizontal summation of the supply curves of the two firms.

It should be noted that the market supply curve has been derived for a fixed number of firms in the market. As the number of firm's changes, the market supply curve shifts as well. Specifically, if the number of firms in the market increases (decreases), the market supply curve shifts to the right (left).

We now supplement the graphical analysis given above with a related numerical example. Consider a market with two firms: firm 1 and firm 2. Let the supply curve of firm 1 be as follows:

$$S_1(p) = \begin{cases} 0 & : p < 10 \\ p-10 & : p \geq 10 \end{cases}$$

Notice that $S_1(p)$ indicates that (1) firm 1 produces an output of 0 if the market price, p, is strictly less than 10, and (2) firm 1 produces an output of $(p - 10)$ if the market price, p, is greater than or equal to 10. Let the supply curve of firm 2 be as follows:

$$S_2(p) = \begin{cases} 0 & : p < 15 \\ p-15 & : p \geq 15 \end{cases}$$

The interpretation of $S_2(p)$ is identical to that of $S_1(p)$, and is, hence, omitted. Now, the market supply curve, $S_m(p)$, simply sums up the supply curves of the two firms; in other words:

$$S_m(p) = S_1(p) + S_2(p)$$

But, this means that $S_m(p)$ is as follows:

$$S_m(p) = \begin{cases} 0 & : p < 10 \\ p - 10 & : p \geq 10 \text{ and } p < 15 \\ (p-10)+(p-15) = 2p - 25 & : p \geq 15 \end{cases}$$

Monopolistic Competition

Monopolistic competition is a market structure which lies in between perfect competition and monopoly and thus it has the features / characteristics of the both. The concept of monopolistic competition is more realistic than perfect competition and monopoly and we can even relate this type of market structure with the one which is prevailing in our current markets. We will look at the model given by Professor E. H Chamberlin in his book "The theory of monopolistic competition" in 1933.

Definition and Characteristics of Monopolistic Competition

By definition, monopolistic competition refers to a market structure in which a large number of sellers sell differentiated products, which are close substitutes for one another. Here, a close substitute is one whose cross-elasticity is close to unity or greater. Monopolistic competition combines the basic elements of both perfect competition and monopoly.

The element of monopoly in monopolistic competition arises from the fact that each firm has an absolute right to produce and sell a branded or patented product. Other firms are prevented by laws from producing and selling a branded product of other firms. This gives a firm monopoly power over production, pricing and sale of its own-branded product. For example, consider toilet soap industry. Similarly, Ford Motor Company has monopoly power for producing and selling cars under the brand name Ford Motor Company. No other car manufacturing company can produce and sell cars under this brand name. So is the case with all other car manufacturing companies.

The element of competition comes from the fact that each branded product has several close substitutes and firms selling branded products of the same generic category have to compete for the market share. Considering again our example of toilet soaps,, all the companies producing and selling these branded toilet soaps are in intensive competition for capturing the largest possible market share. One index of the competition between them is the amount that they spend advertising their product. These features of the toilet soap industry make it monopolistically competitive. Toothpaste industry with a number of branded product names (e.g. Binaca, Colgate, Close-up, Pepsodent, Forhans, Cibaca, Neem, Meswak, Signal, Promise, Prestige and so on) is another example of monopolistic competition. So is the case with major industrial products, e.g., electrical tubes and bulbs, TV sets, refrigerators, air conditioners, personal computers, textile goods, tea, coffee, cigarettes, soft drinks, cold creams, shampoos, detergents, shaving blades, shaving cream, hair oils, hair dyes, shoes, wrist watches, steel, cement, mobile phones and so on.

Let's now have a look at the characteristics of monopolistic competition:

- Large number of buyers and sellers: In monopolistic competitive market, there exist large number of both the buyers and sellers of the product. This is the same feature as of the perfect competition. However there is one difference that competitive firms are very small relative to the size of the market whereas in monopolistic competition, the firms are not so small in relation to the size of the market.

- Product differentiation: Since various firms under monopolistic competition compete with each other, thus, they compete by selling differentiated products that are either similar or close substitutes of each other. Hence the prices of the products are not too much different from each other. Moreover the cross price elasticity of demand for the products is large but not infinite.

- Freedom of entry and exit: It is relatively easy for the new firms to enter a monopolistic competition market industry and for the existing firms to leave the industry. If the industry is profitable, new firms will enter the industry and similarly any firm can leave the industry if it incurs losses. This feature of free entry and exit is based on the low startup costs and no exit cost.

- Market power: Firms under monopolistic competition face downward sloping demand curve (AR) and marginal revenue (MR) curve lies below it because the firms sell differentiated products (which are and can be close substitutes), and any reduction in the price by the seller would attract the customers of the other product towards it. Therefore, fall in the price of one product will increase the demand of that product; hence, firms under monopolistic competition have some influence on the price. Moreover, the demand curve is comparatively more elastic in this market structure but it is not perfect elastic.

- Non-price competition: Firms under monopolistic competition compete not only in terms of prices but also on other non-price variables which the firm spends on advertising like marketing cost, sales promotion expenses etc.

- Absence of interdependence among firms: In monopolistic competition, each firm acts more or less independent and have their own price policies regarding price and output. Hence, the change in the pricing policy of one firm does not have a significant effect on the price and output of the other firm.

- Concept of industry under monopolistic competition: Industry is defined as the number of firms selling homogeneous/identical products. However with product differentiation, the definition of industry becomes ambiguous. Hence, Professor Chamberlin has replaced the concept of industry with "group of firms" producing differentiated products which are close substitutes of each other and have high cross price elasticity of demand.

Comparison of Monopolistic Competition with Perfect Competition and Monopoly

S. No.	Monopolistic competition	Perfect competition	Monopoly
1.	Large number of firms	Ok	
2.	Monopoly power- face downward sloping demand and MR curves		Ok
3.	Free entry and exit	Ok	
4.	Firms can earn super normal profits in short run		Ok
5.	Economic profits are zero, P=AC in the long run	Ok	
6.	Non pricing competition – advertising		Ok
7.	Pricing – P > MC (MR = MC) (deadweight loss)		Ok

Short run Equilibrium of the Monopolistic Competitive Firm

Chamberlin has made the following explicit and implicit assumptions to develop his theory of monopolistic competition:

- There are a large number of firms selling slightly differentiated products, which are close substitutes for one another.

- The number of firms in a product group is so large that their activities, especially, maneuvering of price and output, go unnoticed by the rival firms.

- Demand and cost curves for all the products and for all the firms of the group are uniform, i.e., firms face identical demand (including perceived one) and cost curves.

- Consumer's preferences are evenly distributed among the different products and product differentiations are not such that they make a difference in cost.

Since monopolistically competitive firms have downward sloping demand curve, so they have some market power and can influence the price as each firm sells differentiated product which is not exactly similar to the product of the other firm but yes somewhat substitute to the product of the other firms. Moreover there exist no major barriers to entry or exit in monopolistic competition, thus, this feature puts a limit on the profits of the firms.

Now because of the free entry, the new firms will keep entering a monopolistic competition market until economic profits are driven to zero.

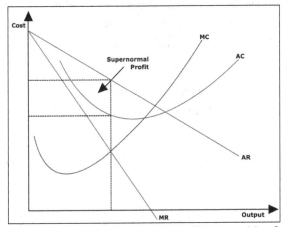

Short run equilibrium of monopolistically competitive firm.

Here, AR is the demand curve of the monopolistic competitive firm which is downward sloping because they sell differentiated products. MR is the corresponding marginal revenue curve. MC is the marginal cost curve and AC is the Average cost curve of a monopolistic competitive firm. A profit maximizing firm will produce where it's MR = MC. In this case, P>AC so firms earn super normal profits, as indicated by the rectangle area in figure.

Here the second order condition is also satisfied at the equilibrium i.e. dMR/dQ < dMC/dQ.

Long Run Equilibrium of a Monopolistically Competitive Firm

The long-run conditions differ from the short-run conditions because in the long run: (i) new firms enter the industry, (ii) firms indulge in price competition, (iii) changes (i) and (ii) take place simultaneously and (iv) firms advertise their product more vigorously.

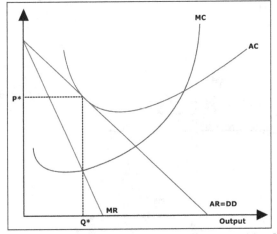

Long run equilibrium of a monopolistically competitive firm.

When monopolistically competitive firms earn positive or supernormal profits in short run, then this attract new firms to enter the market and hence new potential firms start producing their own differentiated product in the market. This reduces the economic profit of the market as the existing firms lose their market share and their demand curve shifts down. This will go on till all the firms earn only normal profits and the economic profits comes to zero.

In order to maximize profits, firms will produce where MR = MC. Here one point to note is that the demand curve is tangent to the firms AC curve which implies P = AC and economic profits = 0.

Hence we can write the following long run equilibrium conditions under monopolistic competition:

- MR = MC

- dMC/dQ < dMR/dQ

- P = AC

Monopolistic Competition and Economic Efficiency

Perfectly competitive firms are economically efficient because they maximize the sum of producer and consumer surplus, whereas monopoly leads to a loss in the social welfare of the society. Let's see here if the monopolistically competitive firms are efficient or not and how are they compared with the competitive firms.

There are basically two sources of inefficiencies in monopolistic competitive firms:

1. Under monopolistic competition, equilibrium price exceeds marginal cost, whereas under perfect competition P=MC.

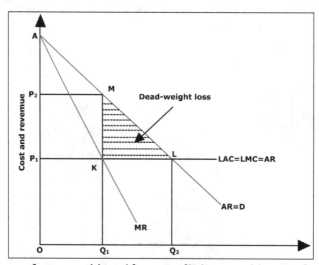

Comparing perfect competition with monopolistic competition: Deadweight loss.

Since under monopolistic competition P>MC, this means that value to the consumers of the additional units of output exceeds the cost of producing that output. The sum of consumer and producer surplus can be maximized if the output was expanded up to the point where P = MC by the MKL region in figure. Hence, MKL region is the deadweight loss under monopolistic competition that arises due to the existence of monopoly power (downward sloping demand curve). Hence social welfare is not maximized under monopolistic competition.

2. Because of the free entry and exit assumption under perfect competition and monopolistic competition, long run equilibrium occurs where P = AC, i.e., economic profits = 0 in the long run. However, there is one important difference in both types of market, i.e., in case of a competitive firm, zero profits occurs at the minimum of the average cost curve, however, under monopolistic competition, the zero profits occurs on the falling portion of the average cost curve, and not at its minimum. This happens because firms face downward sloping demand curve and therefore the zero point occurs to the left of the minimum of the average cost curve. Hence, firms under monopolistic competition operate with excess capacity.

The Concept of Excess Capacity

Excess capacity is defined as the difference between the ideal output and the actual output attained in the long run, where ideal output is the output which is produced by the firms where the long run average cost is at its minimum. Under monopolistic competition, the firms though earns zero economic profits but there always exists the problem of excess capacity because the monopolistically competitive firms output does not coincide with the output at the minimum of LAC curve.

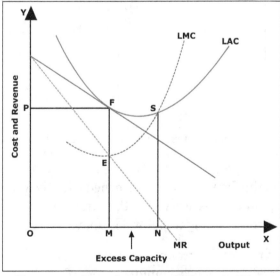

Excess capacity under monopolistic competition.

As we can see in figure, a monopolistic firm produces M output which is less than the ideal output N. This difference is termed as excess capacity because each firm is producing its output at an average cost that is higher than it could achieve by producing its capacity output. Excess capacity is a kind of inefficiency of the firms which reduces social welfare and makes the consumers worse off.

Excess Capacity under Chamberlin Model

Prof. Chamberlin's explanation of the theory of excess capacity is different from that of ideal output under perfect competition. Under perfect competition, each firm produces at the minimum on its LAC curve and its horizontal demand curve is tangent to it at that point.

Its output is ideal and there is no excess capacity in the long-run. Since under monopolistic competition the demand curve of the firm is downward sloping due to product differentiation, the long-run equilibrium of the firm is to the left of the minimum point on the LAC curve. According to Chamberlin, so long as there is freedom of entry and price competition in the product group under monopolistic competition, the tangency point between the firm's demand curve and the LAC curve would lead to the "ideal output" and no excess capacity.

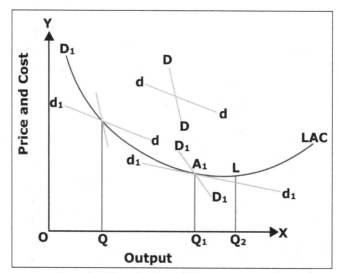

Excess capacity under Chamberlin model of monopolistic competition.

When there is no price competition due to the prevalence of these factors, the curve dd is of no significance and the firms are only concerned with the group DD curve. Suppose the initial short-run equilibrium is at S where the firms are earning supernormal profits because the price OP corresponding to point S is above the LAC curve.

With the entry of new firms in the group, super-normal profits will be competed away. The new firms will divide the market among themselves and the DD curve will be pushed to the left as d_1d_1 in figure where it becomes tangent to the LAC curve at point A_1, This point A_1 is of stable equilibrium in the absence of price competition for all firms in the group and they are earning only normal profits. Each firm is producing and selling OQ output at QA (= OP) price.

In Chamberlin's analysis, O_1 is the 'ideal output'. But each firm in the group is producing OQ output in the absence of price competition. Thus OQ_1 represents excess capacity under non-price monopolistic competition.

Monopolistic Competition Versus Perfect Competition: A Comparison

The monopolistic competition given by Chamberlin, is characteristically closer to perfect competition. There are, however, significant differences between the two kinds of markets in respect of (i) the number of firms, (ii) the nature of products, (iii) the nature of competition, (iv) efficiency in production and (v) capacity utilization.

1. The Number of Firms: The number of firms in both monopolistic competition and perfect competition is very large. But the number of firms under perfect competition is much larger than that under monopolistic competition. The number of firm in perfect competition is so large that an individual firm has absolutely no control on the price of its product: price is determined by the market forces and is given to the firm.

However under monopolistic competition, the number of firms is only so large that an individual firm does have power to change price of its product especially under the condition of product differentiation. A firm can increase the price of its product and still retain some of its buyers (which are not possible under perfect competition) and if a firm cuts down the price of its product, it captures a part of the market of the rival firms. On the contrary, if a firm in perfect competition cuts down the price, it goes out of the market itself.

Moreover, the competitive firms are very small relative to the size of the market whereas in monopolistic competition, the firms are not so small in relation to the size of the market.

2. The Nature of the Product: Under perfect competition, product is homogeneous and, therefore, the product of each seller is treated as a perfect substitute for the product of other firms. Under monopolistic competition, on the other hand, there is product differentiation and the product of each firm is a close substitute for that of the others.

3. The Nature of Competition: Under perfect competition with homogeneity of products, there is practically no competition. Each firm faces a horizontal demand curve and sells any quantity without affecting the market share of other firms. On the other hand, under monopolistic competition, the firms face a downward sloping demand curve due to product differentiation. Competition between the firms may take the form of price competition or non-price competition where non-price competition takes the form of competitive advertising of the product by the firms.

4. Efficiency in Production: Efficiency in production under monopolistic competition and perfect competition is compared on the basis of their equilibrium output. Though the rules for profit maximization are the same for the firms in both the kinds of the markets (i.e., MR = MC with MC rising), but still the equilibrium output under perfect competition is higher than that under monopolistic competition. Moreover the production under perfect competition is more efficient than under monopolistic competition.

5. Capacity Utilization: In continuation with the issue of efficiency in production, it has been shown that capacity utilization under monopolistic competition is lower than that under perfect competition. It means that under monopolistic competition, there is underutilization of capacity i.e. there is excess capacity under monopolistic competition whereas there is none under perfect competition.

Criticism of Chamberlin's Theory of Monopolistic Competition

- Chamberlin's Theory has Low Predicting Power.

- Chamberlin's Model is challenged on Theoretical Grounds.

- Chamberlin's Model Makes Unrealistic Assumptions like assuming identical cost and revenue curves are not justified, assuming no interdependence is not reasonable, assuming that firms do not learn is not correct.

- Chamberlin's Measure of Excess Capacity is logically inconsistent.

- Chamberlin's Model Lacks Empirical Validity.

Despite these damaging criticisms, Chamberlin's theory of monopolistic competition is regarded as a significant contribution to the theory of value and remains a subject matter of microeconomics for analytical rigour and insight that it provides in analyzing a monopolistically competitive market.

Oligopoly

Non-collusive models of oligopoly explain the price and output determination in an oligopolistic market. Suppose Chamberlin's model of oligopoly consisting of an "small group" of firms and Sweezy's Kinked demand curve models are regarded as most important models of this category.

Equilibrium under Independent Action

In 1939, Prof. Sweezy presented the kinked demand curve analysis to explain price rigidities in oligopolistic markets. Sweezy found that if the oligopolistic firm lowers its price, its rivals will lower the price in order to avoid losing their customers. Thus the firm lowering the price will not be able to increase its demand much. This portion of its demand curve is relatively inelastic.

On the other hand, if the oligopolistic firm increases its price, its rivals will not follow it and change their prices. Thus the quantity demanded of this firm will fall considerably. This portion of the demand curve is relatively elastic. In these two situations, the demand curve of the oligopolistic firm has a Kink at the prevailing market price which explains price rigidity.

Assumptions

The kinked demand curve hypothesis of price rigidity is based on the following assumptions:

- There are few firms in the oligopolistic market.

- The product produced by one firm is a close substitute for the other firms.

- The product is of the same quality. There is no product differentiation.

- No advertising expenditures.

- There is an established or prevailing market price for the product at which all the sellers are satisfied.

- Each seller's attitude depends on the attitude of his rivals.

- Any attempt on the part of a seller to push up his sales by reducing the price of his product will be counteracted by other sellers who will follow his move.

- If he raises the price others will not follow him, rather they will stick to the prevailing price and cater to the customers, leaving the price-raising seller behind.

- The marginal cost curve passes through the dotted portion of the marginal revenue curve so that changes in marginal cost do not affect output and price.

Following these assumptions, the price-output relationship in the oligopolist market is given in figure. In this figure, KPD is the kinked demand curve and OP_0 the prevailing price in the oligopoly market for the OR product of one seller. Starting from point P, corresponding to the current price OP (OP_0) any increase in price above it will considerably reduce his sales, for his rivals are not expected to follow his price increase.

This is because the KP portion of the kinked demand curve is elastic, and the corresponding portion KA of the MR curve is positive. Therefore, any price-increase will not only reduce his total sales but also his total revenue and profit.

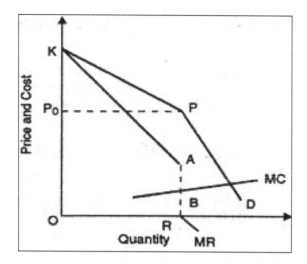

On the contrary, if the seller reduces the price of the product below OP_0 (or P), his rivals will also reduce their prices. Though he will increase his sales, his profit would be less than before. The reason is that the PD portion of the kinked demand curve below P is less elastic and the corresponding part of marginal revenue curve below R is negative. Thus in both the price- raising and price-reducing situations the seller will be a loser.

He would stick to the prevailing market price OP_0 which remains rigid. In order to understand the working of the kinked demand curve, let us analyze the effect of changes in cost and demand conditions on price stability in the oligopolistic market.

Changes in Costs

In oligopoly under the kinked demand curve analysis changes in costs within a certain range do not affect the prevailing price. Let us suppose the cost of production falls so that the new MC curve is MC_1 to the right, as in figure.

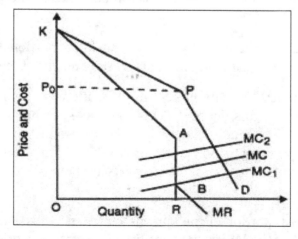

It cuts the MR curve in the gap AB so that the profit- maximizing output is OR which can be sold at OP_0 price.

It should be noted that with any cost reduction the new MC curve will always cut the MR curve in the gap because as costs fall, the gap AB continues to widen due to two reasons:

(1) As costs fall, the upper portion KP of the demand curve becomes more elastic because of the greater certainty that a price rise by one seller will not be followed by rivals and his sales would be considerably reduced.

(2) With the reduction in costs the lower portion PD of the kinked curve becomes more inelastic, because of the greater certainty that a price reduction by one seller will be followed by the other rivals.

Thus the angle KPD tends to be a right angle at P and the gap AB widens so that any MC curve below point A will cut the marginal revenue curve inside the gap. As a result there is the same output OR at the same price OP_0 and large profits for the oligopolistic sellers.

In case the cost of production rises the marginal cost curve will shift to the left of the old curve MC as MC_2. So long as the higher MC curve intersects the MR curve within the gap up to point A, the price situation will be rigid.

However, with the rise in costs the price is not likely to remain stable indefinitely and if the MC curve rises above point A, it will intersect the MC curve in the portion KA so that a lesser quantity is sold at a higher price.

Thus there may be price stability under oligopoly even when costs change so long as the MC curve cuts the MR curve in its discontinuous portion. Therefore, chances of the existence of price-rigidity are greater where there is a reduction in costs than there is a rise in costs.

Changes in Demand

We now explain price rigidity where there is a change in demand with the help of figure. D_2 is the original demand curve. MR_2 is its corresponding marginal revenue curve and MC is the marginal cost curve. Suppose there is a decrease in demand shown by D_1 curve and MR_1 is its marginal revenue curve. When demand decreases, a price-reduction move by one seller will be followed by other rivals.

This will make LD_1, the lower portion of the new demand curve, more inelastic than the lower portion HD_2 of the old demand curve. This will tend to make the angle at L approach a right angle.

As a result, the gap EF in MR_1 curve is likely to be wider than the gap AB of the MR_2 curve. The marginal cost curve MC will, therefore, intersect the lower marginal revenue curve MR_1 inside the gap EF, thus showing a stable price for the oligopolistic industry.

Since the level of the kinks H and L of the two demand curves remains the same, the same price OP is maintained after the decrease in demand. But the output level falls from OQ_2 to OQ_1. This case can be reversed to show increase in demand by taking D_1 and MR_1 as the original demand and marginal revenue curves and D_2 and MR_2 as the higher demand and marginal revenue curves respectively.

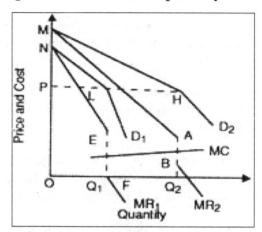

The price OP is maintained but the output rises from OQ_1 to OQ_2. So long as the MC curve continues to intersect the MR curve in the discontinuous portion, there will be price rigidity.

However, if demand increases, it may lead to a higher price. When demand increases, a seller would like to raise the price of the product and others are expected to follow him.

This will tend to make the upper portion MH of the new demand curve elastic than the NL portion of the old curve. Thus the angle at H becomes obtuse, away from the right angle.

The gap AB in the MR_2 curve becomes smaller and the MC curve intersects the MR_2 curve above the gap, indicating a higher price and lower output. If, however, the marginal cost curve passes through the gap of MR_2, there is price stability.

The whole analysis of the kinked demand curve points out that price rigidity in oligopolistic markets is likely to prevail if there is a price reduction move on the part of all sellers. Changes in costs and demand also lead to price stability under normal conditions so long as the MC curve intersects the MR curve in its discontinuous portion. But price increase rather than price rigidity may be found in response to rising cost or increased demand.

Reasons for Price Stability

There are a number of reasons for price rigidity in certain oligopoly markets:

- Individual sellers in an oligopolistic industry might have learnt through experience the futility of price wars and thus prefer price stability.

- They may be content with the current prices, outputs and profits and avoid any involvement in unnecessary insecurity and uncertainty.

- They may also prefer to stick to the present price level to prevent new firms from entering the industry.

- The sellers may intensify their sales promoting efforts at the current price instead of reducing it. They may view non-price competition better than price rivalry.

- After spending a lot of money on advertising his product, a seller may not like to raise its price to deprive himself of the fruits of his hard labour. Naturally, he would stick to the on-going price of the product.

- If a stable price has been set through agreement or collusion, no seller would like to disturb it, for fear of unleashing a price war and thus engulfing himself into an era of uncertainty and insecurity.

- Lastly, it is the kinked demand curve analysis which is responsible for price rigidity in oligopolistic markets.

Criticism

Kinked demand curve given by Prof. Sweezy has been criticised on the following grounds:

- Not proper explanation of price determination: The kinked demand curve is criticised on the ground that it does not explain how the prevailing price is determined. It merely helps to explain why oligopolistis will not change the prevailing price if it yields them reasonable profit.

- According to Prof. Baumol, "the kinked demand curve theory is not designed to deal with oligopolistic price and output determination. Rather, it seeks to explain why, once a price quantity combination has been decided upon, it will not readily change." Therefore, the kinked demand curve only explains price rigidity but not price itself.

- Wrong assumptions: The theory of kinked demand curve is based on the assumption that other firms will follow price decrease but not price increase. The said assumption of Kinked Demand Theory could not be proved empirically. Oligopoly prices are not as rigid particularly in an upward direction as the kinked demand theory implies. According to Prof. Stigler, "There is little historical basis for a firm to believe that price increases will not be matched by rivals and that price decreases will be matched".

- It ignores Non-Price competition: The price rigidity theory given by Prof. Sweezy does not take into consideration non-price competition. The oligopolist may charge the prevailing price but at the same time allow several concessions to the customers. It makes the real price flexible even if money price remains rigid. Moreover, Swcezy model ignores, credit facilities, concessions and other promotional facilities given to the customers.

- It Fails to Consider Competitive Reaction: The Kinked Demand Curve of Prof. Sweezy fails to consider competitive reaction patterns. Prof. Baumol found that the Kinky demand curve does not show how the oligopolistic firm's view of competitive reaction patterns can affect the change ability of whatever prices it charges from the consumer.

Cartel Model

In a model of collusive oligopoly, firms get together and agree to set prices and outputs so as to maximise total industry profits, they are known as a cartel.

Assumptions of the Cartel Model

For the sake of simplicity, we shall make here the following assumptions:

- There are only two firms in the oligopolistic industry, i.e., here we have a case of duopoly.

- Each firm produces and sells a product that is a perfect substitute for that of the other.

- The product is perishable.

- There are many knowledgeable buyers of the product.

- Each firm knows the market demand for the product.

- The two firms have different cost curves.

- Both the firms have the same expectations about the prices and productivities of the inputs which they use.

- The price of the product is the sole parameter of action of each firm.

- The two firms are contemplating whether or not to form a cartel and agree upon a price that will promise the maximum maximorum of profits per period to both of them jointly.

Analysis of the Cartel Model

Let us discuss the choice of this price and its implications with the help of figure. Here, in part (a), the average and marginal cost curves of duopolist A are given to be AC_A and MC_A, and those of duopolist B are given to be AC_B and MC_B in part (b).

As is seen in these figures, the cost levels of A have been assumed here to be lower than those of B. The curve DD in part (c) of the figure is the market demand curve for the product produced by the duopolists.

Here the dupolists A and B are exploring the possibility of jointly producing and selling the product and earning the maximum maximorum of profits. Henceforth, we shall call the duopoly firms A and B that have come under collusion, the firms A + B (the "plus" sign indicates collusion).

In our attempt to analyse the price-output-profit policy of the firms A + B, we shall first see how the firms would distribute the production of any particular quantity (q) of their product between the plants of A and B, so that the cost may be minimum. We may call the plants of the two firms plant A and plant B.

Now, the total cost (C) of producing any particular quantity of output, q is:

$$c = C_A(q_A) + C_B(q_B) = C(q_A, q_B)$$

Subject to:

$$q = q_A + Q_B = \text{constant}$$

Where,

- q_A = quantity of output to be produced in plant A.

- q_B = quantity of output to be produced in plant B.

- C_A = cost of production in plant A.

- C_B = cost of production in plant B.

Given these, the first-order conditions (FOCs) of producing the output quantity, q, in the two plants at minimum cost, i.e., the FOCs for minimising C, are:

$$\left.\begin{array}{l} \dfrac{\partial C}{\partial q_A} = 0 \\[2mm] \dfrac{\partial C}{\partial q_B} = 0 \end{array}\right\}$$

Now, $\dfrac{\partial C}{\partial q_A} = 0 \Rightarrow \dfrac{\partial C_A}{\partial q_A} + \dfrac{\partial C_B}{\partial q_B} \cdot \dfrac{\partial q_B}{\partial q_A} = 0$

$\Rightarrow MC_A - MC_B = 0 \left[\because \dfrac{\partial q_B}{\partial q_A} = -1 \text{ because } q_A + q_B = q = \text{constant} \right]$

$\Rightarrow MC_A = MC_B$

Similarly, we would obtain:

$$\dfrac{\partial C}{\partial q_B} = 0 \Rightarrow MC_A = MC_B$$

Conditions ($MC_A = MC_B$) and ($\dfrac{\partial C}{\partial q_B} = 0 \Rightarrow MC_A = MC_B$) give us that two (or more) oli-gopoly firms under collusion (here firms A + B) would distribute the production of any particular quantity of output between their plants in such a way that the marginal cost (MC) in each plant may become the same.

We may easily understand the economic significance of this condition. Instead of MC_A being equal to MC_B, if we have $MC_A > MC_B$ (in the two-firm case), then the firms A + B would reduce the quantity of production in the higher cost plant A and increase the quantity in the lower cost plant B, total output remaining the same.

The firms would do this because then they would be able to produce the same quantity of total output (q) at a lower cost.

Now, as we know, for the sake of profit maximisation, and, therefore, for the sake of efficient production, firms A + B would operate along the upward sloping segments of the MC curves of plants A and B that correspond to the second stage of production. That is why, as the firms decrease and increase q_B, MC_a will fall and MC_B will rise, and ultimately, at some distribution, MC_A will become equal to MC_B.

This distribution is the cost-minimising distribution of the output quantity, q, between the two plants. For if $MC_A = MC_B$, then it will not be possible for the firms to reduce the cost further by transferring output production from plant A to plant B, or, the other way round.

On the other hand, if $MC_A < MC_B$, the firms A + B will reduce output in plant B and increase it in plant A, till MC_A rises and MC_B falls to become equal to each other.

Thus, we come to the conclusion that the duopoly firms under collusion (i.e., firms A + B) will distribute the production of any particular quantity of output over the two plants in such a way that the MC in each plant may become the same; only then it would be able to produce the said quantity at the minimum cost.

Therefore, that at each quantity of output, q, there is a problem of cost- minimisation, or, profit-maximisation (the price, p, and, therefore, total revenue, p x q, being given by the demand curve). Here equilibrium will be obtained at that quantity, q*, at which profit is maximum among the maximums, or, maximum.

We may now proceed to explain how the equilibrium output, q*, of the firms A + B with maximum of profit is obtained. It follows from ($MC_A = MC_B$) or ($\dfrac{\partial C}{\partial q_B} = 0 \Rightarrow MC_A = MC_B$) that, at any output, $q = q_A + q_B$, the condition $MC_A = MC_B$ ensures cost-minimising of profit-maximising distribution of q between the two plants.

Now, at any $q = q_A + q_B$, the MC of firms A + B is $MC_A = MC_B$. This is because, here the

q_Ath unit of output is either the q_Ath unit of output in plant A or the q_Bth unit of output in plant B, and the additional cost of producing that unit is either MC_A or MC_B, and $MC_A = MC_B$.

On the revenue side, the firms A + B sell any quantity, q, of their product at the price given by the demand curve, DD. Now, if at any q, the firms A + B have $MC = MC_A = MC_B < MR$ (marginal revenue), then they would be able to earn a positive profit on the margin, and so, they would increase the output to push up the maximum maximorum of profit.

But as q increases the MR, being a decreasing function of q, would diminish, and MC ($= MC_A = MC_B$) would increase, since in the relevant range, both MC_A and MC_B are increasing functions of q. Therefore q, while increasing, would eventually assume a value (say, q^*) at which we would have $MR = MC$ ($= MC_A = MC_B$).

At this $q = q^*$, the firm would acquire the maximum maximorum of profit. For, now its profit on the margin is zero, and so it will not be able to increase its profit by increasing q.

On the other hand, if at some q, the firms have $MC = MC_A = MC_B > MR$, then it would suffer losses on the margin and would now want to shed the loss-earning marginal units, i.e., it would now want to decrease q to maximise its profit. But as q decreases, the firm's MC ($= MC_A = MC_B$) would also decrease, and its MR would increase.

Eventually, at $q = q^*$, the firm would have $MR = MC$ ($= MC_A = MC_B$), and this $q = q^*$ would be its q with maximum of profit. For, now the firms' losses on the margin are zero, and so it is no longer required of the firms to decrease their output in order to maximise profit.

It follows from the above analysis that the necessary or the first order condition (FOC) for profit maximisation under collusive oligopoly (here duopoly) is:

$$MR = MC_A = MC_B$$

However, condition (previous equation) is not the sufficient condition or the second order condition (SOC) of profit maximisation. For, if at the $MR = MC_A = MC_B$ point, the firms A + B find that a further increase in output would result in MC ($= MC_A = MC_B$) being less than MR, (which can of course happen in an inefficient stage of production), then the firms would not settle at this point, rather they would go on increasing the output quantity, for, by doing that, they would be able to increase the profit level.

Therefore, the SOC for profit maximisation states that at the point where the FOC is satisfied, i.e., at the $MR = MC_A = MC_B$ point, further increase in output should result in $MC = MC_A = MC_B$ being greater than MR. In that case, there would be a loss on the margin and so the firms A + B would not venture beyond the point (where the FOC is satisfied).

In other words, the SOC for profit maximisation under collusive oligopoly states that, at the point of intersection between the MC curve and the MR curve, where the FOC has been satisfied, the slope of the MC curve viz., the MC_{A+B} curve in figure (c), which, as we shall see, is the lateral summation of the MC_A and MC_B curves, should be greater than that of the MR curve.

It may be noted that, since the firms operate in the stage of efficient production, they would operate along the positively sloped portion of their respective MC curves, and, therefore, along the positively sloped portion of the MC_{A+B} curve. Here the SOC for profit maximisation would be automatically satisfied, for the MR curve of the firms A + B is negatively sloped, by definition.

We may now illustrate the profit-maximising equilibrium of the collusive oligopoly under discussion with the help of figure. The MC_{A+B} curve in figure (c) is the MC curve of firms A + B.

It is obtained by laterally adding together the MC_A and MC_B curves given in figures (a) and (b). The curve MC_{A+B} shows us what would be the total output of the firms A + B at any particular amount of MC in both the plants.

Thus, if the MC in both the plants is to be OC, ($MC_A = MC_B = OC$), plant A should produce OM_A of output and plant B should produce OM_B. The combined output in this case would be $OM_A + OM_B = OM$.

Conversely, we would also know from the curve MC_{A+B} what would be the MC = MC_A = MC_B at any particular output. For example, at q = OM, the MC = MC_A = MC_B would be OC, provided the distribution of this q between the two plants is $q_A = OM_A$ and $q_B = OM_B$.

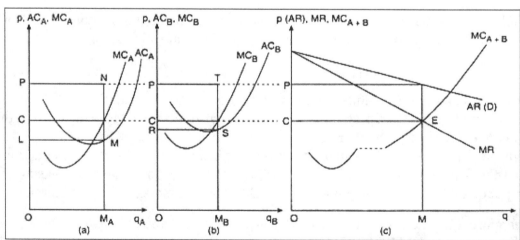

Equilibrium under collusive oligopoly.

Now, the total output for which the firms A+ B would be jointly earning the maximum maximorum of profits is obtained at the point of intersection, E, of the MR and MC_{A+B}

curves in figure (c). For at the point E, or at the total output of OM, the FOC for profit maximisation, viz., MR = MC$_A$ = MC$_b$ (- OC), has been satisfied.

Also, the SOC for maximum profit has been satisfied at point E, for here the MR curve is negatively sloped and the MC$_{A+B}$ curve is positively sloped.

It is obtained from the AR curve in figure (c) that the output OM of firms A + B can be sold at the price OR The output OM and the price OP are called, respectively, the monopoly output and price, for they would form the equilibrium price-output combination if the firms A and B merged into a single monopolistic firm.

The duopolists in this collusive oligopoly model will plan to sell OM units of their product at a price of OP per unit and firm A will produce and sell OM$_A$ units per period and firm B, OM$_B$ per period. The distribution of the 'monopoly' output of OM between the two firms implies a distribution of the maximum joint profits.

In the solution given in figure, firm A may expect to earn LMNP of profits per period and firm B may expect to earn RSTP of profit per period. The sum of LMNP and RSTP will be the maximum maximorum of profits that the two firms will be able to earn jointly.

Mathematical Derivation of the Condition for Maximum Profit

We may also derive the conditions for maximum maximorum of profit under collusive oligopoly with the help of calculus.

The profit (π) function of the firms A + B is:

$$\pi = R(q) - C_A(q_A) - C_B(q_B) = \pi(q_A, q_B)$$

Here,

- π = Profit of the firm A + B.
- R = The Total Revenue of the Firms.
- q = Quantity Produced = Quantity Sold = $q_A + q_B$.

All other symbols are already known to us.

Now, the FOCs for Maximum Maximorum of Profit are:

$$\frac{\partial \pi}{\partial q_A} = \frac{\partial R}{\partial q}\frac{\partial q}{\partial q_A} - \frac{\partial C_A}{\partial q_A} = 0$$

$$\text{and } \frac{\partial \pi}{\partial q_B} = \frac{\partial R}{\partial q}\frac{\partial q}{\partial q_B} - \frac{\partial C_B}{\partial q_B} = 0$$

Which imply,

$$\frac{\partial R}{\partial q} = \frac{\partial C_A}{\partial q_A} = \frac{\partial C_B}{\partial q_B} \left[\because \frac{\partial q}{\partial q_A} = \frac{\partial q}{\partial q_B} = 1 \right]$$

$$\Rightarrow MR = MC_A = MC_B$$

Which is the same as the first order condition ($MR = MC_A = MC_B$) that we have already obtained. It may be noted that condition (previous equation) is perfectly general; if the number of collusive firms be n, then also we would have the condition to be:

$$MR = MC_1 = MC_2 = ... = MC_n$$

Let us now come to the SOC for the maximum maximorum of profit. This condition states that the principal minors of the following determinant (D) would alternate in sign starting from the negative:

$$D = \begin{vmatrix} \dfrac{\partial^2 \pi}{\partial q_A^2} & \dfrac{\partial^2 \pi}{\partial q_A \partial q_B} \\ \dfrac{\partial^2 \pi}{\partial q_B \partial q_A} & \dfrac{\partial^2 \pi}{\partial q_B^2} \end{vmatrix}$$

In other words, the SOCs would be:

$$\frac{\partial^2 \pi}{\partial q_A^2} < 0 \Rightarrow \frac{\partial^2 R}{\partial q^2} - \frac{\partial^2 C_A}{\partial q_A^2} < 0$$

$$\Rightarrow \frac{\partial}{\partial q}\left(\frac{\partial R}{\partial q}\right) - \frac{\partial}{\partial q_A}\left(\frac{\partial C_A}{\partial q_A}\right) < 0$$

$$\Rightarrow \frac{\partial}{\partial q}(MR) - \frac{\partial}{\partial q_A}(MC_A) < 0$$

$$\Rightarrow \frac{\partial}{\partial q}(MR) - \frac{\partial}{\partial q_A}(MC_A)$$

and $\dfrac{\partial^2 \pi}{\partial q_A^2} \dfrac{\partial^2 \pi}{\partial q_B^2} - \left(\dfrac{\partial^2 \pi}{\partial q_A \partial q_B}\right)^2 > 0 \left[\because \text{in general, } \dfrac{\partial^2 \pi}{\partial q_A \partial q_B} = \dfrac{\partial^2 \pi}{\partial q_B \partial q_A} \right]$

$$\Rightarrow \frac{\partial^2 \pi}{\partial q_A^2} \frac{\partial^2 \pi}{\partial q_B^2} > 0 \left[\because \left(\frac{\partial^2 \pi}{\partial q_A \partial q_B}\right)^2 \gtrsim 0 \right]$$

$$\Rightarrow \frac{\partial^2 \pi}{\partial q_B^2} < 0 \left[\because \frac{\partial^2 \pi}{\partial q_A^2} < 0 \right]$$

$$\Rightarrow \frac{\partial}{\partial q}(MR) < \frac{\partial}{\partial q_B}(MC_B)$$

Previous both equations give us the SOCs for maximum maximorum of profit under collusive oligopoly. These conditions state that at the MR = MC_A = MC_B point, i.e., at the point of intersection of the MR and MC_{A+B} curves in figure (where the FOC has been satisfied), the slope of the MR curve of firms A + B should be less than the slopes of both MC_A and MC_B curves.

This implies, as we have already asserted, that the slope of the MR curve should be less than the slope of the MC_{A+B} curve. We have also mentioned the significance of these conditions. Like the FOC, the SOCs are also perfectly general.

That is, if the number of collusive firms is n, then these conditions give us that, at the point where the FOC is satisfied, the slope of the MR curve should be less than the slope of the MC curve of each of the firms.

Comparison between the Collusion Solution and the Quasi-competitive Solution:

The profit of the two firms taken together, or, the industry profit, is given by:

$$\pi = \pi_A + \pi_B = \left|100 - 0.5(q_A + q_B)\right|(q_A + q_B) - 5q_A - 0.5q_B^2$$
$$\Rightarrow \pi = 100(q_A + q_B) - 0.5(q_A + q_B)^2 - 5q_A - 0.5q_B^2$$
$$= \pi(q_A \cdot q_B)$$

Setting the partial derivatives of π equal to zero:

$$\frac{\partial \pi}{\partial q_A} = 95 - q_A - q_B = 0$$

$$\frac{\partial \pi}{\partial q_B} = 100 - q_A - 2q_B = 0$$

Solving (previous equation) for q_A and q_B and substituting in equations previous both equations, we have the following collusive solution:

$$q_A = 90 \text{ (units)}, q_B = 5 \text{ (units)}, p = 52.5 \text{ (Rs)}, \pi_A = 4,275 \text{ (Rs)}, \pi_B = 250 \text{ (Rs.)}$$

After comparing previous equation, we find that, under collusion, total output is much lower (95 < 190), price is much higher (52.5 > 5) and profits are much higher (4,275, 250 > 0, 12.5).

Cartel Instability

The problem with agreeing to form a cartel in the real world is that there is always a temptation for the participating firms to act contrary to the agreement, i.e., to cheat. We may elaborate the problem as follows. Let us rewrite the profit function as:

$$\pi = p(q)[q_A + q_B] - C_A(q_A) - C_B(q_B)$$
$$= \pi(q_A, q_B) \quad [\text{Where, } q = q_A + q_B]$$

The FOCs for maximum maximorum of profits are obtained from (previous equation) as:

$$\frac{\partial \pi}{\partial q_A} = \frac{\partial p}{\partial q}\frac{\partial q}{\partial q_A}(q_A + q_B) + p\frac{\partial q}{\partial q_A} - \frac{\partial C_A}{\partial q_A} = 0$$
$$\Rightarrow \frac{\partial p}{\partial q}(q_A + q_B) + p - MC_A = 0 \left[\because \frac{\partial q}{\partial q_A} = 1\right]$$

And

$$\frac{\partial \pi}{\partial q_B} = \frac{\partial p}{\partial q}\frac{\partial q}{\partial q_B}(q_A + q_B) + p\frac{\partial q}{\partial q_B} - \frac{\partial C_B}{\partial q_B} = 0$$
$$\Rightarrow \frac{\partial p}{\partial q}(q_A + q_B) + p - MC_B = 0 \left[\because \frac{\partial q}{\partial q_B} = 1\right]$$

That is, the FOCs are:

$$p = \frac{\partial p}{\partial q}(q_A + q_B) = MC_A$$

And

$$p = \frac{\partial p}{\partial q}(q_A + q_B) = MC_B$$

We also have the profit function of firm A as:

$$\pi_A = p(q)q_A - C_A(q_A)$$

Where, q = q_A + q_B, or, q_B = q - q_A

And from (previous equation), we have:

$$\frac{\partial \pi_A}{\partial q_A} = p(q) + \frac{\partial p}{\partial q}\frac{\partial q}{\partial q_A}q_A - MC_A(q_A)$$

Now, from ($p = \frac{\partial p}{\partial q}(q_A + q_B) = MC_A$ and $p = \frac{\partial p}{\partial q}(q_A + q_B) = MC_B$), we have:

$$p(q) + \frac{\partial p}{\partial q}q_A - MC_A = -\frac{\partial p}{\partial q}q_B > 0 \left[\because \frac{\partial p}{\partial q} < 0 \right]$$

From previous both equations, we obtain:

$$\frac{\partial \pi_A}{\partial q_A} > 0$$

That is, if firm A believes that firm B will keep its output fixed, then it will also believe that it can increase profits (π_A) by increasing its own production (q_A). It may be shown in a similar way that the firm B will also believe accordingly.

And herein lays the temptation for a member of the cartel to increase his own profits by unilaterally expanding his output beyond the output level that maximises joint profits. The situation becomes grave for the existence of the cartel if each firm comes to know that the other firm is not going to keep its output at the agreed level.

Therefore, in order to make the cartel effective and operational, its members must be able to detect and punish cheating. Otherwise, temptation to cheat would break the cartel.

In order to renew our understanding of the cartel solution, let us assume that the costs of production are zero and the demand curve for the product is linear.

Then the total revenue (R) function of the cartel will be:

$$R = (a - bq)q = aq - bq^2 = R(q) \text{ where } q = q_A + q_B$$

And here the MR = MC condition, or the FOC for maximum profit, will be:

$$a - 2bq = 0$$

$$\Rightarrow a - 2b(q_A + q_B) = 0$$

$$\Rightarrow q_A + q_B = a/2b$$

Since marginal costs are zero here, the division of output between the two firms does not matter. All that is important here is the total industry output which is this solution is shown in figure. In this figure, q_A is measured along the horizontal axis and q_B along the vertical axis.

Since $q_A + q_B = a/2b$, here we have $q_A = a/2b$, given $q_B = 0$ and $q_B = a/2b$, given $q_A = 0$, or here we would have any other combination of positive values of both q_A and q_B provided it lies on the straight line joining the points L (a/2b, 0) on the horizontal axis and M (0, a/2b) on the vertical axis.

Now, at any point on this line, the industry's profit is maximum, i.e., the profit of A is maximum given the profit of B and the profit of B is maximum given the profit of A, i.e., the iso-profit curve of A is the lowest, given the iso-profit curve of B and the iso-profit curve of B is the lowest, given the iso-profit curve of A, i.e., at any point on the line LM, the iso-profit curves of the two firms are tangent to each other.

Hence, the (q_A, q_B) combinations that maximise total industry profits and give us the alternative cartel solutions are those that lie on the line LM in figure.

Figure also helps us to understand how the temptation to cheat is present at the cartel solution. Let us consider, for example, the point N at the midpoint of the line segment LM.

At this point, the two firms share the market equally between themselves, each producing and selling half of the total quantity sold in the market. Let us now suppose that firm A decides to increase its output believing that B would keep its output unchanged.

Consequently, A would now move towards right of the point N along a horizontal straight line and would reach a lower iso-profit curve which implies that he would now be on a higher level of profit.

Similarly, if firm B decides to increase its output at the point N, believing that A would keep its output constant, it would move upward from N along a vertical straight line and reach a lower iso-profit curve or a higher level of profit. Thus both the duopolists are in temptation to increase their respective outputs in violation of the cartel agreement.

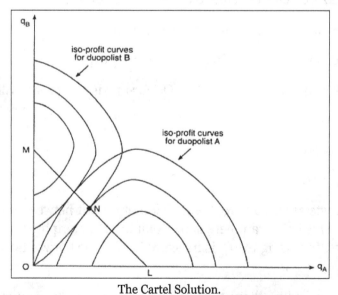

The Cartel Solution.

Punishment Strategies

We have seen above that a cartel is fundamentally unstable for its members are always tempted to increase their output quantities beyond their maximising levels. If the cartel is to continue its operations successfully, the behaviour of its members must conform to the agreement made by them. One way to ensure this is for the firms to threaten to punish each other for violating the cartel agreement.

This is known as a punishment strategy. For example, let us consider a duopoly with two identical firms. If the firms come to an understanding and produce the monopoly output, then the share of each firm will be half the monopoly output (= 1/2 x 1/2 a/b = 1/4 a/b) and the total profit of the duopolists will be maximised.

Let us suppose that the profit accruing to each firm, now, is π_m. In an effort to make this position stable, one of the firms, say, firm A, may threaten firm B that if it violated the output agreement, then it would punish firm B by producing the Cournot level of output forever.

Now, since the optimal response to Cournot behaviour is Cournot behaviour, both the firms now would operate at the Cournot equilibrium point which is the point of inter-section, I, of the reaction functions of the two firms. In other words, the point of oper-ation of the firms would shift from the point N to the point I.

Consequently, both the firms would move to a higher iso-profit curve, i.e., both of them would move to a lower level of profit. It may be noted also that in the cartel solution, total amount of output produced by the duopolists was 1/2 of competitive output and each of them had an equal share which was 1/4 of the competitive output.

Now, in the Cournot solution, total amount of output is larger being equal to 2/3 of competitive output and each firm had an equal share, equal to 1/3 of competitive out-put. Therefore, as the cartel breaks down, the firms now produce a larger quantity of output and sell at a lower price, since the demand curve for the product is negatively sloped, and earn a lower level of profit.

The economics here is very simple. Let us suppose that the two firms have agreed to produce an equal share of the collusive, monopoly level of output. Now, if one of the firms produces more output than its quota, it makes profit, say, π_d where $\pi_d > \pi_m$.

That is, here the two firms agree to enter into a cartel. They agree to restrict production. Consequently, the price goes up. Now one of them decides to produce more output to take advantage of the high price. This is the standard temptation that a cartel member is easily susceptible to.

Let us now look at the benefits and costs of cheating as opposed to those of normal car-tel behaviour. If each firm produces the cartel amount, then it gets a steady stream of payoffs of Tin. The present value (PV) of this stream is given by PV of Cartel behaviour = $\pi_m + \pi_m/r$.

On the other hand, if the firm produces more than the cartel amount, it gets a one-time benefit of profits π_d, but then the cartel breaks up, and it would have to revert to the Cournot behaviour to get a stream of payoffs of π_c. Therefore, we have:

PV of cheating $= \pi_d + \pi_c/r$

Obviously, the PV of cartel amount would be greater than the PV of cheating if,

$$\pi_m + \frac{\pi_m}{r} > \pi_d + \frac{\pi_C}{r}$$

$$\Rightarrow \frac{\pi_m}{r} - \frac{\pi_C}{r} > \pi_d - \pi_m$$

$$\Rightarrow \pi_m - \pi_C > r\left(\pi_d - \pi_m\right)$$

$$\Rightarrow r < \frac{\pi_m - \pi_C}{\pi_d - \pi_m}$$

$$\Rightarrow r\left(\pi_d - \pi_m\right) < \pi_m - \pi_C$$

The above inequality implies that so long as the interest rate (r) is sufficiently small, the expected return from cheating (i.e., the LHS of the inequality) is smaller than the expected return of cartel over the Cournot return (i.e., the RHS of the inequality), and therefore, if the above inequality is satisfied, the tendency to violate the provisions of the cartel agreement would be eliminated. That is, the firms would now stick to their cartel quotas.

Monopoly

Monopoly is rare and an extreme opposite of perfectly competitive market structure. In a monopoly, there exists only a single seller where he/she sells the products to a large number of buyers. For this he/she may charge a uniform price or may indulge into price discrimination. The main advantage to a monopolist is that it has no competitors or rivals in the market and hence, it earns profits even in the long run.

Meaning and Characteristics of Monopoly

Monopoly means single seller of a product but it is really a very rare condition to have a monopoly in a market structure, especially in the private sector. Since a monopolized industry is a single firm industry therefore there is no distinction between a firm and an industry in a monopolistic market structure. Hence the demand curve of a monopolistic firm is same as the market demand curve.

Characteristics of monopoly:

- Single Seller of a product.

- Barriers to entry and exit.

- No close substitute of the product is available in the market.

- Imperfect knowledge about the product and market between buyers and seller.

- Price discrimination.

- No supply curve of a monopolistic firm.

However the main source of the emergence of monopoly is barriers to entry like legal restrictions, patent rights, sole control over the scarce resources, efficiency etc.

Short Run Equilibrium of the Monopoly

The equilibrium of a firm is attained at a point where the firm earns maximum profit. The short run equilibrium of a monopolistic firm can be studied through two approaches:

TR – TC Approach

According to the Total revenue (TR) and Total cost (TC) approach, a monopolistic firm is in equilibrium at the price and output where TR – TC = profit is maximum. For instance, in the following figure, the firm faces a cubic TC function $TC = F + bQ - cQ^2 + dQ^3$ (where F = fixed cost) and the demand function $Q = a - bP$. When we graph the TC function then we get a Total cost curve as follows, similarly from the demand curve we can get a revenue function by multiplying it with price and hence when we plot it then we get the following TR curve:

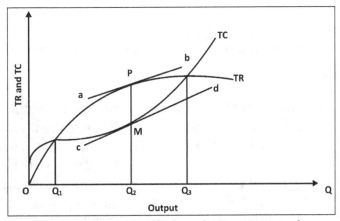

Equilibrium of monopoly through TR - TC approach.

As can be seen from the above figure that till OQ_1 and after OQ_3, a monopolistic firm faces loss as its TC > TR. Hence a monopolistic firm earns positive profits only between OQ_1 and OQ_3. Now the main question is that at which point or output does it maximizes its profit in this range? This question can be answered in two ways. First is that the point or output where the vertical distance between the TR and TC is maximum is the point or output where the monopolist earns maximum profit. Another way of finding out the maximum profit is through the tangency points on TR and TC. As it can be seen from the above figure, if we draw two parallel lines both at TR and TC then the parallel lines are tangent on TR at point P and at TC on point M. now if we analyze this then this is the same point where the distance between the TR and TC is maximum too. Hence the corresponding output at this point corresponds to maximum profit. Hence, a profit maximizing monopoly reaches its equilibrium at output OQ_2.

MR – MC Approach

As we know that Marginal revenue (MR) is the slope of TR and Marginal cost (MC) is the slope of TC, therefore this approach is in-turn an extension of the previous approach. The equilibrium under this approach is shown in the following diagram.

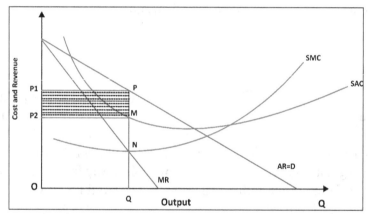

Equilibrium of the monopoly through MR – MC approach.

The Average revenue (AR) curve of a monopolist is downward sloping like a demand curve and is also the demand curve for the monopolist firm because TR = P*Q:

$$AR = P*Q/Q = Q$$

Hence AR is the demand curve of the monopolist firm. Correspondingly the MR is also downward sloping and have twice the slope of the AR, therefore it cuts the x axis at exact the half of the AR. SMC is the short run marginal cost of the firm which is U- shaped because in short run some factors are fixed and some are variable and when we increase the production then the cost initially reduces because of economies of scale but after reaching a minimum point of cost when the production is gain increased then the cost also increases due to diseconomies of scale. Hence SMC is U- shaped. Moreover, SMC is the differentiation of TC so when we plot this on a graph we get the SMC curve as above. Similarly, SAC is the Short run average cost curve of the monopolistic firm which is again U- shaped but it is below the SMC, because SMC cuts SAC from below and SAC is the combination of short run average fixed cost and short run average variable cost i.e. AC = AVC + AFC.

Now in order to be in equilibrium, a firm has to fulfill the following two conditions:

- MR = MC.

- Slope of MR > slope of MC, i.e. MR should cut MC from below.

Looking at the above figure, MR = MC at point N, correspondingly the profit maximizing point or the equilibrium point of the firm is N where a monopolistic firm produces OQ quantity and sells it at OP1 price and thus maximizes its profit.

Now in order to find out whether at this point the monopolistic firm earns a positive profit or a normal profit or a loss, we draw SAC and the point where it cuts PQ line, i.e. at point M, shows the cost of producing OQ output. So as per this, the price of selling OQ output is OP and the cost of producing OQ is OM. In other way, the total revenue from selling OQ output is OP_1PQ and the corresponding cost of producing this output is OP_2MQ. Here, clearly the cost of producing the output is much less than the revenue which the monopolist earns after selling it to its consumers. Hence the rectangle P_2P_1PM is the positive profit or the super normal profit which a monopolistic firm earns in the short run.

The next question which arises at this point is that "Does a monopoly firm always make positive profit in the short run?" the answer of this is NO, because there is no pure certainty that a monopoly firm will always earn positive profits in the short run. Actually it depends upon the cost which it bears for the production of its output and correspondingly the cost curve i.e. the curvature of the SAC determined whether the monopoly firm will earn a normal profit, positive profit or loss. Hence, given the level of output the three possibilities can be:

- If AR > AC, there is economic profit for the firms.

- If AR = AC, the firm earns only normal profit.

- If AR < AC, the firm makes losses: a theoretical possibility in the short run.

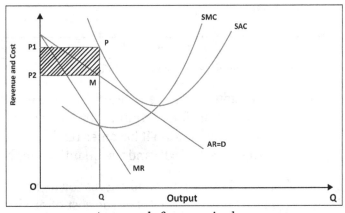

A monopoly firm accruing loss.

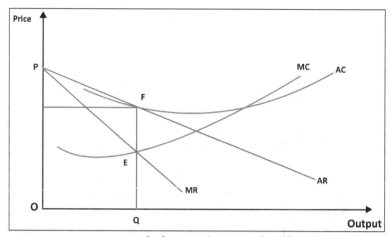

A monopoly firm earning normal profit.

No Supply Curve of a Monopoly Firm

Economists have found out that a monopoly firm do not faces a certain or unique supply curve because a monopolist has a power to discriminate price, i.e. he can sell same quantity of output at different price and can sell different quantity of output at same price. In order to show this, let us draw a diagram depicting a monopolist selling same quantity at two different prices.

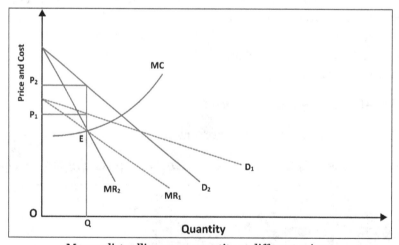

Monopolist selling same quantity at different prices.

As we know that a supply curve shows a unique relationship between the price and the output and a monopoly firm the equilibrium output is attained at a point where MR = MC and P>MC. Therefore under this condition it becomes really very difficult to trace a unique relationship between the Price (AR=P) and the quantity supplied.

Now, suppose a monopoly firm faces two demand curves for its product as D_1 and D_2, then correspondingly it will face two MR also. Since the cost of production is the same therefore, it faces a single MC which is upward sloping as usual.

Now MC cuts both MR at the same point at E, depicting the same OQ level of quantity to produce but when we stretch this point to their respective AR curves then we can see that the price for the same quantity is coming out to be different. The consumer, whose demand curve is D_1, gets the same quantity at price OP_1 and those facing D_2 get it for OP_2. Hence the monopolist can sell the same quantity of goods to the different users having different demand curves at different prices.

Similarly, he can sell different output at the same price as follows:

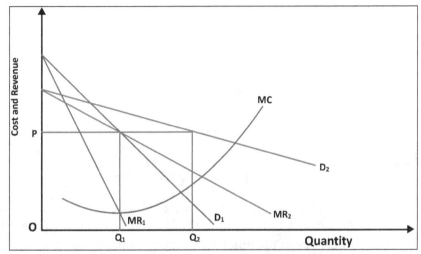

Monopolist charging same price for different quantity.

In the above case also, the monopolist sells different quantities i.e. OQ_1 (to the people having D_1 demand curve) and OQ_2 (to the people having demand curve D_2) at the same price OP.

Hence in both the cases, a monopoly firm finds it very difficult to get a unique relationship between the price and output of the firm; hence it has no certain supply curve.

Long Run Equilibrium of a Monopoly Firm

The long run equilibrium condition of a monopoly firm is quite different as compare to the other types of the market structure, as in monopoly there is no free entry or exit of the firms and hence has barriers to entry and exit like patent, economies of scale, legal protection etc., whereas in other competitive market, new firms can easily enter and exit in case of super normal profits or losses.

A monopolist always has option to close down in long run if he incurs losses in short run and can continue production in case of profits. If SAC> AR, then the monopolist makes loses in short run and will go out of business in long run if the market size is so small that no plant size can ensure pure profits in the long run. However, if AR> SAC, then it earns a short run profit given by Q_1 output in the following diagram, then the monopolist will continue production and can even expand in order to maximize its profits.

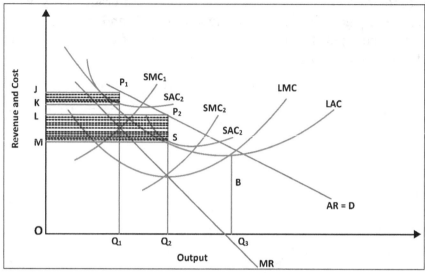

Long run equilibrium of a monopoly firm.

As shown in the above diagram, AR, MR, SAC and SMC shows the short run conditions of a monopoly firm and LAC and LMC shows the long run conditions. The intersection point of LMC and MR curves determines the equilibrium output at Q_2 and given the AR curve, the price is determined at P_2Q_2, which is also the long run equilibrium of the monopolist firm as the monopolist maximizes its long run profits at this point. However er the total long run profit is shown by the area $LMSP_2$. Note that, P_1Q_1 price and OQ_1 output is the short run equilibrium where its short run profit is shown by the smaller shaded area.

Multi-plant Monopoly

A monopoly produces homogeneous product and can expands its firm size by operating in more than one plant. This is a case of multi plant monopoly, where the monopolist can produce its output in more than one plant. For this we can assume that:

- A monopoly firm has two plants A and B.

- The cost conditions of both the plants are different.

- The firm is aware of its AR and MR.

The cost conditions of the two plants are given and shown in the following diagram. Total MC can be determined by horizontal summation of both $MC_A + MC_B$, which is shown in panel c of the following diagram. If the monopolist knows it's MR and MC then it can easily determines its profit condition as shown by output OQ in panel c of the following diagram:

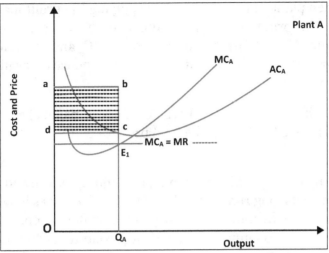

Plant A: Equilibrium under multi-plant monopoly firm.

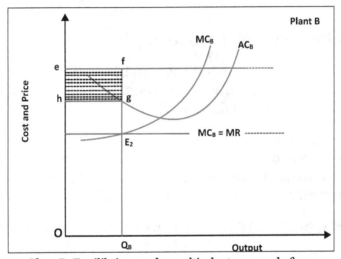

Plant B: Equilibrium under multi-plant monopoly firm.

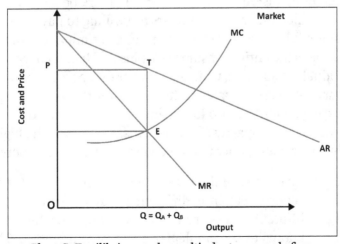

Plant C: Equilibrium under multi-plant monopoly firm.

The output for each plant can be obtained by applying the profit maximizing rule, i.e. $MR = MC_A = MC_B$. The profit maximizing output of each plant can be obtained by drawing a horizontal line $MR = MC$ from point E through MC_A and MC_B. Now this line intersects the respective MC of each plant at E_1 and E_2 and hence determines the output in each plant as OQA and OQB.

Now the profit maximization price is OP (determined at panel c) and that of plant A is Oa and that of plant B is Oe. Hence, the total profit of plant A is abcd and that of plant B is efgh.

However in the long run, a multi plant monopoly adjusts its size and number of plants in order to maximize its long run profits. The monopolist makes long-run adjustments when the existing size of the minimum-cost-plant is smaller compared to the size of the market, and there exist economies of scale. If such conditions do exist, the monopolist would adjust the size of each plant in the long run, so that the minimum of SAC coincides with the minimum of MC.

Price Discrimination Under Monopoly

A monopolist always have the option to charge different prices of the same product form different consumers or group of consumers, as he is the sole producer of the product. This is known as price discrimination.

Consumers are discriminated in respect of price on the basis of their income or purchasing power, geographical location, age, sex, quantity they purchase, their association with the seller, frequency of purchases, purpose of the use of the commodity or service, and also on other grounds which the monopolist may find suitable.

There exist three types of price discrimination exercised by a monopolist, which is given below:

- First degree price discrimination: When the monopolist sells its output at different prices which different consumers are willing to pay then this kind of price discrimination is known as first degree price discrimination. In this type, the monopolist extracts the entire consumer surplus and hence charges that price which each individual consumer is willing to pay for that product because he knows the demand curve of each consumer, so he can charge the maximum price which each consumer can pay for that product to buy. For instance, a doctor, who knows or can guess the paying capacity of his patients, can charge the highest possible fee from visibly the richest patient and the lowest fee from the poorest one.

- Second degree price discrimination: When the monopolist divides the entire market or the consumers into different groups, sections or categories and then charges different prices from each section, then this type of price discrimination is known as second degree price discrimination. This type of price discrimination is also known as block pricing system, as the monopolist divides the entire market in blocks and hence charges different prices from each block.

- Third degree price discrimination: When a profit maximizing monopoly firm sets different prices in different markets having demand curves with different elasticity, it is using third-degree price discrimination. A monopolist is often faced with two or more markets, completely separated from each other—each having a demand curve with different elasticity. Therefore, a uniform price cannot be set for all the markets without losing the possible profits. The monopolist, therefore, allocates total output between the different markets and fixes different prices, so that profit is maximized in each market. Profit in each market would be maximum only when MR =MC in each market. The monopolist, therefore, allocates its total output between the markets in such proportions that in each market MR = MC.

Suppose, there are two markets A and B with different demand and MR curves. The horizontal summation of both demand curves and MR curves gives the total demand curve and total MR curve as represented in panel c of the following figure:

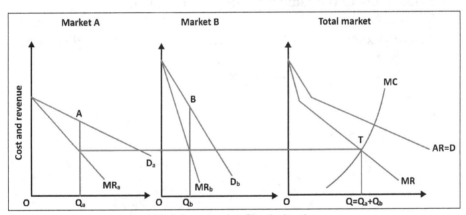

Third degree price discrimination.

Given the MC curve of the firm, the point where MR=MC gives the profit maximizing output OQ of the monopolist in panel c at point T.

Now the main question is how to allocate OQ output in both the markets in such a way so that the monopolist can maximize its profits in both the markets. The profit maximizing output for each market can be obtained by drawing a line from point T, parallel to X-axis, through MR_b and MR_a. The points of intersection on curved MR_a and MR_b determine the optimum share for each market. The monopolist maximizes profit in market A by selling OQ_a units at price AQ_a and by selling OQ_b units in market B at price BQ_b.

The firm's total equilibrium output is $OQ = OQ_a + OQ_b$. Since at OQ_a, $MR_a = MC$ in market A, and at OQ_b, $MR_b = MC$ in market B,

$$MC = TQ = MR_a = MR_b$$

Thus, the equilibrium condition is satisfied in both the sub-markets and the monopoly firm adopting the third degree method of price discrimination maximizes its profits.

The third degree method of price discrimination is most suitable where the total market is divided between the home and the foreign markets. However, it may be suitably practiced between any two or more markets separated from each other by any two or more of such factors as geographical distance, transport barriers, cost of transportation, legal restrictions on the inter-regional or inter-state transfer of commodities by individuals, etc.

The Deadweight Loss Under Monopoly

Monopoly not only causes loss of social welfare but also distortions in resource allocation. The suboptimal allocation of resources and loss of social welfare is known as deadweight loss, as represented in the following figure. Suppose, there is a constant-cost industry which has LAC =LMC, given AR and MR curves, a perfectly competitive industry will produce OQ_2 at which LAC = LMC =AR at price OP_1.

On the other hand, under the same cost and revenue conditions, the equilibrium of a monopoly firm will be at point K with OQ_1 of output at price OP_2. The comparison of prices and outputs under monopoly and perfect competition gives the measure of the loss of social welfare.

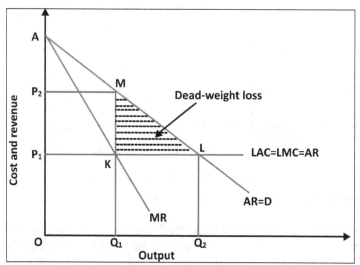

Deadweight Loss under Monopoly.

Loss of Social Welfare Under Monopoly

The loss of social welfare is measured in terms of loss of consumer surplus. The total consumer surplus equals the difference between the total price which a society is willing to pay for the consumption of a commodity and the total price that it pays for that commodity. If an industry is perfectly competitive, the total output available to the society will be OQ_2 at price OP_1 The total price which the society pays for OQ_2 is given by the area $OP_1LQ_2 = OP_1 \times OQ_2$. The total price which it is willing to pay for the output OQ_2 is given by the area $OALQ_2$ which is the value which society would be willing to pay for output OQ_2. Thus,

$$\text{Consumer's surplus} = OALQ_2 - OP_1LQ_2 = ALP_1$$

If the industry is monopolized, the equilibrium output is set at OQ_1 and price at OP_2. This leads to a loss of a part of consumer surplus:

$$\text{Loss of consumer surplus under monopoly} = ALP_1 - AMP_2 = P_2MLP_1.$$

Of this total loss of consumer surplus (P_2MLP_1), P_2MKP_1 goes to the monopolist as monopoly profit or pure profit. The remainder $MKL = P_2MLP_1 - P_2MKP_1$ goes to none. Therefore, it is termed as deadweight loss to the society caused by monopoly.

References

- Non-collusive-model-modern-version-model-of-oligopoly-7386: economicsdiscussion.net, Retrieved 18, April 2020

- Collusive-oligopoly-or-cartel-model-microeconomics: economicsdiscussion.net, Retrieved 06, January 2020

Theories of Firm

The theories of firm primarily state that a firm exists and takes decisions in order to maximize profits. A few of the prominent theories of firm are Baumol sales maximisation model, Williamson's model of managerial discretion, Robin Marris' model of managerial enterprise, etc. The topics elaborated in this chapter will help in gaining a better perspective about these theories of firm.

Baumol Sales Maximisation Model

The Sales maximization model is based on the following assumptions:

- There is a single period time horizon of the oligopolistic firm.

- The firm aims at maximizing its total sales revenue in the long run subject to a minimum profit constraint.

- The firm's minimum profit constraint is set competitively in terms of the current market value of its shares.

- The oligopolistic firm is facing cost curves which are of normal U-shaped and the demand curve is downward sloping possessing a negative relationship between price and output. Its total cost and revenue curves are also of the conventional type.

Let us determine the price and output under oligopolistic firm in Baumol sales maximization model graphically. It is shown in figure1. In the figure, Total revenue, total cost and total profits are measured on Y-axis and output is measured on X-axis. TC is the total cost curve in the long run as it starts from the origin. TR is the total revenue curve faced by the oligopolistic firm. OP is the total profit curve which starts from the origin, reaches a maximum and then falls thereafter as the level of output increases. Total profit is defined as the difference between total revenue and total cost at various levels of profit. Thus, total profit curve measures the vertical distance between total cost and total revenue curve at various levels of output. Profit is maximum when firm is producing OB level of output. So, if an oligopolistic firm wants to maximize profit it should produce OB units of output.

Oligopolistic firm under Baumol sales maximization model seeks to maximize sales subject to a minimum profit constraint. If the firm wants to maximize sales then it would produce OD level of output which is greater than profit maximizing level of output OB. It is clear from the figure that sales maximizing output is greater than profit maximizing output. At OD level of output, total revenue is maximum as shown by point TR_2. At this level of output, the firms are earning total profit equal to HD which is less than the maximum total profit BF. Suppose the minimum profit constraint is denoted by line TL which indicates the minimum total profits which a firm wants to obtain. This minimum profit line TL cuts the total profit curve at point G. If the firm seeks to maximize sales subject to a minimum profit constraint OT then it would produce and sell OC units of output. The total revenue at output level OC is CTR_1. The total revenue that is earned at output level OC is less than the maximum total revenue TR_2. But the total revenue that is earned at output level OC is the maximum obtainable revenue with respect to the minimum profit constraint as shown by minimum profit line TL.

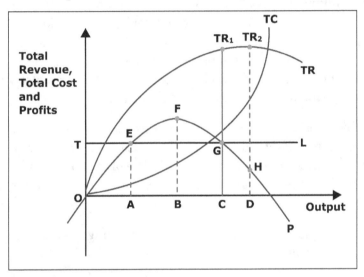

The firm can earn minimum profit OT as shown by the minimum profit line TL even by producing OA units of output but the total revenue earned at output level OA is less than at output level OC. If the objective of the oligopolistic firm is to maximize sales subject to minimum profit constraint then it would not produce OA units of output. The output associated with maximum sales is larger than profit maximizing output OB but less than total revenue maximizing output OD. The oligopolistic firm under Baumol sales maximization model would be in equilibrium at output level OC. At this output, firms are earning total profits equal to GC. In Baumol sales maximization model, firms are maximizing sales subject to minimum profit constraint will lead to lower prices and greater output in comparison to profit maximization. The price would be lower in sales maximization model because output is greater and demand curve and average revenue faced by oligopolistic firm is negatively sloped.

The price that is charged at output level OC is calculated by dividing total revenue with units of output produced. The total revenue earned by producing OC units of output is CTR_1. The price that is charged for output level OC is CTR_1/OC.

Baumol's Sales Maximization Model: Non Price Competition

Under sales maximization model, another most important feature of the firm is non-price competition. We have seen under oligopoly that oligopolistic firms are reluctant to change price as it can give wrong signal to their competitors. Firms rather than engaging in price competition indulge themselves in maximizing sales by promoting their products with the help of advertisement, banners, posters, giving free samples, product modification, introduction of special services for the customer's etc. It has been widely observed by many economists that oligopolistic firm is often very much reluctant to use price cutting to promote their sales. The greater the intensity with which oligopolistic firms indulge in nonprice competition can be better explained with sales-maximization objective rather than with profit-maximization objective. This increase in non-price competition expenditure increases the volume of sales and thus increases the total revenue earned by the oligopolistic firms. On the other hand, the effect of changes in price on total revenue is doubtful. This happens because of nature of demand, whether it is elastic or not elastic. Any reduction in price increases the total revenue in that it usually adds to the number of units which can be sold; simultaneously it also works in the opposite direction by reducing the revenue on each unit sold.

The effect of reduced prices on profits is more uncertain because if it fails to raise total revenue, it will most probably reduce profits because the increase in output as a result of reduction in price will increase total costs. On the other hand, while the profitability of advertising, product modification improved service is doubtful, their favorable effect on the sales is quite certain.

Let us now turn to explain how much optimal advertising expenditure a firm will undertake under Baumol sales maximization model.

Optimal Advertising Outlay under Baumol Sales Maximization Model

Under Baumol sales maximization model, firms seeks to maximize sales subject to a minimum profit constraint. The important question is how much optimal advertising expenditure would be incurred by a firm so as to achieve this objective. This is shown in figure. In the figure, Total revenue, total cost and total profits are measured on Y-axis and advertisement outlay is measured on X-axis. TC is the total cost curve faced by the firm. TR is the total revenue curve faced by the oligopolistic firm which shows the change in total revenue as the advertising outlay is raised given the price of the product. OP is the total profit curve which starts from the origin, reaches a maximum and then falls thereafter as the level of output increases. The curve OD is the advertisement cost incurred by the firm and it is drawn so as to make 45° angle with X-axis.

Baumol based on his empirical evidence assumed that increase in advertising outlay by a firm will always raise the physical volume of sales up to a point and after reaching at this point sales are increasing at a diminishing rate. Given the price of the product, as a result of increase in advertising outlay, the total revenue will increase in proportion to the increase in the physical value of sales. Thus, this increase in advertising outlay will cause the total revenue to increase up to a certain point and beyond these point diminishing returns likely to sets in. The cost that a firm is incurring on fixed and variable costs are taken to be independent of the advertisement outlay. The total cost TC is obtained by adding a fixed amount of other costs (OM) to the advertising cost curve OD. Total profit is defined as the difference between total revenue and total cost at various levels of profit. Thus, total profit curve measures the vertical distance between total cost and total revenue curve at various levels of output.

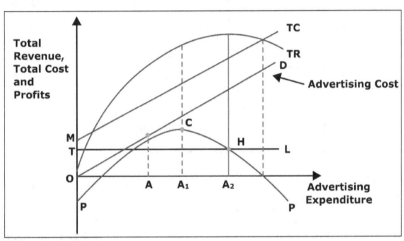

If the firm seeks to maximize its profit then to earn GA_1 units of profit, it would have to incur advertising expenditure equal to OA_1. If the firm seeks to maximize sales subject to a minimum profit constraint TL, then it should spend OA_2 advertisement expenditure. This sales maximization advertisement expenditure OA_2 is more than the profit maximizing expenditure OA_1. The objective of sales maximization subject to a constraint leads to a greater level of advertisement expenditure than the profit maximization objective.

Baumol's Sales Maximization Model: Change in Overhead Cost

The important aspect of Baumol sales maximization model is the effect of changes in overhead cost on the prices of the product. Under profit maximization theory, if the overhead cost do not vary with output then changes in overhead cost does not affect the prices of the product and nor even output produced of the products. But in general changes in overhead costs do affect the price of the product and the output. "This piece of received doctrine is certainly at variance with business practice where an increase in fixed costs is usually the occasion for serious consideration of a price increase".

Firms seek to maximize sales subject to minimum profit constraint. Under Baumol sales maximization model, we can rationalize the change in price of the product as a result of change in overhead costs. Suppose oligopolistic firms are in equilibrium that is they are maximizing sales subject to a minimum profit constraint, any increase in overhead costs would result in increase in total cost of production. This increase in total cost of production would result in fall in the profit level below the minimum acceptable profit level. In order to prevent this fall in the profit level below the minimum acceptable profit level and to be in equilibrium, oligopolistic sales maximization firms would reduce the production of the product so as to raise the price of the product. It is shown in figure.

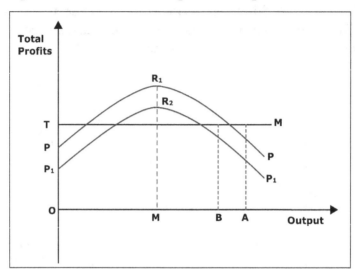

In the figure, total profits are measured on Y-axis and output is measured on X-axis. OP is the total profit curve which starts from the origin, reaches a maximum and then falls thereafter as the level of output increases. Now suppose for certain revenue and cost function, the total profits curve PP as shown as in the figure. Suppose the minimum profit constraint is denoted by line TM which indicates the minimum total profits which a firm wants to obtain. The oligopolistic firm who seeks to maximize sales subject to a minimum profit constraint TM is in equilibrium at OA level of output. Now suppose there is an increase in overhead cost by the amount PP_1. With any increase in overhead cost there is an increase in total cost of production and thus a reduction in the profit earned by the firm. This increase in overhead cost would shift the total profit curve uniformly downward by the amount PP_1. After increase in overhead cost, the new profit curve is PP_1. This increase in the overhead cost does not affect the profit maximizing level OM. This is so because any increase in overhead cost reduces the height of the profit curve uniformly downward with no change in the location of its peak. But the sale maximizing output with TM minimum profit constraint will reduce output from OA to OB. This reduction in the profit would induce firms to raise the price of the product. So, under Baumol sales maximization model, any increase in overhead cost would result in increase in the price of the product.

Baumol Sales Maximization Model: Corporation Income Tax

Under sales maximization model of Baumol, we can easily explain the impact of corporation tax on the price of the product and the output. Corporate income tax is defined as tax on the profits of the public limited companies. The same can be explained as like changes in overhead cost. It is shown in figure. Let us suppose that the corporation income tax of amount PP_1 has been imposed. The profit maximizing firm cannot do anything to shift any part of the corporate income tax to the consumer. Profit maximizing firm cannot even gain anything by raising the price of the product or changing its output as a result of imposition of corporate income tax. Hence, the price of the product and the output remain unaltered as a result of the imposition of the corporate income tax. The corporation income tax reduces the height of the total product curve from PP to PP_1 but it does not make peak of the curve to move either left or right. For the sales maximization firm with minimum profit constraint, the price of the product will be raised and output would decline as a result of corporate income tax.

Williamson's Model of Managerial Discretion

Williamson has developed managerial-utility-maximisation theory as against profit maximisation. It is also known as the 'managerial discretion theory'. In large modem firms, shareholders and managers are two separate groups. The shareholders want the maximum return on their investment and hence the maximisation of profits. The managers, on the other hand, have consideration other than profit maximisation in their utility functions. Thus the managers are interested not only in their own emoluments but also in the size of their staff and expenditure on them.

Thus Williamson's theory is related to the maximisation of the manager's utility which is a function of the expenditure on staff and emoluments and discretionary funds. "To the extent that pressure from the capital market and competition in the product market is imperfect, the manager, therefore, has discretion to pursue goals other than profits".

The managers derive utility from a wide range of variables. For this Williamson introduces the concept of expense preferences. It means "that managers get satisfaction from using some of the firm's potential profits for unnecessary spending on items from which they personally benefit".

To pursue his goal of utility maximisation, the manager directs the firm's resources in three ways:

- The manager desires to expand his staff and to increase their salaries. "More staff is valued because they lead to the manager getting more salary, more prestige and more security." Such staff expenditures by managers are denoted by S.

- To maximise his utility, the manager indulges in "featherbedding" such as pretty secretaries, company cars, too many company phones, 'perks' for employees, etc. Such expenditures are characterised as 'management slack', M by Williamson.

- The manager likes to set up "discretionary funds" for making investments to advance or promote company projects that are close to his heart. Discretionary profits or investments D are what remains with the manager after paying taxes and dividends to shareholders in order to retain an effective control of the firm.

Thus the manager's utility function is:

$$U = f(S, M, D)$$

Where U is the utility function, S is the staff expenditure, M is the management slack and D the discretionary investments. These decision variables (S, M, D) yield positive utility and the firm will always choose their values subject to the constraint, S $\geq$ o$\geq$Mo, D$\geq$o. Williamson assumes that the law of diminishing marginal utility applies so that when additions are made to each of S, M and D, they yield smaller increments of utility to the manager.

Further, Williamson regards price (P) as a function of output (X), expenditure on staff (S), and the state of environment which he calls 'a demand shift parameter' (E), so that P = f (X, S, E).

This relationship is subject to the following constraints:

(a) The demand function is assumed to be negatively sloping: $\partial P / \partial X < $o; (b) staff expenditures help increase the demand for the firms product: $\partial P / \partial S > $o; and (c) increases in the demand shift parameter E, tend to raise demand: $\partial P / \partial E > $o.

These relationships reveal that the demand for X is negatively related to P, but is positively related to S and E. When the demand increases, the output and expenditure on staff will also increase which will push the costs of the firm, and consequently the price will rise, and vice versa.

In order to formalise his model, Williamson introduces four different types of profits: actual, reported, minimum required and discretionary profits. Denoting R = revenue, C = total production costs and T = taxes, then actual profits π_A =R-C-S.

If the amounts of managerial slack or emoluments (M) are deducted from the actual profits, we get reported profits.

$$\pi_R = \pi_A = M = R - C - S - M$$

The minimum required profits, π_o, are the lowest level of profits after paying taxes which the shareholders must receive in order to hold shares of the firm.

Since discretionary profits (D) are what remains with the manager after paying taxes and dividends to shareholders, therefore,

$$D = \pi_R - \pi_0 - T$$

To explain Williamson's utility maximisation model diagrammatically, it is assumed for the sake of simplicity that U=f (S, D) so that discretionary profits (D) are measured along the vertical axis and staff expenditures on the horizontal axis in figure.

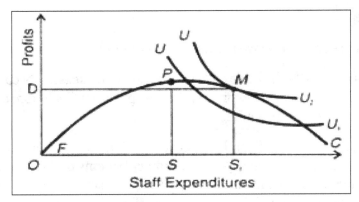

FC is the feasibility curve showing the combinations of D and S available to the manager. It is also known as the profit-staff curve. UU$_1$ and UU$_2$ are the indifference curves of the manager which show the combination of D and S. To begin, as we move along the profit-staff curve from point F upwards, both profits and staff expenditures increase O till point P is reached. P is the profit maximisation point for the firm where SP is the maximum profit levels when OS staff expenditures are incurred.

But the equilibrium of the firm takes place when the manager chooses the tangency point M where his highest possible utility function UU$_2$ and the feasibility curve FC touch each other. Here the manager's utility is maximised. The discretionary profits OD (=S$_1$M) are less than the profit maximisation profits SP.

But the staff emoluments OS are maximised. However, Williamson points out that factors like taxes, changes in business conditions, etc. by affecting the feasibility curve can shift the optimum tangency point, like M in the Figure. Similarly, factors like changes in staff, emoluments, profits of stockholders, etc. by changing the shape of the utility function will shift the optimum position.

Critical Appraisal

Williamson has supported his utility-maximisation hypothesis by citing a number of evidences which are generally consistent with his model. Thus his theory is empirically sound as compared with other managerial theories.

This model is also superior to Baumol's sales-maximisation model because it also explains the facts involved in Baumol's theory. Williamson does not treat sales maximisation as a single criterion like Baumol but as a means of the manager for increasing his staff and emoluments. This approach is rather more realistic.

Further, in Williamson's model output is higher, and price and profits are lower than in the profit maximisation model. Silbertson has shown that Williamson's model preserves the results of the normal profit-maximisation model in conditions of pure or perfect competition.

Weaknesses

But there are some conceptual weaknesses of this model:

- He does not clarify the basis of the derivation of his feasibility curve. In particular, he fails to indicate the constraint in the profit-staff relation, as shown by the shape of the feasibility curve.

- He lumps together staff and manager's emoluments in the utility curve. This mixing up of non- pecuniary and pecuniary benefits of the manager makes the utility function ambiguous. But these difficulties can be overcome by introducing a three-dimensional diagram. But it will make the analysis more complex.

- This theory does not deal with oligopolistic interdependence and of oligopolistic rivalry.

- Most economists are reluctant to pursue Williamson's utility-maximisation theory "due to the knowledge that so many factors (e.g., profit, sales, output, growth, number of staff and expenditure on plush offices and cars) are likely to give utility to people in industry that they shall end up with a model incapable of yielding any definite results."

Robin Marris' Model of Managerial Enterprise

The Marris model of managerial enterprise was developed by Robin Marris in 1964. Like Willaimson, Marris approach is also based on the fact that whenever the difference between ownership and control exist, then the self-interest of agent makes profits lower than in a situation where principals act as their own agents. In other words, the Marris model is also based on the fact the ownership and control of the firm are in the hands of two different people.

He, like Williamson, also assumed that the managerial utility function includes variables such as salary, status, prestige, job security and other monetary compensation. Out of these, salary is the only quantitative variable which is measurable. On the other hand, all other variables except salary are non- quantifiable i.e. not measurable. The utility function of managers is a function of salary, monetary expenditure on the staff and the discretionary investment:

$$U_M = f(S, M, I_D)$$

Where,

- U_M is the Utility of the Managers.

- S is monetary expenditure on the staff.

- M is the Management slack.

- I_D is Discretionary investment.

Here, the variables expenditure on staff salary, management slack and discretionary investment is used the unquantifiable concepts like power, status, job security, dominance etc. The variable expenditure on staff, management slack and disinvestment can be assigned some nominal values. The goal of the managers is the maximization of their own utility. On the other hand, the goal of the owners of the firm i.e. shareholders is to maximize profits, market share, capital, output, public image etc.

$$U_O = f(P, MS, K, Y)$$

Where,

- U_O is the utility of the owners.

- P is Profit.

- MS is Market share.

- K is Capital.

- Y is output.

Here the goal of the manager is the maximization of their own utility.

In contrast to Williamson, Marris argues that the difference between the goal of the managers and the goals of the shareholders is not as wide as other managerial theories claim. This is so because most of the variables appearing in both functions are strongly correlated with a single variable: the size of the firm. He assumes that managers are basically concerned with rate of growth of size. There are various measures (indicators) of size exist, like capital, output, revenue, market share, and there is no consensus about which of these measures is the best. Marris defines size in terms of corporate capital which is sum total of book value of fixed assets, inventory, net short term assets including cash reserves.

The size and the rate of growth are not necessarily equivalent from the point of view of managerial utility. If they are used interchangeably then there would be high mobility among managers of the firm: the managers would be indifferent between being employed and promoted within the same growing firm (enjoying higher salaries, power and prestige), and moving from a smaller firm to a larger firm where they would have the same earnings and status. But in world the mobility of managers is low. Various studies have proved that managers prefer to be promoted within the same organization rather than move to a larger one, where the environment might be hostile to the 'newcomer' Hence managers aim at the maximization of the rate of growth rather than the absolute size of the firm.

Goal of the Firm

The goal of the firm is the maximisation of the balanced rate of growth of the firm, that is, the maximisation of the rate of growth of demand for the products of the firm and of the growth of its capital supply. This can be written as:

Maximise $g = g_D = g_C$

Where,

- g is balanced growth rate.

- g_D is growth of demand for the products of the firm.

- g_C is the growth of the supply of capital.

Let us understand the growth of demand for the products of the firm and growth of supply of capital in detail. The utility function of owners can be written as:

$$U_O = f(g_C)$$

Where,

- U_O is the Utility of the Owners.

- g_C is the rate of growth of capital.

On the other hand, the utility function of the managers may be written as follows:

$$U_M = f(g_D, S)$$

Where,

- U_M is the Utility of the managers.

- g_D is the rate of growth of demand for the products.

- S is Job Security.

Marris's assumes the utility function of managers is a function of rate of growth of demand for the products and Job security. He assumes that salaries, status and power of managers are strongly correlated with the growth of demand for the products of the firm. Hence, managers will enjoy higher salaries and will have more prestige the faster the rate of growth of demand for the products.

Marris recognizes that the drive for the rate of growth is not without constraints. Thus in the model there are two constraints – the managerial team constraint and the job security constraint.

The Managerial Constraint

Marris adopts Penrose's thesis of the existence of a definite limit on the rate of efficient managerial expansion. At any one time period the capacity of the managerial team determines the upper limit to the growth of the firm. There is a limit to the output increased by hiring new managers because of their lack of experience and time lag involved in attaining required skill.

Penrose's theory is that planning and execution of the operations of the firm are the result of teamwork which requires the co-operation and coordination of all managers. There is a time lag when a new manager is fully ready to join the teamwork necessary for the efficient functioning of the firm. Thus, although the 'managerial ceiling' is receding gradually, the process cannot be speeded up.

Similarly, the other factor that also limits the rate of growth of the firm is 'research and development'. Research and Development implies any new ideas or innovation which affect the growth of demand for the products of the firm. The work in the R & D department is a slow process and it cannot be expanded quickly. In order to enhance research and development you need to hire new scientists and designers which require time to contribute efficiently. Research and development also cannot expand output continuously. The managerial constraint and research and development capacity of the firm set limits both to the rate of growth of demand (g_D) and the rate of growth of capital supply (g_C).

The Job Security Constraint

This is natural that the managers want job security. This desire of security by managers is reflected in their preference for service contracts, generous pension schemes, and their dislike for policies which endanger their position by increasing the risk of their dismissal by the owners. The risk of dismissal of managers arises if their policies lead the firm towards financial failure (bankruptcy) or render the firm attractive to be take-over by other competitors. In the first case the shareholders may replace the old staff in the hope that by appointing new management the firm will be run more successfully whereas in the second case, if the take-over is successful, the new owners may decide to replace the old management.

Marris suggests that managers would like to seek job security by adopting a cautious and prudent financial policy. The prudent financial policy would consist of:

a) Non-involvement with risky investments. The managers should choose projects which guarantee a steady performance. They should not involve in ventures that are risky i.e. highly profitable if successful but will endanger the managers' position if they fail.

b) Financing growth mainly from the profit levels being generated by the present set of products.

To judge the prudence of a financial policy, Robin Marris proposed the concept of financial constraint (a). This financial constraint is determined by the risk attitude of the top management. The management who is a risk lover would like to prefer high value of a, while the management who is a risk averse would like to prefer low value of a. The financial constraint a is the weighted average of the three security ratios i.e. the leverage (or debt ratio), the liquidity ratio, and the retention ratio.

1. Leverage Ratio: The leverage or debt ratio is defined as the ratio of value of debt to the total assets of the firm:

$$\text{Leverage or Debt Ratio}(a_1) = \frac{\text{Value of Debts}}{\text{Total Assets}}$$

The leverage ratio measures the extent of reliance on borrowing for expansion purpose. A lower leverage ratio would retard growth and a higher leverage ratio would invite takeover bids and increases the rate of failure.

2. The liquidity ratio is defined as the ratio of liquid assets to the total assets of the firm:

$$\text{Liquidity Ratio}(a_2) = \frac{\text{Liquidity Assets}}{\text{Total Assets}}$$

Low liquidity ratio implies the possibility of insolvency of the firm whereas high liquidity ratio increases the security. If the liquidity ratio is too high then it would have an adverse effect on the rate of growth. Therefore to ensure security the management should choose the value of a_1 which is neither too high nor too low. In his model Marris assumed that the firm operates in the region where there is a positive relation between liquidity and security.

3. The retention ratio is defined as the ratio of retained profits to total profits:

$$\text{Retentaion Ratio}(a_3) = \frac{\text{Retained Profits}}{\text{Total Profits}}$$

Retained profits are the most important financial source for the growth of capital. The high level of retained profits cannot keep shareholders happy. And a too high retained profit implies that management is taking a risk of displeasing the shareholders.

The two characteristics of the financial constraint are:

- Marris assumed that the financial constraint is negatively related to a_2, and positively related to a_1 and a_3.

- Marris also assumed that there is a negative relation between 'job security' (s) and the financial constraint a. It implies that if a is increased, the job security of managers declines and if a is decreased the job security of managers increases. Thus, the financial constraint determines the level of job security and hence limits the rate of growth of the capital supply and also the rate of growth of the size of the firm.

Equilibrium of the Firm

The goal of the firm is the maximization of the balanced rate of growth of the firm, that is, the maximization of the rate of growth of demand for the products of the firm and of the growth of its capital supply. This can be written as:

Maximize $g = g_C = g_D$

Where,

- g is balanced growth rate.

- g_D is growth of demand for the products of the firm.

- g_C is the growth of the supply of capital.

Rate of Growth of the Demand

The rate of growth of demand for the products depends on:

- The rate at which new products are tried-Diversification rate.

- The percentage of successful new products.

$$g_D = f(d, k)$$

Where,

- d is the diversification rate.

- k is the proportion of successful new products.

The two forms of diversification are:

- Differentiated Diversification: The firm may introduce a completely new product whose close substitutes are not available. These new products create new demand and thus compete with other products for the income of the consumer. This is the most important form in which the firm seeks to grow.

- Imitative Diversification: The firm may introduce a product whose close substitutes are available by existing competitors. It is almost certain to induce competitors' reactions. Given the uncertainty regarding the reactions of competitors the firm prefers to diversify with new products. There exist a positive relationship between diversification and the rate of growth of demand.

The proportion of successful new products, k, depends on the rate of diversification d, the advertising expenses, Price of new successful products, the research & development expenditure and on the intrinsic value of the products.

$$k = f(d, A, P, R\&D, \text{int rinsic value})$$

The proportion of successful new products, k, is positively related to advertisement expenditure and research and development expenditure. Marris has used average profit margin (m) as a proxy for advertisement and research and development expenditure. The average profit margin m is negatively related to advertisement and R&D expenditure, the proportion of successful new products is also negatively related with the average profit margin. The proportion of successful new products depends on diversification as well, the rate of new products introduced in each period if too many new products are introduced too fast, the proportion of fails increases.

Thus, the rate of growth of demand, g_D, is a function of diversification d and average profit margin m.

$$g_D = f_3(d, m), \frac{\partial g_d}{\partial d} > 0 \text{ and } \frac{\partial g_d}{\partial m} < 0$$

The growth rate of demand is positively correlated with the diversification rate (d) and negatively related with average profit margin.

Rate of Growth of Capital Supply

The rate of growth is financed from two sources: internal and external. The internal source of finance is profits. The external source of finance may be obtained by the issue of new bonds or from bank loans. Marris assumed that the main source of finance for growth is profits. This is because of two reasons:

- The issue of new shares as a means of obtaining funds is, for prestige and other reasons, not often used by an established firm.

- The external source of finance is limited by the security attitude of managers, that is, from their desire to avoid mass dismissal.

The rate of growth of capital supply is proportional to the level of profits.

$$g_c = a.P$$

Where,

- g_c is the growth rate of corporate capital.

- P is the net rate of profits, after depreciation and tax, earned on productive assets.

- a is the financial security coefficient.

The level of total profits P depends on the average rate of profit, m, and on the capital output ratio, O, which is the efficiency of the performance of the firm. So, P is a function of average profit rate and overall capital output ratio.

$$P = f(m, O)$$

Where,

$$\frac{\partial P}{\partial m} > 0$$

The overall capital output/ratio is not a simple arithmetic average of the capital/output ratios of the individual products of the firm, but is a function of the diversification rate d. It can be written as:

$$O = f(d)$$

For a given capital, the relationship between capital output ratio and diversification is up to a certain level of d positive, reaches a maximum, and then starts falling as the number of new products increases the overall output. Output is at maximum when the d is at its optimum level allowing the optimal use of the managerial team and the R & D personnel. Beyond the optimal point, the total output decreases with further increases in d. Hence the success rate for new products falls and efficiency declines.

Substituting for capital output function in the profit function we obtain:

$$P = f(m, d)$$

Now substitute the profit function P in the g_c function we obtain:

$$g_c = a.f(m, d) = a.P$$

The rate of growth of capital is determined by three factors the financial policies of the managers, the average rate of profit and the diversification rate. If all the security constraints on leverage, liquidity and retention ratio are operative, the value of a becomes unique. This unique value of a then becomes a constraint in the model. This can be written as:

$$a \leq a^*$$

And

$$g_C \leq a^*.P$$

Where, a^* is the value of a associated with financial policies in which all the security constraints are effective.

The Complete form of Marris Model

The complete summarization of the above equations is as follows:

$$g_D = f(m, d) \, (\text{Demand Growth Equation})$$
$$P = f(m, d) \, (\text{Profit Rate Equation})$$
$$g_C = a.f(m, d) = a.P \, (\text{Supply of Capital Equation})$$
$$a \leq a^* \, (\text{Security Constraint})$$
$$g_C = g_D \, (\text{Balanced Growth Equation})$$

The firm is in equilibrium where $g_D = [f(m, d)] = g_C = [a.f(m, d) = a.P]$. Here the equilibrium equation depends upon two unknown variables m and d. The model cannot be solved unless one of the variables m or d is subjectively determined by the managers. Once the managers define a and one of the other two policy variables, the equilibrium rate of growth can be determined.

Sylos-Labini's Model

Sylos-Labini developed a model of limit-pricing based on scale-barriers to entry. His model is clumsy, due to its unnecessarily stringent assumptions and the use of arithmetical examples.

However, his analysis of the economies-of-scale barrier is more thorough than that of Bain. He highlighted the determinants of the limit price and discussed their implications, thus providing the basis for Modigliani's more general model of entry-preventing pricing.

Sylos-Labini concentrated his analysis on the case of a homogeneous oligopoly whose technology is characterised by technical discontinuities and economies of scale.

Assumptions

1. The market demand is given and has unitary elasticity. The product is homogeneous and will be sold at a unique equilibrium price.

2. The technology consists of three types of plant a small plant with a capacity of 100 units of output; a medium-size plant with a capacity of 1000 units of output; a large-size plant with a capacity of 8000 units of output. Each firm can expand by multiples of its initial plant size only. That is, a small firm may expand by installing another small plant a medium firm may expand by setting up a second medium-size plant, and so on. There are economies of scale cost decreases as the size of the plant increases. However, with this rigid technology we cannot construct a continuous LRAC curve. We have three cost lines corresponding to the three plant sizes.

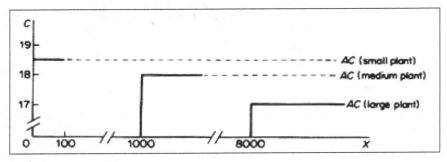

3. The price is set by the price leader who is the largest firm, with the lowest cost (ex-hypothesis) at a level low enough to prevent entry. The smaller firms are price-takers. Each one individually cannot affect the price. However, collectively they may put pressure on the leader by regulating their output. Thus the largest firm does not have unlimited discretion in setting the price it must set a price that is acceptable to all the firms in the industry as well as preventing entry.

4. There is a normal rate of profit in each industry. Sylos, in his example, assumed that the rate of normal profit is 5 per cent.

5. The leader is assumed to know the cost structure of all plant sizes, and the market demand.

6. The entrant is assumed to come into the industry with the smallest plant size.

7. The established firms and the entrant behave according to what Modigliani called the 'Sylos's Postulate'. This includes two behavioural rules, one describing the expectations of the established firms and the other the expectations of the entrant. Firstly, the existing firms expect that the potential entrant will not come into the market if he thinks that the price post-entry will fall below his LAC.

Secondly, the entrant expects that the established firms will continue in the post-entry period to produce the same level of output as pre-entry. Under these assumptions, as entry takes place the market price falls and the whole of the resulting increase in the quantity demanded accrues to the new entrant. Clearly this is the same as Bain's Model B.

Sylos does not give any reason for this behavioural pattern.

The Model

Sylos-Labini presents his model with a numerical example. He starts with the market structure shown in table which is assumed to be created at random, and proceeds to examine how equilibrium is attained in this market. The equilibrium at price 20 is not stable, because the market output is too small and the price is too high, so entry will take place.

Table: Initial Market Structure.

Plant Size	Capacity (Units of X)	Number of Firms	Total Outout X	Initial Price (Arbitrary Units)	Market Demand (Value)
Small (X_s)	$X_s = 100$	20	2000	20	40, 000
Medium (X_m)	$X_m = 1000$	2	2000	20	40, 000
Large (X_l)	$X_l = 8000$	1	8000	20	160, 000
Total Market		23	12, 000		240, 000

This is due to the fact that, given the cost structure of the three plants in the industry, the profits are too high for all firms at the price of 20. From table it is apparent that the profit rate of the small firms is 8.1 per cent of the medium firms 11.1 per cent and of the large firms 17-6 per cent. These rates are higher than the minimum profit rate (normal profit) of the industry which is assumed to be 5 per cent. The excess profits will attract entry. Under the above rigid assumptions regarding technology, the possibility of expansion of the existing firms by multiples of their initial plant size and the unitary elasticity of demand, the following results emerge.

Table: Cost Structure of Firms, with the assumed technology.

Plant Size	Capacity Output	TFC	AFC	TVC	AVC	TC	ATC	Profit Rate % on ATC	Unit Profit	Price	Total Revenue
Small Firm	100	100	1	1750	17.5	1850	18.5	8.1	1.5	20.0	2000
								5.4	1.0	19.5	1950
								5.0	0.9	19.4	1940

Me-dium Firm	1000	2000	2	16,000	16	18,000	18	11.1	2.0	20.0	20,000
								8.3	1.5	19.5	19,500
								7.8	1.4	19.4	19,400
								5.7	1.2	19.2	19,200
								5.0	0.9	18.9	18,900
Large Firm	8000	24,000	3	112,000	14	136,000	17	17.6	3.0	20.0	160,000
								14.7	2.5	19.5	156,000
								14.1	2.5	19.4	155,200
								12.9	2.2	19.2	153,600
								5.0	0.85	17.85	142,800

No new large firm will enter into the industry. If it did, total sales would rise to 20,000 units and the price would fall to 12, a level lower than the minimum acceptable price to any firm in the industry. The minimum acceptable prices for the three plant sizes are 19-4 (for the small plant), 18-9 (for the medium size plant) and 17-85 (for the large scale plant).

Even the entry of a new medium-size firm is precluded given the costs and the demand in the industry. If a medium-size plant were installed sales would increase to 13,000 units, and the price would fall to 18-4, which is not acceptable by the small and the medium- size firms.

However, up to three small firms can enter the market. Their entry would cause sales to rise to 12,300 units and the price to fall to 19-5, which exceeds the minimum acceptable price of all firms. The entry of a fourth small firm would depress the price to 19-3, a level below the minimum acceptable price (of 19-4) of the small firms.

Thus the entry-forestalling price is just above the minimum acceptable level of the smallest, least efficient firms.

The above results regarding the entry conditions under the given cost and demand conditions are shown in table. The computations are based on the assumption that the demand has unitary elasticity so that the total expenditure is the same (equal to the initial level of 240,000) at all prices.

Table: Prices and level of output yielding a total expenditure of 240, 000.

Output X	Price P	Total Expenditure R = XP (e = 1)
12,000	20.0	240,000
12,100	19.8	240,000
12,200	19.6	240,000

12, 300	19.5	240, 000
12, 400	19.3	240, 000
12, 500	19.2	240, 000
12, 770	18.8	240, 000
13, 000	18.4	240, 000
18, 000	13.3	240, 000
20, 000	12.0	240, 000

Price Determination

The price is set by the largest, most efficient firm. The equilibrium price must be acceptable by all the firms in the industry, and should be at a level which would prevent entry. Given that firms have different costs, there are as many minimum acceptable prices as plant sizes. For each plant the minimum acceptable price is defined on the average-cost principle:

$$P_i = TAC_i(1 + r)$$

Where,

- P_t = the minimum acceptable price for the ith plant size.

- TAC_i = total average cost for the ith plant size.

- r = normal profit rate of the industry.

The minimum acceptable price covers the TAC of the plant and the normal (minimum) profit rate of the industry (in Sylos's example $r = 5$ per cent for all plant sizes, that is, the normal profit of the industry is 5 per cent). The price leader is assumed to know the cost structure of all plant sizes and the normal (minimum) profit rate of the industry. Given this information the leader will set the price that is acceptable by the smallest, least efficient firms, and will deter entry.

The price tends to settle at a level immediately above the entry preventing price of the least efficient firms, which it is to the advantage of the largest and most efficient firms to let live. The price leader, which is the most efficient firm, will set the price at a level acceptable to all existing firms and low enough to forestall entry. Entry takes place with the minimum plant scale which has the highest cost.

In Sylos's model, where differential costs are assumed, the price, in order to be a long-run equilibrium one, apart from preventing entry must also be acceptable by the least efficient firms, allowing them to earn at least the normal industry profit given that the most efficient firm (leader) does not find it worthwhile to eliminate the smaller firms, either because such action is not profitable or because the leader is afraid of attracting government intervention due to high concentration in the industry.

Clearly the medium and large-scale firms, having lower costs, will be earning abnormal profits. But small firms will also normally be earning some abnormal profits without attracting entry. Given the market demand at the minimum acceptable price of the smallest least efficient firm (and given that at that price all established firms work their plants to full capacity), the price leader will set the price at such a level, that, if the entrant decides to enter, the market price will fall below his minimum acceptable price (which is the same as the minimum acceptable price of the smallest, least efficient plant size).

In figure the market demand at the minimum acceptable price P_s of the smallest, least efficient, firm is X. The leader will set the limit price $P_L > P_s$. The price P_L corresponds to the level of output $X_L = X - X_s$ and is the equilibrium price because it satisfies the two necessary conditions: it is acceptable by all firms, and it deters entry, because if entry occurs the total output X_L will be increased at the level $X_L + X_s = X$ and the price will fall to (just below) the minimum acceptable price of the entrant, that is, to a level just below P_s.

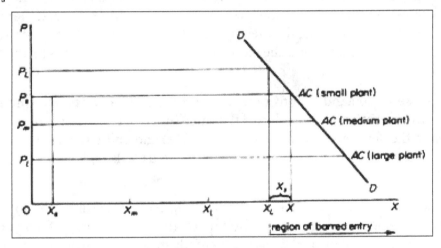

The P_L is indirectly determined by the determination of the total output that the established firms will sell in the market. Given that in the long run price cannot fall below the cost of the least efficient firm, and that the entrant can enter only with the smallest least- efficient plant size, the leader can determine the output X at which all established firms use their plants up to capacity. He next determines the total quantity that the firms will sell in the industry X_L so as to prevent entry.

X_L is such that if the entrant comes into the market with the minimum viable size, X_s, the total post-entry output $(X_L + X_s)$ will just exceed X, and hence will drive price down to a level just below the AC of the entrant (= AC of the small least-efficient firms). Given X_L, the limit price P_L is determined from the market-demand curve DD. The entrant will be deterred from entering the market because (under the Sylos's Postulate) he knows that if he enters he will cause the price to fall below his AC. Any output larger than X_L is entry-preventing, while any output smaller than X_L will not prevent entry.

In Sylos's model all firms earn abnormal profits, which are increasing with plant size and there is an upper and a lower limit of the entry-preventing price: the equilibrium price cannot be higher than P_L nor lower than P_s.

In Sylos's model the determinants of the entry-preventing price are:

- The absolute sizes of the market X.

- The elasticity of market demand.

- The technology of the industry, which defines the available sizes of plant.

- The prices of factors of production, which, together with the technology, determine the total average cost of the firms.

The Absolute Market Size

There is a negative relationship between the absolute size of the market and the limit price. The larger the markets size the lower the entry prevention price. If there is a dynamic increase in the demand, denoted by a shift to the right of the industry-demand curve, the effect on the price and the structure of the industry depends on the size and the rate of increase.

If the increase in demand is considerable and occurs rapidly, the existing firms, if they want to prevent entry, must lower the price (or set a lower price initially, in anticipation of the developments on the demand side) and build up additional capacity to meet the demand (or have adequate foresight so as to keep a continuous reserve capacity).

If the price is high and profits lucrative, and if the established firms cannot build up capacity fast enough to keep up with the rate of growth in demand, then entry from new firms or already established firms in other industries will take place. If we relax the restrictive assumption that the entrant will enter with the smallest optimal plant size, and accept that large firms from other industries manage to enter at a lower cost, some or all of the small firms will be eliminated, and price will fall.

Thus a rapid increase in the absolute market size will tend to reduce price and increase the average plant size in the industry, unless the existing firms can keep their shares constant by keeping continuously adequate reserve capacity. This policy, however, may be very costly. Thus in fast-expanding industries entry is almost certain to occur and price will be reduced.

If the growth of demand is slow, the existing firms will most probably be able to meet the increased demand by appropriate reserve capacity and gradual new investment, and the price will not be reduced unless new techniques with lower costs can be adopted for the larger scales of output to which the established firms are gradually led.

The Elasticity of Market Demand

The elasticity of market demand is also negatively related to the limit price. The more elastic the demand is, the lower the price that established firms can charge without attracting entry. If at the going price there is a considerable increase in the elasticity of demand (for price reductions), and if the firms are able to identify clearly this change in the elasticity of demand, the effects on price and on market structure are the same as in the case of a shift in the market demand.

The detection of changes in the elasticity is almost impossibly difficult in practice, and the established firms will most probably not count (and plan ahead) on such uncertain changes in e. Thus if e does in fact change substantially, new large firms (established elsewhere) will enter into the market, since the existing firms will not be able to cope with such change, and the price will fall.

The Technology and Technical Change

The technology determines the minimum viable plant size. In any given 'state of arts,' the larger the minimum viable plant size, the higher will be the limit price. Thus there is a positive relation between the minimum viable plant and the premium included in the limit price.

If technology changes (technical progress) and benefits all plant sizes, costs will fall and price will decrease. However, if technical progress is such that only large firms have access to it, the limit price will not change. The large firms will have larger actual profits, but under the assumptions of Sylos's model the price need not change. If technical progress is associated with product innovation (rather than process innovation) the price in the market will not normally be affected. One should expect an intensification of non-price competition as all firms in the industry will attempt to imitate the innovation.

Sylos seems to imply that technical progress is accessible only to the large firms who can afford large research and development departments. In the real world the large firms will not have any incentive to lower the price of their commodities despite the reduction in their costs. Under these conditions the large firms will realise higher profits and this will have serious implications for the distribution of income and employment.

The Prices of Factors of Production

Changes in factor prices affect all the firms in the industry in the same way. Thus an increase in factor prices will lead to an increase in the costs and the limit price in the industry. Similarly a reduction in factor prices will lead to a decrease in the limit price.

Differentiated Oligopoly

Sylos extended his analysis to the case of differentiated oligopoly. Sylos argues that when the products are differentiated the entry-barriers will be stronger than in the case of homogeneous oligopoly due to marketing economies of scale. Advertising unit costs and possibly the cost of raw materials per unit of output are likely to fall as the scale of output increases. Hence the overall cost difference between the smaller and larger plants will be greater as compared to the homogeneous oligopoly case. Product differentiation, therefore, will reinforce the scale-barrier.

Sylos's analysis of differentiated oligopoly lacks the rigour of his model of homogeneous oligopoly. He suggests, however, that he is primarily concerned with the implications of technological discontinuities for price and output, and that product differentiation is one of the main concerns of the 'theoreticians of imperfect competition' to whose analysis Sylos's work is complementary.

Behavioral Model of Cyert and March

H. A. Simon, one of the advocates of the behavioral approach to the theory of firm, points out that firms aim at satisficing rather than profit maximization i.e. firms want to achieve satisfactory level of profit. According to him, there is an 'aspiration level' that a firm has. An aspiration level of a firm is based on its goal as well as its past experience. If the firm believes that its actual performance is sufficient enough to achieve a given aspiration level then the aspiration level will be revised upward. On the other hand, if the firm believes that its actual performance is not sufficient enough to achieve a given aspiration level then the aspiration level will be lowered.

Cyert and March have put forth a full scale behavioral theory of the firm. In a modem large multiproduct firm, ownership is separate from management. This is basically the principal agent problem. It explains the relationship between the principal (owner) and the agent (who performs owner's works). The principal agent shows that whenever the difference between ownership and control exist, then the self -interest of agent makes profits lower than in a situation where principals act as their own agents. Here the firm is not considered as a single entity with a single goal of profit maximization. Modern business firm are group of individuals who are engaged in the decision-making process relating to its internal structure. These business firms have multiple goals.

The behavioral theory of the firm, as developed by Cyert and March, focuses on the decision-making process of the 'large multiproduct firm under uncertainty in an imperfect market. In a modem large multiproduct firm, ownership is separate from management. This is basically the principal agent problem. It explains the relationship between the principal (owner) and the agent (who performs owner's works). The principal agent shows that whenever the difference between ownership and control exist, then the self-interest of agent makes profits lower than in a situation where principals act as their own agents. Here the firm is not considered as a single entity with a single goal of profit maximization. Modern business firm are group of individuals who are engaged in the decision-making process relating to its internal structure whose interests may conflict with each other. They call this complex organization an organizational coalition. This organizational coalition may include managers, workers, stock holders, customers and so on. These business firms have multiple goals.

Cyert and March deals not only with the internal structure of the firm but also with the problem of uncertainty. They challenge the assumption of profit maximization and also the omission of the uncertainty from the conventional theory of the firm. Under conditions of uncertainty about demand and cost conditions, it is not possible to judge whether the profit is maximized or not as the information regarding profits is not there.

Unlike the conventional traditional theory of the firm which was based on single goal of profit maximization, the behavioral theory assumes that an organization has multiple goals to achieve. An organization has five goals which the firms generally possess. These are:

- Production goal: There are certain goals that are needed to be achieved at the production level. This goal originates from the production department. It is the main objective of the production manager to smoothen production process. This is possible by managers by distributing production evenly over time irrespective of fluctuations in demand that is possible seasonally. He is also avoiding excess capacity, lying off workers at some periods, overworking the plant and resorting to rush recruitment of workers at other times because of consequence of higher costs, excess capacity, dismissal payments or too frequent breakdowns of machinery and wastes of raw materials in period of 'rush' production. This goal is related to output decisions.

- Inventory goal: The inventory goal originates mainly from the inventory department, if such a department exists, or from the sales and production departments. This goal represents the demands of coalition members who are well connected with inventory. It is affected by pressures on the inventory from customers and salesmen. This goal is related to decisions in output and sales areas.

- Sales goal: The sales goal aims at meeting the demand of coalition members connected with sales, who regard sales necessary for the stability of the organization. The sales department wants an adequate stock of output for the customers. The sales goal originates from the sales department.

- Share-of-the-market goal: The market-share goal is an alternative to the sales goal. It is related to the demands of sales management of the coalition who are primarily interested in the comparative success of the organization and its growth. Like the sales goal, the market-share goal is related to sales decisions. The same department will also normally set the 'sales strategy,' that is, decide on the advertising campaigns, the market research programs, and so on.

- Profit goal: The profit goal is set by the top management so as to satisfy the demands of share- holders and the expectations of bankers and other finance institutions; and also to create funds with which they can accomplish their own goals and projects, or satisfy the other goals of the firm.

The five goals that an organization should possess. The number of goals can be increased but this addition of new goal would result in complexity of decision making process. There exist a negative relationship between efficiency of decision making and the number of goals. The efficiency of decision-making decreases as the number of goals increases and vice versa. The goals of the firm are decided by the top management. This is done through continuous bargaining between the groups of the coalition. The firms while forming goals attempts to satisfy as many demands which it is confronted by various members of the coalition. Some of the goals may be desirable to all members of the coalition. For example, the sales goal is directly desirable to the sales manager and his department, to the top management and most probably to the shareholders. But it is also indirectly desirable to all the other members of the coalition as all the members of the coalition know that unless the firm sells whatever it produces no one will be able to attain his own individual goals.

But except this goal, there are other goals that are desirable only too few members of the groups. For example, profits goal is directly desirable to the shareholders and the top management, but not of the employees in lower administrative levels or of the workers 'on the floor.' The goals of the firm, like the goals of the individual members or groups of the coalition, take the form of aspiration levels rather than strict maximizing constraints. The firm in the behavioral theories seeks to satisfice that is, to attain a 'satisfactory' overall performance, as defined by the set aspiration goals, rather than maximize profits, sales or other magnitudes. The firm is a satisficing organization rather than a maximizing entrepreneur.

1. Conflicting Goals: The goals of the firm, like the goals of the individual members or groups of the coalition, take the form of aspiration levels rather than strict maximizing constraints. The factor that determines these goals within the firm is the aspiration level of the individuals. These aspiration level changes overtime as a result of organizational learning. In the organizational coalition, these goals are regarded as the product of a bargaining- learning process. But it is not necessary that different goals get resolved cordially. There may exist conflicts among goals. The organizational coalition is thus a coalition of conflicting interests. These conflicting interests can be reconciled by the distribution of 'side payments' among coalition members. The actual amount of the side payment that needs to be distributed is not fixed for the coalition. That actual amount basically depends on the form of the coalition and demand of coalition members. In the long run, the demand for coalition members is equal to the side payments. The behavioral theory focuses on the short-run relation between side payments and demands. These side payments can be in the form of cash or in kind. The side payment in kind is mostly in the form of 'policy' that is the right to take part in the policy decisions of the

organization. In the short run, new demands are being constantly generated and the goals of the organization are continuously adapted to take account of these increased demand. The demand for the coalition members in the organization need not be mutually consistent. All this increased demand are not made simultaneously. The organization that is meeting the demand can remain viable by attending the demand in sequence. But the problem can still arise when the organization is not able to accommodate the demand of its coalition member even sequentially. This happens due to lack of resources.

2. Satisficing Behavior: Conflicting goals of the organization can be reconciled by the distribution of 'side payments' among coalition members. Besides distribution of side payments, the conflicting goals of the organization are resolved by subjecting them to a constant review. This constant review is required because aspiration levels of coalition members change with experience. The aspiration levels change with the process of satisficing. Each person in the organization has a satisficing level for each of his goals. If this desired level is achieved then they will not seek for more. But if this desired level is not achieved, the aspiration levels are revised downwards. If they are exceeding the desired amount, the aspiration levels are raised upwards. In both situations, the satisfactory levels of performance are changed accordingly.

3. Organizational Slack: A coalition is sound and workable if payments made to various members of the coalition are adequate. In order to have a workable coalition, enough resources are needed to meet all the demands of members of the coalition in an organization. This is generally not possible because there exists a disparity between the total resources available to the organization and the total payments required to maintain the coalition. The difference between the total resources available and total necessary payments is called organizational slack. The organizational slack arises in payments to coalition members in the organization that is in excess of what is required to maintain the organization.

There are other forms of slack exist when the organization operates under market conditions that are not perfect. There is a possibility that the shareholders may be paid dividends in excess of what is required to keep them in the organization or the customers may be charged lower prices so that they may stick to the products of the firm. The workers may be paid wages in excess of what is needed to keep them in the firm. The executives may be provided with services and personal luxuries more than what is required to keep them. All such expenses in the form of excess payments are slack expenditures for the firm which every member of the coalition obtains from time to time.

Organizational slack is typically not zero. But it is positive. It is possible that some members of the coalition in general obtain a greater share of the slack than do others. In general, those members of the coalition who are full-time tend to get more payments than the other members of the coalition. This organizational slack is very important for the existence of coalition. The organizational slack plays a productive role by enabling the firm to maintain themselves under crisis type situation. It also enables the firm to adjust itself to changes in external environment. It serves as a cushion to absorb abnormal shocks.

These payments increases during boom periods and decreased during bad phases of business. Thus, organizational slack plays both a stabilizing and an adaptive role.

4. Decision-making Process: The important parameter that needs to be discussed is the decision-making process. In the Cyert-March model, the decision making rests with the top management and with the lower levels of administration. It is the top management that sets the organizational goals and allocates the given resources to the various departments. This allocation of resources is based on their share of the total budget of the firm.

The share in the budget depends upon the bargaining power and the skill of each manager. This bargaining power is determined by the past performance of each department and their hard work. In this process of allocation, the top management retains some funds to be allocated at its discretion at any time to any department.

The decision making process at the lower levels provides various degrees of freedom of action to the administration. In the budget is allocated to each department. Once the share is distributed from budget, each manager has considerable discretion in spending the funds at his disposal. All the decisions that are taken by the managers are implemented by the lower level staff based on their experiences and the "blue print" rules lay down earlier.

Another factor that determines the decision making process is information and expectations formed within the organization. Information plays an important role in the decision making process as it is required to facilitate the decision maker. Seeking information is not costless and it is required at each and every step. Search activity is started whenever problem persists as search helps to locate and collect information. This information determines the aspirations of each department which, in turn, helps the top management in setting goals. On the other hand, expectations also play an important role in decision making process as organizational expectations are related to the hopes and wishes of the decision-maker. Given these two parameters that affect the decision making process, the top management examines and decides upon the projects presented by the managers. The top management evaluates the projects presented by the managers on the basis of two grounds. First, Budget constraint which emphasize on the availability of fund for the project. And Second, Improvement criteria which focus on whether the project is better than the existing one? In making decisions, the top management follows the rule that leads to a better state in the future than it was in the past. Thus, the Cyert-March model of behaviorism is thus an adaptive rational system.

The Game Theory

Game theory is extremely useful because it allows us to anticipate the behavior of economic agents within a game and the outcomes of strategic games. Game theory gets its name from actual games. Games like checkers and chess are strategic games where two players interact and the outcome of the game is determined by the actions of both players. In economics, game theory is particularly useful in understanding imperfectly competitive markets like oligopoly because the price and output decisions of one firm affects the demand and therefore profit function of the other firms. Here we will study only non-cooperative games, games where the players are not able to negotiate and make binding agreements within the game. An example of a cooperative game might be one where two poker payers agree to share winnings no matter who actually wins, as a result their strategies are based on how best to maximize the joint expected payoff, not individual payoffs.

All games have three basic elements: players, strategies and payoffs. The players of the game are the agents actively participating in the game and who will experience outcomes based on the play of all players. The strategies are all of the possible strategic choices available to each player, they can be the same for all players or different for each player. The payoffs are the outcomes associated with every possible strategic combination, for each player. Any complete description of a game must include these three elements. In the games that we will study, we will assume that each player's goal is to maximize their individual payoff which is consistent with the rational utility-maximizing agent that is the foundation of modern economic theory.

We begin by separating games into two basic types: simultaneous games and sequential games. Simultaneous games are games in which players take strategic actions at the same time, without knowing what move the other has chosen. A good example of this type of game is the matching coins game where two players each have a coin and choose which side to face up. They then reveal their choices simultaneously and if they match one player gets to keep both coins and if they don't match the other player keeps both coins. Sequential games are games where players take turns and move consecutively. Checkers, chess and go are all good examples of sequential games. One player observes the move of the other player, and then makes their play and so on.

Games can also be single-shot or repeated. Single-shot games are played once and then the game is over. Repeated games are simultaneous move games played repeatedly by the same players. A single-shot game might be a game of rock, paper, scissors played once to determine who gets to sit in the front seat of a car. A repeated game might be repeated plays of rock, paper, scissors with the first player to win five times getting the right to sit in the front seat of a car.

Games can become very complicated when all players do not know all the information about the game. We will assume common knowledge. Common knowledge is when the players know all about the game – the players, strategies and payoffs – and know that the other players know, and that the other players know that they know, and so on ad infinitum. In simpler terms all participants know everything.

Single Play Games

The most basic of games is the simultaneous, single play game. We can represent such a game with a payoff matrix: a table that lists the players of the game, their strategies and the payoffs associated with every possible strategy combination. We call games that can be represented with a payoff matrix, normal-form games.

Let's start with an example of a game among two friends, Erika and Sven, who are competing to be the top student in a class. They have a final exam approaching and they are deciding whether they should be cooperative and share notes or be uncooperative and keep their notes to themselves. They won't see each other at the end of the day so they each have to decide whether to leave notes for each other without knowing what the other one has done. If they both share notes they both will get perfect scores. Their teacher gives a ten point bonus to the top exam score, but only if there is one exam better than the rest so if they both get top score there is no bonus and they both get 100 on their exams. If they both don't share they won't do as well and they will both receive a 95 on their exams. However if one shares and the other doesn't the one who shares will not benefit from the other's notes, so will only get a 90 and the one who doesn't share will benefit from the other's notes, get the top score and the bonus for a score of 110.

All of these facts are expressed in the payoff matrix in figure. Since this is a single-shot, simultaneous game it is a normal-form game and we can use a payoff matrix to describe it. There are two players: Lena and Sven. There are two strategies available to each player. Lena's strategies are in blue and correspond to the rows and Sven's are in red and correspond to the columns and they are the same for both: share or don't share. The payoffs for each strategy combination are given in the corresponding row and column and Lena's payoffs are in blue and Sven's payoffs are in red. We will assume common knowledge – they both know all of this information about the game, and they know that the other knows it, and they know that the other knows that they know it, and so on.

		Sven	
		Share	Don't Share
Lena	Share	100, 100	90, 110
	Don't Share	110, 90	95, 95

The Valedictorian Game.

The payoff matrix a complete description of the game because it lists the three elements: players, strategies and payoffs.

It is now time to think about individual strategy choices. We will start by examining the difference between dominant and dominated strategies. A dominant strategy is a strategy for which the payoffs are always greater than any other strategy no matter what the opponent does. A dominated strategy is a strategy is a strategy for which the payoffs are always lower than any other strategy no matter what the opponent does. Predicting behavior in games is achieved by understanding each rational player's optimal strategy, the one that leads to the highest payoff. Sometimes the optimal strategy depends on the opponent's strategy choice, but in the case of a dominant strategy, it does not and so it follows that a rational player will always play a dominant strategy if one is available to them. It also follows that a rational player will never play a dominated strategy. So we now have our first two principles that can, in certain games, lead to a prediction about the outcome.

Let's look at the Valedictorian Game in figure. Notice that for Lena she gets a higher payoff if she doesn't share her notes no matter what Sven does. If Sven shares his notes, she gets 110 if she doesn't share rather than 100 if she does. If Sven doesn't share his notes, she gets 95 if she doesn't share and 90 if she does. It makes sense then that she will never share her notes. Don't share is a dominant strategy so she will play it. Share is a dominated strategy so she will not play it. The same is true for Sven as the payoffs in this game happen to be completely symmetrical, though they need not be in games. We can predict that both players will choose to play their dominant strategies and that the outcome of the game will be don't share, don't share – Lena chooses don't share and Sven chooses don't share – and they both get 95.

This outcome is known as a Dominant Strategy Equilibrium (DSE), an equilibrium where each player plays his or her dominant strategy. This is a very intuitive equilibrium concept and is the one used in situations where all players have a dominant strategy. Unfortunately many, or even most, games do not have the feature that every player has a dominant strategy. Let's examine the DSE in this game. The most striking feature of this outcome is that there is another outcome that both players would voluntarily switch to: share, share. This outcome delivers 100 to each player and is therefore more efficient in the Pareto sense – there is another outcome where you could make one person better off without hurting anyone else. Games with this feature are known as Prisoner's Dilemma games – the name comes from a classic game of cops and robbers, but the general usage is for games that have this Pareto suboptimal feature.

Why do we get this suboptimal result? It comes from the fact that each agent is purely self-interested, all they care about is maximizing their own payoffs, and if they think the other player is going to play share, their best play is to not share. What is particularly interesting about this result is that it overturns the first welfare theorem of economics that says that a competitive equilibrium is Pareto Efficient. The difference is the strategic nature of the interactions in the game. Here we have much of the same conditions of a competitive market, but because of the strategic nature of the game, one player's actions affect the other players' payoffs.

What if a game lacks dominant strategies? Let's take an example where you are thinking about which party to attend because you want to meet up with friends. Let's simplify the example by saying that there are two friends Malia and Caitlin who both have been invited to two parties, one sponsored by the college international club and another sponsored by the college debate club. Neither of them have a particular preference about which party they want to go to, but they definitely want to see each other and so want to end up at the same party. They talked earlier in the week and so they know that each is considering the two parties and how much each of them like the two parties, so there is common knowledge. The problem is that Caitlin's mobile phone battery has run out of charge and they can't communicate. When asked how much they would enjoy the parties Caitlin and Malia gave similar answers and we will represent them as payoffs in the payoff matrix in figure.

		Malia	
		International Club (IC)	Debate Club (DC)
Caitlin	International Club (IC)	10, 15	2, 1
	Debate Club (DC)	1, 2	15, 10

The Party Game.

This matrix shows Caitlin's strategies on the left in a column and Malia's strategies in a row on top. Each of them has exactly two strategies: International Club and Debate Club. Foe each their payoffs are shown in the boxes that correspond to each strategy pair. For example in the box for International Club, International Club the payoffs are 10 and 10. The first payoff corresponds to Caitlin and the second corresponds to Malia.

We now have to determine each players best response function: one player's optimal strategy choice for every possible strategy choice of the other player. For Caitlin, her best response function is the following:

- Play IC if Malia plays IC.

- Play DC if Malia plays DC.

For Malia, her best response function looks similar:

- Play IC if Caitlin plays IC.

- Play DC if Caitlin plays DC.

Since the best response changes for both players depending on the strategy choice of the other player, we know immediately that neither one has a dominant strategy. What then? How do we think about the outcome of the game? The solution concept most commonly used in game theory is the Nash equilibrium concept. Nash equilibrium is an outcome where, given the strategy choices of the other players, no individual player can obtain a higher pay off by altering their strategy choice. An equivalent way to think about Nash equilibrium is that it is an outcome of a game where all players are simultaneously playing a best response to the others' strategy choices. The equilibrium is intuitive, if, when placed in a certain outcome, no player wishes to unilaterally deviate from it, then equilibrium is achieved – there are no forces within the game that would cause the outcome to change.

In the party game above, there are two outcomes where the best responses correspond: both players choosing IC and both players choosing DC. If Caitlin shows up at the International Club party and finds Malia there, she will not want to leave Malia there and go to the Debate Club party. Similarly if Malia shows up at the International Club party and finds Caitlin there, she will not want to leave Caitlin there and go to the Debate Club party. So the outcome (IC, IC) – which describes Caitlin's choice and Malia's choice is a Nash equilibrium. The outcome (DC, DC) is also Nash equilibrium for the same reason.

This example illustrates the strengths and weaknesses of the Nash equilibrium concept. Intuitively, if they show up at the same party, both women would be content and neither one would want to leave to the other party if the other is staying. However, there is nothing in the Nash equilibrium concept that gives us guidance as to predicting at which party the women will end up. In general, a normal form game can have zero, one or multiple Nash equilibrium.

Consider this different version of the party game where Caitlin really doesn't want to go to the International Club party, so much so that she prefers attending the Debate Club party without Malia to attending the International Club party with Malia.

		Malia	
		International Club (IC)	Debate Club (DC)
Caitlin	International Club (IC)	1, 15	2, 1
	Debate Club (DC)	5, 2	15, 10

The Party Game, Version 2.

Now DC is a dominant strategy for Caitlin. Malia knows Caitlin does not like the International Club party and will correctly surmise that she will attend the Debate Club party no matter what. So both Caitlin and Malia will go to the Debate Club party and (DC, DC) is the only Nash Equilibrium. In this case the Nash equilibrium concept is satisfying, it gives a clear prediction of the unique outcome of the game and it intuitively makes sense.

Another possibility is a game that has no Nash equilibrium. Consider the following game called matching pennies. In this game two players, Ahmed and Naveen, each have a penny. They decide which side of the penny to have facing up and cover the penny until they are both revealed simultaneously. By agreement, if the pennies match Ahmed gets to keep both and if the two pennies don't match, Naveen keeps both. The players, strategies, and payoffs are given in the payoff matrix in figure.

		Naveen	
		Heads	Tails
Ahmed	Heads	1, –1	–1, 1
	Tails	–1, 1	1, –1

The Matching Pennies Game.

Ahmed's best response function is to play heads if Naveen plays heads and to play tails if Naveen plays tails. Naveen's best response is to play tails if Ahmed plays heads and to play heads if Ahmed plays tails. There is no correspondence of best response functions, no outcome of the game in which no player would want to unilaterally deviate and thus no Nash equilibrium. The outcome of this game is unpredictable and no outcome creates contentment for both players.

Finding the Nash equilibrium in normal form games is made relatively easy by following a simple technique that identifies the best response functions on the payoff matrix itself. To do so, simply underline the maximum payoff for a given opponent strategy. Consider the example below. For Chris, if Pat plays Left, the maximum payoff is 65 which come from playing up, so let's underline 65. This is a representation of the best response to Pat playing left, Chris should play up. Moving along the columns we find that Chris should play down if Pat plays Center, and Chris should play down again if Pat plays Right. Switching perspective, if Chris plays Up Pat gets a maximum payoff from playing Left so we underline Pat's payoff, 44, in that box. Continuing on, if Chris plays Middle, Pay should play Right, and if Chris plays Down, Pat should play Center.

		Pat		
		Left	Center	Right
Chris	Up	65, 44	29, 38	44, 29
	Middle	53, 41	35, 31	19, 56
	Down	30, 57	41, 63	72, 27

So now that we have identified each players best response functions, all that remains is to look for outcomes where the best response functions correspond. Such outcomes are those where both payoffs are underlined. In this game the two Nash equilibria are (Up, Left) and (Down, Center).

If we change the payoffs in the game to what is shown below notice that each player has a dominant strategy as see by the thee underlines all in the row 'Down' for Chris and three underlines all in the column 'Center' for Pat. Down is always the best strategy choice for Chris no matter what Pat chooses and Center is always the right strategy choice for Pat no matter what Chris chooses.

		Pat		
		Left	Center	Right
Chris	Up	30, 41	29, 44	44, 24
	Middle	53, 33	35, 56	19, 39
	Down	65, 57	41, 63	72, 27

The dominant strategy equilibrium (Down, Center) also fulfills the requirements of Nash equilibrium. This will always be true of dominant strategy equilibria: all dominant strategy equilibria are Nash equilibria. However, we know the reverse is not true: not all Nash equilibria are dominant strategy equilibria. So dominant strategy equilibria are a subset of Nash equilibria, or to put it in another way, the Nash equilibrium is a more general concept than Dominant Strategy Equilibrium.

Mixed Strategies

So far we have concentrated on pure strategies where a player chooses a particular strategy with complete certainty. We now turn our attention to mixed strategies where a player randomizes across strategies according to a set of probabilities he or she chooses. For an example of a mixed strategy let's return to the matching pennies game in figure.

		Naveen	
		Heads	Tails
Ahmed	Heads	1, -1	-1, 1
	Tails	-1, 1	1, -1

The Matching Pennies Game.

By using the underline strategy to illustrate best responses, there is no Nash equilibrium of this game in pure strategies. What about mixed strategies? A mixed strategy is a strategy itself, for example Ahmed might decide that he will play heads 75% of the time and tails 25% of the time. What is Neveen's best response to this strategy? Well if Naveen plays tails with certainty, he will win 75% of the time. Ahmed's best response to Naveen playing tails is to play tails with certainty, so Ahmed's mixed strategy is not a Nash equilibrium strategy. How about Ahmed choosing a mixed strategy of playing heads and tails each with a 50% chance – simply flipping the coin – can this be a Nash equilibrium strategy? The answer is yes which is evident when we think of Naveen's best response to this mixed strategy. Naveen can play either heads or tails with certainty or the same mixed strategy with equal results; he can expect to win half the time. The pure strategies have best responses as given in the matrix above so only the mixed strategy is Nash equilibrium. If Ahmed decides to flip his coin, Naveen's best response is to flip his too. And if Naveen is flipping his coin, Ahmed's best response is to do the same.

So this game, that did not have Nash equilibrium in pure strategies, does have Nash equilibrium in mixed strategies. Both players randomize over their two strategy choices with probabilities .5 and .5.

Sequential Games

There are many situations where players of a game move sequentially. The game of checkers is such a game, one player moves, the other players observes the move and then responds with their own move. Sequential move games are games where players take turns making their strategy choices and observe their opponents choice prior to making their own strategy choices. We describe these games by drawing a game tree, a diagram that describes the players, their turns, and their choices at every turn, and the payoffs for every possible set of strategy choices. We have another name for this description of sequential games: extensive form games.

Consider a game where two Indian food carts located next to each other are competing for many of the same customers for its Tikka Masala. The first cart, called Jack's, opens first and sets its price, the second cart, called Tridip's opens second and sets its price after observing the price set by Jack's. To keep it simple let's suppose there are three prices possible for both carts: high, medium, low.

The extensive form or game tree representation of this game is given in figure. The game tree describes all of the principle elements of the game: the players, the strategies and the payoffs. The players are described at each decision node of the game, each place where a player might potentially have to choose a strategy. From each node there extend branches representing the strategy choices of a player. At the end of the final set of branches are the payoffs for every possible outcome of the game. This is the complete description of the game. There are also subgames within the full game. Subgames are the all of the subsequent strategy decisions that follow from one particular node.

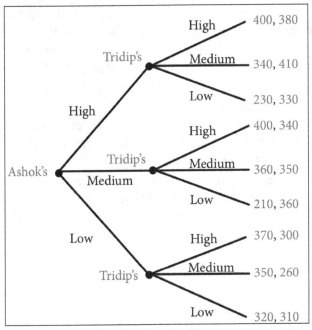

The Curry Pricing Game.

In this game Jack's is at the first decision node so they get to move first. Tridip's is at the second set of decision nodes so they move second. How will the game resolve itself? To determine the outcome it is necessary to use backward induction: to start at the last play of the game and determine what the player with the last turn of the game will do in each situation and then, given this deduction, determine what the payer with the second to last turn will do at that turn, and continue this way until the first turn is reached. Using backward induction leads to the Subgame Perfect Nash Equilibrium of the game. The Subgame Perfect Nash Equilibrium (SPNE) is the solution in which every player, at every turn of the game, is playing an individually optimal strategy.

For the curry pricing game illustrated in figure, the SPNE is found by first determining what Tridip will do for each possible play by Jack. Tridip is only concerned with his payoffs in red and will play Medium if Jack plays High and get 410, will play Low if Jack plays Medium and get 360, and will play Low if Jack plays Low and get 310. Because of common knowledge, Jack knows this as well and so has only three possible outcomes. Jack knows that if he plays High, Tridip will play Medium and he will get 340; if he plays Medium, Tridip will play Low and he will get 210, and if he plays Low, Tridip will play Low and he will get 320. Since 340 is best of the possible outcomes, Jack will pick High. Since Jack picks high, Tridip will pick Medium and the game ends.

Backward induction will always lead to the SPNE of a sequential game.

Credible and Non-credible Threats

Let's consider a famous game where there is an established 'incumbent' firm in a market and another entrepreneur who is thinking of entering the market and competing with the incumbent who we will call the 'potential entrant.' Suppose, for example, that there is just one pizza restaurant in a commercial district just off a university campus that sells pizza slices to the students of the university, let's call it Gino's. Since they face no direct competition, they can sell a slice of pizza for $3 and they make $400 a day in revenue. But there is a pizza maker named Vito who is considering entering the market by setting up a pizza shop in an empty storefront just downs the street from Gino's. When facing the potential arrival of Vito's pizza restaurant, Gino has two choices: accommodate Vito by keeping prices higher (say $2) or fighting Vito by selling his slices below cost in the hope of preventing Vito from opening. The game and the payoffs are given below in the normal form game in figure.

		Vito's (Potential Entrant)	
		Enter	Don't Enter
Gino's	Accommodate	200, 300	400, 0
(Incumbent)	Fight	100, 200	400, 0

The Market Entry Game.

If we follow the underlining strategy to identify best responses we see that this game has two Nash Equilibria: (Accommodate, Enter) and (Fight, Don't Enter). Note that for Gino, both Accommodate and Fight result in the same payoff if Vito chooses don't enter, so we underline both – either one is equally a best response.

		Vito's (Potential Entrant)	
		Enter	Don't Enter
Gino's	Accommodate	200, 300	400, 0
(Incumbent)	Fight	-100, -100	400, 0

But there is something unsatisfying about the second Nash equilibrium – since this is a simultaneous game both player are picking their strategies simultaneously, thus Gino is picking fight if Vito does not enter and so Vito's best choice is not to enter. But would Vito really believe that Gino would fight if he entered? Probably not. We call this a non-credible threat: a strategy choice to dissuade a rival that is against the best interest of the player and therefore not rational.

A better description of this game is therefore a sequential one, where Vito first chooses to open a pizza restaurant and Gino has to decide how to respond.

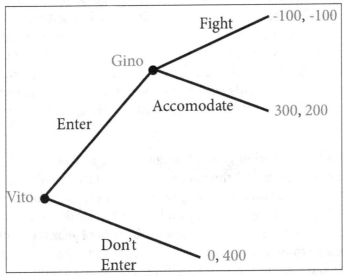

The Sequential Market Entry Game.

In this version of the game, if Vito decides not to enter the game ends and the payoffs are $0 for Vito and $400 for Gino. If Vito decides to enter then Gino can both fight and get $-100, or accommodate and get $200. Clearly the only individually rational thing for Gino to do if Vito enters is to accommodate and, since Vito knows this he will enter.

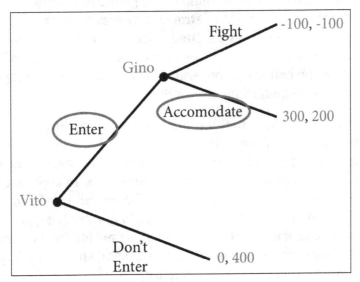

The SPNE of this game is (Enter, Accommodate). What this version of the game does is to eliminate the equilibrium based on a non-credible threat. Vito knows that if he decides to open up a pizza shop, it is irrational for Gino to fight because Gino will make him worse off. Since Vito knows that Gino will accommodate, the best decision for Vito is to open his restaurant.

Repeated Games

Any game can be played more than once to create a larger game. For example, the game "rock, scissors, paper" where two players simultaneously use their hands to form the shape of a rock or a piece of paper or scissors can be played just once, or can be repeated multiple times for example playing "best of 3" where the winner is the first player to win two rounds of the game. This is a normal form game in each round but a larger game when taken as a whole. This raises the possibility that a larger strategy could be employed, for example one contingent on the strategy choice of the opponent in the last round.

Let's return to the Valedictorian game, this game was a prisoner's dilemma, because of individual incentives they find themselves in a collectively suboptimal outcome. In other words there is an outcome that they both prefer but they fail to reach it because of the individual strategic incentive to try and do better for them. But if the same game was repeated more than once over the course of the school year it is quite reasonable to ask if such repetition would lead the players to a different outcome. If the players know they will face the same situation again, will they be more inclined to cooperate and reach the mutually beneficial outcome?

Finitely Repeated Games

If we played the valedictorian game twice, then the strategies for each player would entail their strategy choices for each round of the game. In other words a 'strategy' for a repeated game is the complete set of strategic choices for every round of the game. So let's ask if playing the Valedictorian game twice would alter the outcome in an individual round. Suppose, for example, the two talked before the game and acknowledged that they would both be better off cooperating and sharing. In the repeated game, is cooperation ever a Nash equilibrium strategy?

To answer this question we have to think about how to solve the game. Since this game is repeated a finite number of times, in our case two, it has a last round and similar to a sequential game, the appropriate method of solving the game is through backward induction to find the Subgame Perfect Nash Equilibrium. In repeated games at each round the subsequent games are a subgame of the overall game. So in our case the second and final round of the game is a subgame. So to solve the game we have to first think about the outcome of the final round. Well this final play of the game is the simple normal form game we have already solved, a single-shot, simultaneous play game with one Nash equilibrium: (Don't Share, Don't Share).

Now that we know what will happen in the final round of the game, we have to ask ourselves, what the Nash equilibrium strategy is in the first round of play. Since they both know that in the final round of play the only outcome is for both to not share, they also know that there is no reason to share in the first round either. Why? Well, even if they agree to share, when push comes to shove, not sharing is better individually, and since not sharing is going to happen in the final round anyway, there is no way to create an incentive to share in the first round through a final round punishment mechanism. In essence, after the last period is revealed to be a single-shot prisoner's dilemma game, the second to last period becomes a single-shot prisoner's dilemma game as well because there is nothing in the last round that can alter the incentives in the second to last round, so the game is identical.

		Sven	
		Share	Don't Share
	Share	100, 100	90, 110
	Don't Share	110, 90	95, 95

The Valedictorian Game.

In fact, as long as there is a final round, it doesn't matter how many times we repeat this game, because of backward induction, it simply becomes a series of single-shot games with the Nash equilibrium strategies being played every time.

Infinitely Repeated Games

Things change when normal-form games are repeated infinitely because there is no final round and thus backward induction does not work, there is nowhere to work backward from. This aspect of the games allows space for reward and punishment strategies that might create incentives under which cooperation becomes a Nash Equilibrium.

To see this let's alter the scenario of our Valedictorian game. Suppose that Lena and Sven are now adults in the workplace and they work together in a company where their pay is based partly on their performance on a monthly aptitude test. For simplicity we'll assume that their payoffs are the same as in the Valedictorian game but, this time that represent cash bonuses. The key here is that they foresee working together for as long as they can imagine. In other words they each perceive the possibility that they will keep playing this game for in indeterminate amount of time – there is no determined last round of the game and therefore no way to use backward induction to solve it. Player has to look forward to determine optimal strategies.

So would could a strategy to induce cooperation look like? Suppose Lena says to Sven I will share with you as long as you share with me, but as soon as you don't share, I will stop sharing with you forever – let's call this the 'cooperate' strategy. Sven, in response says, okay, I will do the same; I will share with you until such time as you don't share and then I'll stop sharing together. The question we have to answer is: is both players playing these strategies a Nash equilibrium?

To answer this question we have to figure out the best response to the strategy, are it to play the same strategy or is there a better strategy to play in response? To determine the answer to this question let's think about playing the same strategy and alternate strategies and their payoffs.

If Lena claims she will play the cooperate strategy, what is Sven's outcome if he plays the cooperate strategy in response? Well, in the first period Sven will get 100 because they both share and since they both shared in period one they will both share in period two, Sven will get 100 and it will continue on like this forever. To put a present day value on future earnings, we discount, so Sven's earnings stream looks like this:

Payoff from Cooperate Strategy

$100+100×d+100×d^2+100×d3+100×d^4+...$

What is the payoff from not cooperating? Well in the period in which Sven decides not to share, Lena will still be sharing and so Sven will get 110 but then after that Lena will not share and Sven knows this so he will not share as well and he will therefore get 95 for every round after. Let's call this strategy 'deviate.' Thus his earning stream looks like this:

Payoff from Deviate Strategy

$110+95×d+95×d^2+95×d^3+95×d^4+...$

We are only comparing the two strategies from the moment Sven decides to deviate, as the two payoff steams are identical up to that point and therefore cancel themselves out.

Is to cooperate the best response to the cooperate strategy? Yes, if:

$100+100×d+100×d^2+100×d^3+100×d^4+...$

$>110+95×d+95×d^2+95×d^3+95×d^4+...$

Rearranging:

$5 (d+d^2+d^3+d^4+...) > 10$

This says that cooperation is better as long as the extra 5 a cooperating player gets for every subsequent period after the first is better than the extra 10 the deviating player gets in the first period. To determine if this is true, we have to use the result that:

$$d+d^2+d^3+d^4+...=\frac{d}{1-4}$$

So, $5\left(\frac{d}{1-d}\right)>10$

Or

$$5d > 10(1-d)$$

$$15d > 10$$

$$d > 2/3$$

You can think of d as a measure of how much the players care about future payoffs, and so this says that as long as they care enough about the future payoffs, they will cooperate. In other words if $d > 2/3$, then playing cooperate is a best response to the other player playing cooperate and vice-versa: the strategy pair (cooperate, cooperate) is a Nash equilibrium for the infinitely repeated game.

This type of strategy has a name in economics; it is called a trigger strategy. A trigger strategy is one where cooperative play continues until an opponent deviates and then ceases permanently or for a specified number of periods. An alternate strategy is the tit-for-tat strategy where a player simply plays the same strategy their opponent played in the previous round. Tit-for-tat strategies can also be Nash equilibrium and, in fact, in infinitely repeated games there are often many Nash equilibria, the trigger strategy identified above is but one.

References

- Williamsons-utility-maximisation-theory-marginal-theories-28976: yourarticlelibrary.com, Retrieved 13, May 2020

- The-model-of-sylos-labini-of-limit-pricing-5552: economicsdiscussion.net, Retrieved 21, February 2020

- Intermediate-microeconomics: oregonstate.education, Retrieved 08, August 2020

Permissions

Index

CPSIA information can be obtained
at www.ICGtesting.com
Printed in the USA
BVHW060447110122
625887BV00002B/218